Wildlife of

Lancashire

This book is dedicated to the memory of Rollo Simey who helped to develop the idea of a special book on the wildlife of Lancashire.

Wildlife of Lancashire

Exploring the natural history of Lancashire, Manchester and North Merseyside

Edited by Malcolm Edmunds, Tim Mitcham, Geoff Morries
with a foreword by the President of the Wildlife Trusts, David Bellamy

Carnegie Publishing Ltd
for The Lancashire Wildlife Trust

Wildlife of Lancashire: Exploring the natural history of Lancashire, Manchester and North Merseyside

First published in the UK in 2004 by
Carnegie Publishing Ltd
Carnegie House,
Chatsworth Road,
Lancaster LA1 4SL
www.carnegiepublishing.com

for
The Lancashire Wildlife Trust
The Barn,
Berkeley Drive,
Bamber Bridge,
Preston PR5 6BY
www.wildlifetrust.org.uk/lancashire

ISBN 1-85936-118-8

Copyright © Lancashire Wildlife Trust 2004

Designed and typeset by Carnegie Publishing
Printed and bound by Cambridge University Press

Half title page: Brock Valley. (*Malcolm Edmunds*)

Front cover photograph: Morecambe Bay from Warton Crag (*Lancashire Wildlife Trust*)

Contents

The Wildlife Trust for Lancashire, Manchester and North Merseyside is the leading local environmental charity in this region.

The Trust

*   *Manages Nature Reserves*
    We manage 34 nature reserves covering over 2,000 acres of precious habitats.

*   *Conserves Species*
    We protect both common and rare species in the region and safeguard wildlife sites.

*   *Educates about the Environment*
    We encourage children to learn about and care for their environment through our education centre, visits to schools and wildlife WATCH – the young people's environment club.

*   *Involves the Community*
    We support local action for the environment through community projects and training schemes.

*   *Promotes Urban Wildlife*
    We create green spaces in towns and promote sustainable lifestyles.

*   *Campaigns for Wildlife*
    We work with local authorities, influence decision-makers and resist damaging development.

Can you help us today?

We are extremely grateful for the constant commitment and support of all our members, volunteers and donors. If you are inspired by the wildlife in this book, please help our vital work by becoming a member, volunteering your time or remembering us in your will.

Please contact: The Development Manager, The Wildlife Trust, The Barn, Berkeley Drive, Bamber Bridge, Preston, PR5 6BY. 01772 324129.

Foreword

by David Bellamy,
President of the Wildlife Trusts

Wow! This is a real classic, written by the local experts. And *Wildlife of Lancashire: Exploring the Natural History of Lancashire, Manchester and North Merseyside* does exactly what it says on the tin.

Every sort of living thing is here, whether it swims, slithers, walks, creeps, crawls, flies, or stands resolutely rooted to its appointed spot, safe in the county of the red rose. This is your personal guide to a wonderland overflowing with fascinating, really wild life, there for you and your family to discover.

Only last year, a walk on the not-so-wild side in Blackpool allowed me to see one of Britain's most endangered birds: a Bittern thinking about taking up residence on a caravan park. Not far away in Formby you can see real Red Squirrels, and of course Merseyside generally is a very special place for one particular variety of beetle. In parts of Lancashire you might even bump into the odd Natterjack Toad or two on the golf links! You never really know what you are going to see next, but whatever it is this book will give you all the fascinating facts you could want.

From the dizzy heights of Leck Fell to deep under the sea in Morecambe Bay, you are in for lots of surprises, big and small. The same goes for the ancient woods that still cover parts of the clints and grykes of the limestone karst country. Wherever you wander, this book is a must for you and your library. Read it and a walk in town or countryside will never be the same again.

The Wetlands are, of course, my favourites, and the cleaned-up Mersey estuary is home ground to an array of different sorts of beaks, each one adapted to allow wading birds to feed in the mud. Yes it does rain quite a lot, and not just in Manchester! But then that's why there are still exciting remnants of raised bogs, one of the rarest types of vegetation in the world. No wonder the Wildlife Trusts have taken them into their care and are putting them back into working order.

If you are already a member of the Wildlife Trust I am sure you will have ordered your copy of this book. If you're not then the most natural thing you can do is to join today. But be warned: like this book, being a member of the Trust is a lifetime vocation. For a start, you will be volunteering to help look after some of the 34 reserves the Trust manages, and you could even find yourself contributing to a book like this. After all, some of the experts who wrote this book are, like me, getting a bit long in the tooth and new blood will definitely be needed in the future.

What will the wild places of Lancashire be like then? One thing I can tell you is that without the expertise, vision, care and sheer hard work of the Wildlife Trust, many of the things that the natural historians of the past took for granted would be in grave danger.

Thank you for caring.

DAVID BELLAMY
BEDBURN MAY 2004

Preface and Acknowledgements

This book aims to introduce anyone with an interest in natural history to the wealth of wildlife that can be found in Lancashire, north Merseyside and Greater Manchester. Specialist authors have contributed so that each chapter is written by one or more experts. For groups such as birds and butterflies, the text covers a great many common and rare species and indicates where one can search with a good chance of finding them. For others, including fungi, mosses and moths, the number of species is much greater and our knowledge is much less, so the text introduces the reader to just a few of the species that occur here.

English names have been used for all organisms, where they exist, and these have been given capital letters e.g. Holly, Red Admiral, but common names that include several species have usually been written in lower case e.g. dandelion, wasp. Scientific names have been given where a species is first mentioned or in the chapter dealing with that particular group, and there is cross-referencing of English and scientific names in the index. The book is not intended to be a key to identification – readers can go to specialist books or societies for this – but it is hoped that it will stimulate interest in the fascinating world around us.

Although the book covers north Merseyside and Greater Manchester as well as Lancashire, we have referred to the whole area variously throughout the chapters as 'the Trust area', 'our area' or 'Lancashire'. To include all three every time would be cumbersome for the reader.

We have tried to avoid too many technical words, but this is not always possible so a glossary is included at the end of the book. Not every site of wildlife importance mentioned in the text has public access, but many of the sites that can be visited are listed after the glossary. If you want to see some of the marvellous animals and plants described here there is no alternative to a trip into the field to search them out.

The Wildlife Trust has been working for the past 40 years to try to ensure that the wildlife of both town and countryside will be cherished by future generations. This book is a celebration of what we have and what we hope will still be here for our grandchildren to enjoy.

Malcolm Edmunds, Tim Mitcham, Geoff Morries

Acknowledgements

This book has been made possible by the generous support of Lancashire County Council and of Canatxx Energy Ventures Ltd – we thank them both.

It is a pleasure to thank all of the authors who have contributed for the work they have done, for responding to numerous queries, and for their patience and co-operation with the red pencil of the editors. We are also privileged to have had so many people who have taken excellent photographs and donated them free (or at a much reduced price) for this book, so that we have had to buy in just the last few dozen. Phil Smith and Peter Smith deserve special thanks for the large number of superb pictures they have provided; so, too, does Barbara Craig who kindly let us use photographs by her late husband Stan.

A great many other friends and colleagues both within and outside the Wildlife Trust have assisted and we would like to thank them too, especially: David Bellamy, Nik Bruce, Rosslyn Colderley, Susan Dunning, Dave Earl, Janet Edmunds, Anna Goddard, Aimee Hesp, Alistair Hodge, Keely Isherwood, Peter Jepson, June Pollard, Anne Selby, Judith Smith and Peter Smith. We are grateful for the information and cooperation provided by the Lancashire County Council Environment Directorate, Anne Greatrex at the Greater Manchester Ecology Unit, Christine Bennett at the Environmental Advisory Service, and the Fitzherbert-Brockholes family for data on the Brock Valley heronry.

Credits for Artwork

Nik Bruce for maps: xii, 2, 4, 6, 62, 77, 81, 89, 95, 162, 236, 277, 300

Malcolm Edmunds and Lucy Day: 24–5, 26–7, 30-1

Malcolm Edmunds: 190, 200

Credits for Photographs

Tony Aldridge/English Nature: 83

Miran Aprehamian: 193

Mike Atkinson: 172, 174, 177, 185, 215, 221, 224, 229 (2), 230, 234, 250, 252, 255, 259, 264

Steve Austin/Woodfall Wild Images: 119

Mick Baines/Woodfall Wild Images: 131

Bernard Bedworth: 195

Darren Bedworth: 192, 193

G.I. Bernard/NHPA: 181, 218

Ken Blamire: 206 (2), 209, 215, 228, 251, 253 (2), 258, 265, 266

Kevin Butt: 200, 201 (2), 202, 203

N.A. Callow/NHPA: 262 (2)

Eddie Campion: 114

David Chapman/Woodfall Wild Images: 261

Steve Colclough: 36

Stan Craig: 138, 140 (2), 146, 147, 148, 149, 151, 155 (2), 156, 160, 163, 164, 165, 166, 167

Stuart Crofts: 182 (2), 186 (2), 187, 188

Stephen Dalton/NHPA: 218, 254 (2), 256

Malcolm Edmunds: i, 9, 41, 53, 57, 58, 60 (2), 61, 63 (2), 64 (2), 65, 66, 69 (2), 71 (2), 73, 82, 86, 117, 123, 125, 127, 205, 207, 227 (3), 230, 232, 240, 242 (2), 245, 258, 259 (2), 260, 268, 276, 286

Inigo Everson/Woodfall Wild Images: 106

Harry Fox/OSF/Photolibrary.com: 239

Paul Frear: 194

Fylde Borough Council: 275

Chris Gardner: 196

Bob Gibbons/Woodfall Wild Images, 238, 256

Ray Gibson: 184

Lance Gorman: 240 (2), 241 (3), 242, 260

Eric Greenwood: 20, 59, 64, 72, 88

R.A.Haley: 274

Andy Harmer: 179, 180, 184, 185, 186, 187, 188, 189

Jon Hickling: 8, 10, 13, 14, 22, 23, 46, 50, 59, 60, 75, 273, 284

Geoff Higginbottom: 213

Dorothy Holt: 168

Peter Jepson: 11, 42, 44, 61, 67, 76, 80, 83, 87, 88, 91

Mike Lane/Woodfall Wild Images: 129

Michael Leach/Woodfall Wild Images: 118

Derek Lippett: 192 (2), 196, 197

Pat Livermore: 109, 110, 111, 112 (2), 113, 216

Bob Marsh: 204, 206, 221, 263, 267 (2), 269

Tim Mitcham: 101, 185, 275, 279, 280, 285, 290, 292

Geoff Morries: 79, 86, 90, 97

David Mower: 282

National Gallery of Canada, Ottawa: 19

National Museums Liverpool, Board of Trustees: 17

Jennifer Newton: 216, 248, 252, 255, 266

Oldham Local Studies and Archives: 281

Oxford Bee Company: 246

Jackie Parry: 191 (2)

OSF/Photolibrary.com: 35, 198, 199

Peter Perfect/Woodfall Wild Images: 243, 257

Richard Revels/Woodfall Wild Images: 239, 245

Neil Robinson: 7, 246, 247, 248, 249

Mark Seaward: 105, 107, 108

Laura Sivell: 73, 223, 225, 230, 231, 232, 233, 235, 237 (2)

Jason Smalley: 15, 102 (3)

Peter Smith: 111, 112, 115, 118, 119, 120 (3), 121, 122, 126 (2), 127, 128, 129, 130, 134 (2), 138, 139, 141 (2), 143, 144 (2), 150 (2), 153, 154 (2), 157 (2), 158 (2), 159, 160, 161, 163 (2), 164, 165, 167, 173, 174, 178 (2), 196, 210, 211 (2), 212, 214, 224, 225, 226, 231, 251, 278, 291

Phil Smith: 46, 47 (2), 48, 49, 51, 52 (2), 53, 54 (4), 55, 56 (3), 57 (2), 58, 65, 67, 68, 69, 70 (2), 74 (2), 76 (3), 78, 79, 80, 84, 85 (2), 87 (2), 93, 96, 98, 176, 177, 209, 213, 217, 220, 222, 225, 233, 251, 289

Graham Standring: 276

Paul Thompson/Woodfall Wild Images: 131

Peter Wakely: 5, 40

Roy Waller/NHPA: 183

Warrington Borough Council: 16

Mick Weston: 12

Wildlife Trust: 287, 288

Peter Wilson/Woodfall Wild Images, 199, 204, 217

David Woodfall: 286

Mark Woombs: 25, 28, 31, 32 (2), 33, 34, 36, 37 (2), 38, 39, 132

Dan Wrench: 103, 104 (3)

Steve Young: 137, 142, 152, 168, 170

xi

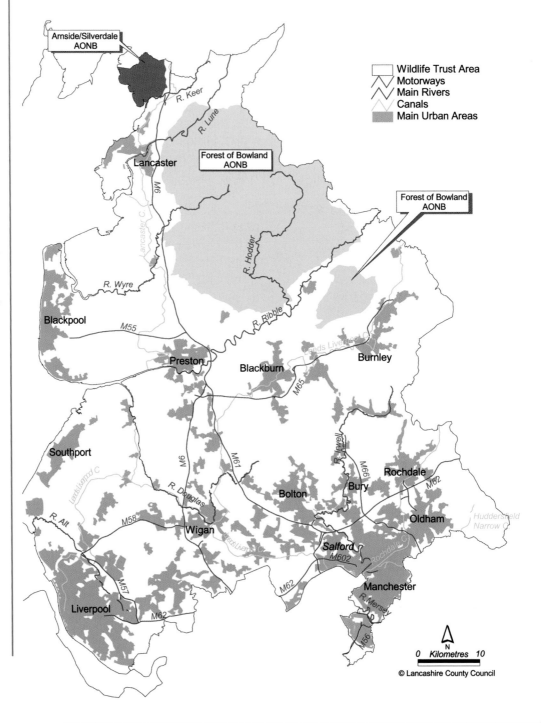

Map 1.
The Wildlife Trust Area.
This book deals with wildlife in the area covered by the Lancashire Wildlife Trust, i.e. the current counties of Lancashire, Greater Manchester and North Merseyside. Also shown are the two Areas of Outstanding Natural Beauty.
(Nik Bruce)

Arnside/Silverdale AONB

Forest of Bowland AONB

Forest of Bowland AONB

Wildlife Trust Area
Motorways
Main Rivers
Canals
Main Urban Areas

R. Keer

R. Lune

Lancaster

M6

Lancaster C.

R. Hodder

R. Wyre

Blackpool

M55

R. Ribble

Preston

Blackburn

Leeds Liverpool C.

Burnley

M65

Southport

Leeds Liverpool C.

M6

M61

R. Irwell

M66

Rochdale

M62

R. Douglas

Bolton

Bury

R. Alt

M58

Wigan

Leeds Liverpool C.

Oldham

Huddersfield Narrow C.

Salford

M602

Rochdale C.

M57

M62

M62

Manchester

R. Mersey

Liverpool

M62

M56

N

0   *Kilometres*   10

© Lancashire County Council

Wildlife of Lancashire

Chapter 1

Lancashire: Setting the Scene

Jon Hickling

The county of Lancashire, including the metropolitan areas of Manchester and North Merseyside, covers approximately 4,670 km² of land; it has a wide variety of habitats, and supports some of the most important wildlife sites in Britain, many of which are of European importance. This chapter presents an overview of the area, its climate, underlying rocks and main wildlife habitats. Then the work of some of the early naturalists who discovered many of the wildlife riches of our area is presented. The next series of chapters look in more detail at the various animals and plants that live here, starting with a look at life in our seas, then working through the plants and fungi and ending with the invertebrate animals. The final chapter looks at how these wildlife riches are being conserved and at what further steps need to be taken to safeguard them for future generations.

The area is one of stark contrasts: it includes almost every major habitat type in the country from the wild, wind-swept, heather dominated upland of the Bowland Fells and South Pennine Moors to the flower-rich sand dunes of the Lytham and Sefton coasts. The Pennine plateau has considerable areas over 200 m, but the highest area in Lancashire is in the extreme north-east, on Leck Fell, which reaches 627 m at Gragareth Fell. The peat-capped moors with their covering of cottongrass and heather are drained by steep-sided river valleys with a scattering of bluebell woodlands and rare flower-rich hay meadows. The extensive mud and sand flats of the Lune, Wyre, Ribble and Alt estuaries are of European importance for over half a million wildfowl and wading birds that overwinter or pass through during migration from their arctic breeding grounds to Africa. The limestone hills of the Silverdale area and the extensive reed bed at Leighton Moss are a magnet for naturalists searching for rare and localised plants and

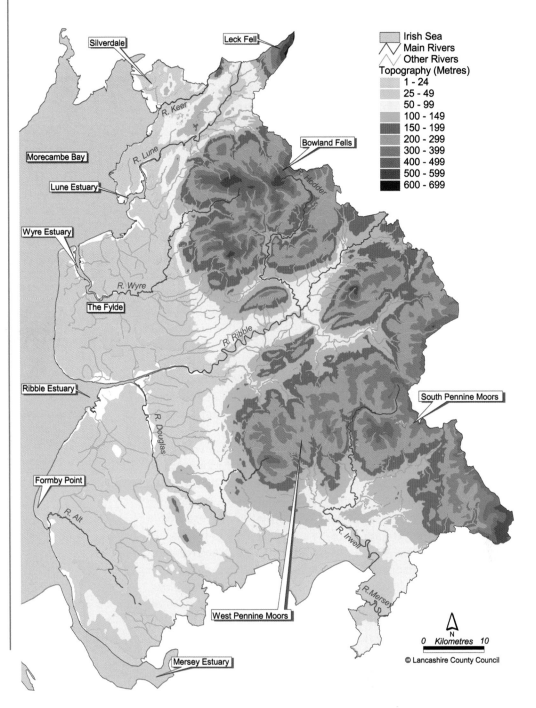

Map 2.
Topography and watercourses of the Wildlife Trust Area.
(Nik Bruce)

Silverdale

Leck Fell

Morecambe Bay

Bowland Fells

Lune Estuary

R. Keer

R. Lune

Hodder

Wyre Estuary

R. Wyre

The Fylde

R. Ribble

Ribble Estuary

South Pennine Moors

R. Douglas

Formby Point

R. Alt

West Pennine Moors

R. Irwell

R. Mersey

Mersey Estuary

Irish Sea
Main Rivers
Other Rivers
Topography (Metres)
1 - 24
25 - 49
50 - 99
100 - 149
150 - 199
200 - 299
300 - 399
400 - 499
500 - 599
600 - 699

N
0   Kilometres   10

© Lancashire County Council

2

Wildlife of Lancashire

animals. These surviving areas of semi-natural vegetation form an integral part of the natural heritage of England's 'Wild North-West' that is irreplaceable and enhances the overall quality of life of Lancashire's inhabitants.

The distribution of Lancashire's wildlife habitats, species and natural features are determined by its climate, topography, geology, past land use patterns and cultural history. Agriculture has shaped the face of the landscape over the centuries and has had a profound effect upon the vegetation. During the past 50 years intensive farming practices have led to a rapid decline in wildlife habitats and associated species, but several key species of national importance still survive in the intensively farmed areas of west Lancashire and the Fylde. Man-made habitats, including areas of 'encapsulated' countryside, also feature prominently within the densely populated industrial areas of central and eastern Lancashire, and in the metropolitan areas of Greater Manchester and North Merseyside, where 3 to 4 million people live and work. Some of these habitats, including mill lodges, old clay pits and field ponds, support nationally important populations of Great Crested Newts, whilst the Rochdale canal has a population of Floating Water-plantain, a plant of European importance.

Many species of wildlife in Lancashire are close to their northern or southern limits in North West England, and some of these are also fast disappearing from the countryside due to the intensification of farming practices, neglect, and the effects of encroaching development. Concerted efforts are required to halt this decline and restore their populations and associated habitats.

Climate

Lancashire's climate is strongly influenced by the height of the land, especially the effect of hills on the prevailing south-westerly air flow from the Atlantic and Irish Sea. Coastal areas tend to have warm summers and mild winters with an annual rainfall of 900 to 1000 mm. Further inland it is warmer in summer and colder in winter, although still generally mild. On the exposed upland plateaux of the Pennine fells, however, the climate is much colder, with parts of Bowland receiving more than 2000 mm of rain per year while Rochdale and Oldham receive over 1400 mm. Snowfall is light in coastal areas but increases away from the sea, occasionally being severe in some upland areas. The recent series of milder winters herald the onset of global warming which will have profound effects on wildlife.

Map 3.
Important sites for wildlife in the Wildlife Trust Area.

Areas of exceptional wildlife and natural history interest are recognised internationally as:

Special Protection Areas (SPAs) – classified under the European Commission Conservation of Wild Birds Directive 1974 for protecting the habitats of rare, vulnerable and migratory bird species.

Special Areas of Conservation (SACs) – classified under the European Habitats Directive 1992 for protecting scarce and threatened habitats of European importance.

Ramsar Sites – designated under an International Convention by governments that met in Iran in 1971 for protecting 'Wetlands of International Importance' supporting migratory, rare, and threatened populations of birds and other animals.

Areas of wildlife interest recognised nationally are **Sites of Special Scientific Interest (SSSIs)** (some of which are recognised internationally as well).

(Nik Bruce)

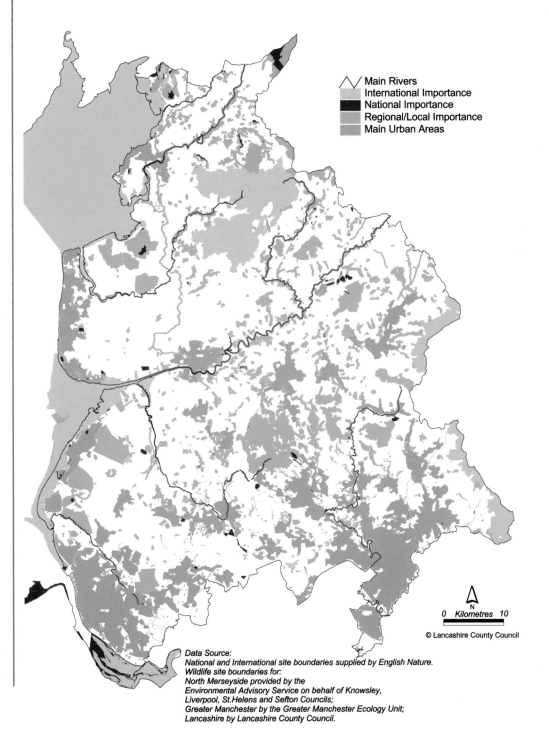

Main Rivers
International Importance
National Importance
Regional/Local Importance
Main Urban Areas

N

0   *Kilometres*   10

© Lancashire County Council

Data Source:
National and International site boundaries supplied by English Nature.
Wildlife site boundaries for:
North Merseyside provided by the
Environmental Advisory Service on behalf of Knowsley,
Liverpool, St.Helens and Sefton Councils;
Greater Manchester by the Greater Manchester Ecology Unit;
Lancashire by Lancashire County Council.

Geological history

Lancashire's landscape has had a complex history over the past 340
million years: at different periods it was covered by deep seas,
shallow tropical lagoons with coral atolls, large deltas and swamps,
deserts, ice sheets and lakes.

Limestones, shales and especially sandstone rocks formed 340 to
280 million years ago in the Carboniferous period tend to form the
high ground of north and east Lancashire, including the hills around
Morecambe Bay, Leck Fell and the Bowland fells, in addition to the
moorlands on Pendle Hill and in the Forests of Trawden and
Rossendale to the south-east. The main limestones were deposited
in shallow tropical seas. These occur around Morecambe Bay and in
the Ribble valley near Clitheroe, where they are quarried for hardcore
and for the manufacture of cement. At the same time limestones,
sandstones, calcareous shales and reef forming limestones were

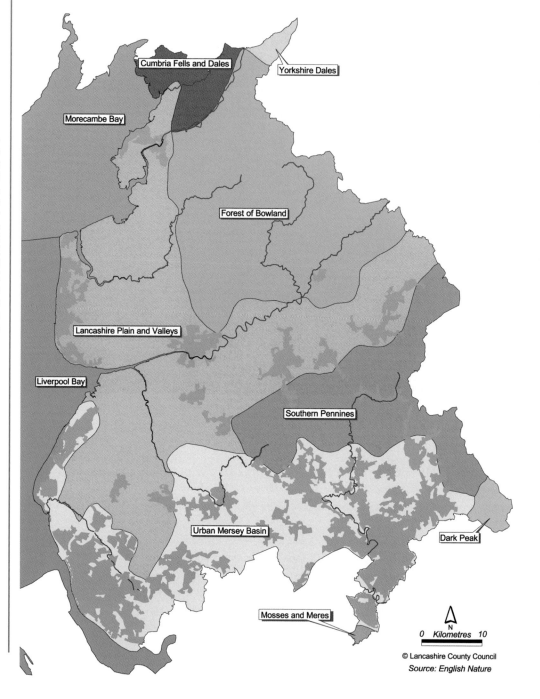

Map 4.
English Nature's Natural Areas in the Wildlife Trust Area.
These provide a framework for describing the landscape and ecological importance of wildlife habitats and species throughout the area, as well as targeting future biodiversity action priority work.
(Nik Bruce)

Cumbria Fells and Dales

Yorkshire Dales

Morecambe Bay

Forest of Bowland

Lancashire Plain and Valleys

Liverpool Bay

Southern Pennines

Urban Mersey Basin

Dark Peak

Mosses and Meres

N
0   Kilometres   10

© Lancashire County Council
Source: English Nature

Wildlife of Lancashire

deposited in layers in the Bowland area and the Ribble valley, and today the reef-forming limestones form the isolated rounded hills and rocky knolls around Clitheroe.

Millstone grits were then deposited above the limestones in a periodically subsiding delta of what is now the Ribble valley area. These rocks were later uplifted and today they outcrop in the high ground of the Bowland Fells and the Rossendale Moors. Different sequences of rocks were laid down in these two areas: in the north alternating beds of limestones, sandstones and shales predominate, whilst in the south massive beds of sandstones with alternating bands of gritstones, shales and coals are present. These latter occur today in the West Pennines and the Forests of Trawden and Rossendale, where a tropical delta and swamps once occurred resulting in the formation of coal. Coal Measures outcrop between Chorley and Skelmersdale, and along the Calder and

Box 1.1
Morecambe Bay Limestones (part of the Cumbria Fells and Dales Natural Area)

Rounded limestone hills clad in deciduous woodlands

Extensive limestone pavements with water worn clints and grikes

Mixed ash woodland with juniper scrub and Yew

Lowland calcareous grassland and herb rich neutral pastures with drystone walls

Calcareous lakes and reed beds (Hawes Water and Leighton Moss)

Remnant lowland raised bogs.

Wildlife to look out for include Dark-red Helleborine, Bird's-eye Primrose, Lancashire Whitebeam, High Brown Fritillary, Pearl-bordered Fritillary, Northern Brown Argus, Purse Web Spider, Bittern, Marsh Harrier, Bearded Tit, Otter, Common Dormouse.

Limestone pavement, wooded hills and Leighton Moss reed beds from Cringlebarrow Wood, Silverdale. *(Neil Robinson)*

Box 1.2 *Forest of Bowland Natural Area*

Extensive areas of blanket bog and heather moorland, managed for grouse

Purple Moor-grass and rushy pastures on upland fringes with breeding waders

Upland oak and mixed ash woodlands in cloughs and valleys, and conifer plantations

Fast-flowing streams and rivers including the Hindbum, Roeburn, Lune, Wyre, Brock, Calder, Ribble, and Hodder

Fragments of herb-rich hay meadows and small areas of upland limestone grassland

Wildlife to look out for include Cranberry, Cloudberry, Great Wood-rush, Emperor Moth, Red Grouse, Hen Harrier, Merlin, Pied Flycatcher, Wood Warbler, Redstart, Grey Wagtail, Dipper (*Cinclus cinclus*), Common Sandpiper (*Actitis hypoleucos*).

Darwen valleys where the industrial towns of Blackburn, Accrington and Colne developed. The remains of old mine workings survive here as a reminder of the once extensive coal industry which was used to power the cotton mills of East Lancashire. Coal was formed inter-bedded with sandstones, shales, mudstones and fireclays which formerly provided building stone and clay for the manufacture of bricks.

*Wildlife of
Lancashire*

Box 1.3 Leck Fell (part of the Yorkshire Dales Natural Area)

Limestone rock ledges, crevice and gorge vegetation

Upland calcareous grassland on limestone outcrops

Upland mixed ash woodlands in cloughs and valleys

Wet and dry upland heathland

Frequent springs and flushes

Wildlife to look out for include Wood Crane's-bill, Green Spleenwort, Merlin, Whinchat, Ring Ouzel.

The Permian and Triassic periods that followed, 280 to 200 million years ago, have rocks which were laid down in shallow seas and surrounding deserts. The oldest rocks from this period are calcareous mudstones, or marls, which occur north west of the Coal Measures towards Chorley. Sandstones extend north to Heysham, and include the younger silty red clays deposited in a shallow sea that went through phases of evaporation. This resulted in the creation of rock salt deposits upon which the chemical industry at Thornton Cleveleys and Preesall was founded.

During the Pleistocene and Recent periods, less than two million years ago, deposits of unconsolidated clay, sands and gravels were

9

Lancashire:
Setting the Scene

Box 1.4
Lancashire Plain and Valleys Natural Area

Arable farmland, field margins, ditches and boundary hedgerows

Isolated fragments of species-rich neutral grasslands

Small pockets of lowland heathland and acid grassland

Fragments of lowland raised bogs (mossland)

Reservoirs, lakes, canals and numerous small field ponds with associated swamp and fen

Rivers, streams and ditches

Semi-natural ancient woodland along river valleys and plantations

Wildlife to look out for include Bog-rosemary, Corn Marigold, Purple Ramping-fumitory, Dyer's Greenweed, Speckled Wood butterfly, Great Crested Newt, Bewick's Swan, Whooper Swan, Pink-footed Goose, Tree Sparrow, Corn Bunting, Daubenton's Bat, Water Vole.

Farmland and woodland, Samlesbury, near Preston. *(Jon Hickling)*

left by retreating glaciers, ice sheets, meltwater, and later, incursions by the sea across most of western Lancashire as the climate warmed. Glacial till (formerly called boulder clay) is spread across the central and western parts of Lancashire with areas of hummocky drumlins north of Lancaster, in the Fylde, and north east of Barnoldswick.

In the last 15,000 years since the end of the last Ice Age in North West England, frequent changes in sea level have caused unconsolidated sands and silts to be deposited along the Fylde and Sefton

Wildlife of Lancashire

Box 1.5 *Southern Pennines Natural Area*

Extensive areas of blanket bog on moorland tops

Impoverished areas of wet and dry upland heath

Large areas of upland acid grassland

Frequent springs and flushes

Fast flowing streams and rivers, canals and reservoirs

Some upland hay meadows in valleys

Upland oak and mixed ash woodlands in valleys

Wildlife to look out for include Common Butterwort, Round-leaved Crowfoot, Marsh Hawk's-beard, Northern Dart moth (*Xestia alpicola*), Red Grouse, Golden Plover, Dunlin, Merlin, Wood Warbler, Pied Flycatcher, Twite.

coast, the Ribble estuary and the River Douglas. Coarse-grained sands were deposited at approximately the same time, forming sandy beaches and dunes which are found today thinly and sporadically in beds throughout West Lancashire.

More recently wind blown sand deposits built up along the coasts of West Lancashire and the Fylde to form extensive sand dune systems. Only a remnant now remains due to agricultural and urban development, especially the holiday resorts of Southport, Lytham, St

11

Lancashire:
Setting the Scene

Moston Fairway Nature Reserve close to industrial area. (Mick Weston)

Annes, Blackpool, and Fleetwood. Elsewhere deposits of lowland peat formed in low lying, water-logged coastal areas, particularly across South and West Lancashire. Peat was also deposited on the high moorlands in the West Pennines, Trawden, Rossendale and the Forest of Bowland, where blanket bog developed in the damp climate. Streams and rivers had their drainage patterns changed at the end of the last Ice Age when they transported large amounts of sand and silt forming the alluvial terraces and flood plains of the rivers Wyre, Lune, Ribble, Darwen and Calder, which now support lush agricultural grassland.

Box 1.7 Morecambe Bay Natural Area

Ungrazed salt marsh on the Wyre estuary

Grazed salt marsh on the Lune estuary and Morecambe Bay

Occasional brackish pools on the landward side of sea walls

Extensive areas of inter-tidal sand and mudflat (the second largest in the United Kingdom)

Intertidal and subtidal boulders, cobble skears with mussel beds

Vegetated shingle

Rocky limestone sea cliffs

Wildlife to look out for include Yellow Horned-poppy, Sea-holly, Sea Beet, Honeycomb Worm,
Edible Cockles, Common Mussels, Shelduck, Wigeon, Knot, Bar-tailed Godwit, Dunlin,
Turnstone, Sanderling.

Lancashire:
Setting the Scene

Natural areas

This fascinating landscape history has been used by English Nature to divide up Lancashire, including Greater Manchester and North Merseyside, into nine 'Natural Areas', each with its distinctive geology, past land use, cultural history and wildlife habitats. (There are actually ten, but the Mosses and Meres has been omitted because it only includes a very small area which is almost entirely taken over by Manchester airport.) These nine Natural Areas are outlined in the accompanying boxed sections.

bottom Liverpool across the Mersey.
(Jon Hickling)

Box 1.8 Liverpool Bay Natural Area

Large expanses of salt marsh within the Ribble estuary (some of the most extensive in the country)

Extensive areas of inter-tidal sand and mudflat

Sand dunes, extensive along the Sefton coast, fragmented on the Fylde coast

Fragmented areas of soft coastal cliffs and impoverished rocky shore

Sedimentary shore and sea bed

Saline lagoons

Coastal waters

Wildlife to look out for include Marsh Helleborine, the dune variety of Narrow-lipped Helleborine, Sharp Club-rush (*Schoenoplectus pungens*), Round-leaved Wintergreen, polychaete worm *Ophelia bicornis*, Natterjack Toad, Sand Lizard, Red-throated Diver, Wigeon, Pintail, Common Scoter, Black-tailed Godwit, Knot, Little Gull, Red Squirrel, Harbour Porpoise, Bottle-nosed Dolphin.

Box 1.9 *Saddleworth Moor (part of the Dark Peak Natural Area)*

Dwarf shrub upland heath

Blanket bog and basin mire

Plantation, wet and semi-natural upland woodland

Neutral and wet grassland, and acid grassland with bracken

Flushes, streams, pools, ponds and reservoirs

Enclosed pasture

Gritstone edges, cloughs and boulder slopes

Wildlife to look out for include Cross-leaved Heath, Common Cottongrass, Hare's-tail Cottongrass, Crowberry, Labrador-tea (*Ledum palustre*), Brown Hare, Mountain Hare, Golden Plover, Curlew, Redshank, Merlin, Twite.

Dovestone Reservoir and Saddleworth Moor.
(Jason Smalley)

Further reading

English Nature (1997a). *Cumbria Fells and Dales – Natural Area Profile.* English Nature, Cumbria Team, Kendal.

English Nature (1997b). *Forest of Bowland – Natural Area Profile.* English Nature, North West Team, Wigan.

English Nature (1997c). *Morecambe Bay – Natural Area Profile.* English Nature, Cumbria Team, Kendal.

English Nature (1997d). *Southern Pennines – Natural Area Profile.* English Nature, Humber to Pennines Team, Wakefield.

English Nature (1997e). *Urban Mersey Basin – Natural Area Profile.* English Nature, North West Team, Wigan.

English Nature (1997f). *Yorkshire Dales – Natural Area Profile.* English Nature, Yorkshire Dales Team, Leyburn.

English Nature (1998a). *Lancashire Plain and Valleys – Natural Area Profile.* English Nature, North West Team, Wigan.

English Nature (1998b). *Cheshire Meres and Mosses – Natural Area Profile.* English Nature, West Midlands Team.

English Nature (1999). *Liverpool Bay – Natural Area Profile.* English Nature, North West Team, Wigan.

Lancashire:
Setting the Scene

Chapter 2

The Lancashire Naturalists

Eric Greenwood

Family portrait of
John Blackburne in
1741 from a
painting reproduced
in J. P. Ryland's *Hale
Hall* (1881). Anna
Blackburne is on the
far right of the
picture.
*(Reproduced by
permission of
Warrington Borough
Council – Library &
Information Services)*

The study and recording of wildlife has long held a fascination for Lancastrians. From the earliest days it involved all levels of society, but we can only speculate on what provided the impetus for such involvement.

During the second half of the eighteenth century there was a general rise in prosperity. This was the start of the industrial revolution with inventions giving rise to new industrial processes and the beginnings of the factory system. At the same time exciting new discoveries were being made on pioneering voyages of discovery. Strange exotic plants and animals were discovered and some of these were brought back live to our shores.

The early naturalists

In the Mersey basin area of Lancashire this spirit of discovery caused great excitement. Wealthy landowners and merchants like John Blackburne (1693–1786) at Orford Hall near Warrington invested in stove houses (heated greenhouses) for the cultivation of tropical plants. Inspired by their cultivation his daughter, Anna Blackburne (1740–93), became a well-known collector whose worldwide correspondents included Carl Linnaeus (1707–78), Thomas Pennant (1726–98) (who visited the Blackburnes in 1768), and Simon Pallas (1741–1811). Among her friends was J. R. Forster (1729–98), for a short time tutor at the non-conformist Warrington Academy and botanist on Captain Cook's second voyage of discovery. Unfortunately she did not publish and her collections were lost, although several plants and animals were named after her.

One of the visitors to Warrington Academy was a Liverpool non-conformist, William Roscoe (1753–1831). He was a market gardener's son but through his own endeavours became a banker and scholar. He was one of the most influential men in early nineteenth-century Liverpool, a founder member of the Liverpool Literary and Philosophical Society, and was instrumental in founding the Liverpool Botanic Garden and the Liverpool Royal Institution. Through Roscoe's efforts and those of the curators at the Botanic Garden, John (1764–1836) and his nephew Henry Shepherd (c. 1783–1858), an important collection at the Garden was built up, including an herbarium, the remains of which are at the Liverpool Museum, now part of National Museums Liverpool. Roscoe recruited John Shepherd on the recommendation of J. L. Phillips of Manchester. One of the most important of these collections was that gathered by J. R. Forster and his son on their voyage with Captain Cook. Henry Shepherd was also noteworthy for being one of the first to grow ferns from spores. In addition the herbarium contains plants of the Liverpool area collected by local botanists from the late eighteenth and early nineteenth centuries. Many of these early records were brought together in Hall's A *Flora of Liverpool* published in 1839.

The 13th Earl of Derby in 1837, aged 61, from a painting by William Derby.
(Reproduced by permission of The Right Hon. the Earl of Derby)

Another early naturalist or collector was the 13th Earl of Derby (1775–1851). Like Anna Blackburne, he is not known for original field-work, but as a collector who not only bought at auction but also financed others to collect for him. His collection consisted of both living and preserved specimens and his menagerie at Knowsley was particularly famous. His animal collections were used extensively by taxonomists for the descriptions of new species, often illustrated by paintings of living specimens in the menagerie. By the time he died his collection, especially of birds, was internationally important. However, he had taken care before his death to find a home for it, and on advice he bequeathed it to the City of Liverpool. This collection became the foundation of the Liverpool Museum and survives as an important component of the collections (Fisher 2002).

Artisan naturalists

The early exploration of Lancashire's wildlife is best known for the part played by artisan naturalists or by men in humble life. Little contemporary information about them remains, but some of their observations survive in the form of collections, archives and published records, although much has been lost. Towards the end of the nineteenth century accounts by near contemporaries were written

Box 2.1 *The Quakers*

Non-conformism, and especially the Religious Society of Friends (Quakers), took an important, but often unremarked, place in the initial discoveries and descriptions of British natural history. Founded by George Fox (1624–91) in the mid-seventeenth century, what was then the Lancashire–Westmorland– West Riding border country was one of the most important centres of the early Quaker movement. Motivated by a desire to seek the truth, meticulous record keeping and education were key parts of their practice. Fox and others were keenly interested in medicine and medicinal plants, and encouraged their study as part of the school curriculum.

Thomas Lawson (1630–91) was one of the first to widen his interest to wild plants generally, and whilst most of his records were from Cumbria some were from Lancashire. North West England remained a stronghold for the Quakers, and the Yealand–Kendal area in particular was associated with several important naturalists including John Dalton. Professor John Dalton FRS (1766–1844) was President of the Manchester Literary and Philosophical Society and was especially prominent in fostering interest in natural

history in Manchester and what was to become Manchester University. His herbarium of mainly Kendal plants was destroyed in World War 2. Others included the Backhouse family, who were to become prominent botanists and horticulturists in Yorkshire and Durham. Further afield in Wensleydale lived the Fothergills, one of whom, Dr John Fothergill FRS (1712–80), who as a boy lived for a while in Warrington, was a London botanist of international repute. More locally James Jenkinson (1738–1808), schoolmaster at Yealand Conyers, provided the first list of plants for the Silverdale area. The Crosfields (George senior, 1754–1820; George junior, 1785–1847) knew both Jenkinson and the Fothergills and provided further records for the Lancaster and Warrington areas of the county.

The Fothergills and Crosfields were in business and represented a rising middle class of entrepreneurs that owed its origins to a large group of small landowning or yeomen farmers of the seventeenth and eighteenth centuries. As the nineteenth century approached and with increasing mechanisation many yeomen diversified into other forms of business activity.

including *Where There's a Will There's a Way* by James Cash of Warrington (1839–1909) in 1873, *Manchester Walks and Wild Flowers* by Leo Grindon (1818–1904) in 1858 (and many other books subsequently), a series of articles in the *Manchester City News* by William Axon in 1874–5 and a long series of articles in the *Heywood Advertiser* by J. S. Rouse in and around 1910. Further recent research has confirmed their importance to natural history and their significance in social history (Percy 1991; Secord 1994a, 1994b).

One of the earliest references to these early naturalists is by Holt who lived at Walton, Liverpool, and wrote a report for the Board of Agriculture in 1795. He refers to the Oldham Society that was in existence as early as 1775. Similarly there was a society in Eccles in the 1770s. Perhaps the best contemporary account of the times of the artisan naturalists is the autobiography of Richard Buxton.

The occupations of artisan naturalists were diverse. Apart from Buxton they included George Crozier (1792–1847), a saddler of Eccleston and Manchester; John Dewhurst (c.1750s–1835), a Manchester fustian cutter; Edward Hobson (1782–1830), a Manchester grocer's assistant who compiled Musci Britannica in 1818 and 1822 (a bound set of mounted mosses arranged in systematic order); James Crowther (1768–1847), a Manchester porter and weaver; John Horsefield (1792–1854), a Prestwich handloom weaver and John Nowell (1802–67), a Todmorden handloom weaver. Many of these early naturalists seemed to have occupations based on handloom weaving and were located in south eastern Lancashire in and around Manchester. Overwhelmingly their interests were botanical, especially flowering plants, ferns, mosses and liverworts, but William Helme (1784–1834), a Preston cotton warper, was interested in entomology. On his death his collection was acquired by public subscription for the Preston Institution for the Diffusion of Knowledge but subsequently lost. A few others collected fossils, and later Manchester became an important centre for palaeontology, and the Manchester Museum contains important locally collected material.

While other towns and cities had artisan naturalists, the unique features of Lancashire naturalists were their numbers and organisation into societies. Quite small hamlets had their own groups and traditionally these groups or societies met on Sundays in their local 'pub'. Here they elected a President whose position was onerous. He was possibly the only one who could read and write and it was to him that the others turned to learn about their local flora. Typically at each meeting the President would name plants brought to him by members of the group and this would lead to a more general discussion. A subscription was levied and apart from liquor this was spent on acquiring books for a library. Later the idea of meeting on a Sunday in a 'pub' caused some problems and a few temperance societies were formed. In addition each society formed a collection. In 1795 Holt suggests the Oldham society had twenty books and a collection of 1500 specimens.

The Lancashire working men naturalists were known to eminent botanists of the day. The story of Sir James Edward Smith is well known: he came to Manchester in search of a rare plant and asked his porter if he could be directed to someone who might help him, only to find that the porter was James Crowther, one of the most knowledgeable artisan naturalists. Occasionally these contacts led a few artisan naturalists to become professional plant collectors. The most notable of these was George Caley (1770–1829), originally a stable boy from Craven, Yorkshire, but later a weaver, who was

Richard Buxton, aged 62, from a daguerreotype by J. B. Dancer (1812–87).
(Reproduced by permission of the National Gallery of Canada, Ottawa)

The Ring O' Bells, Middleton: a public house of the Manchester area where Middleton Botanical Society met in an upstairs room until the mid 1960s. The Society was founded prior to 1800, possibly as early as 1760. By the time the photograph was taken in 1969 only the rotting remains of mounted birds and Lepidoptera were found in the basement, and the last blank pages of the minute book were being used for bar orders. There was no sign of the library or herbarium. George Caley was a member and was greatly influenced by the Society. (*Eric Greenwood*)

introduced to the Manchester botanists through Dr William Withering – another of the great botanists of the time. In 1799 Sir Joseph Banks employed Caley as a collector and subsequently he had a botanical career mostly in Australia and the West Indies. John Bradbury (1768–1823) from Stalybridge was employed by Liverpool Botanic Garden in 1809–11 to explore parts of North America where he died in 1823.

It is intriguing to speculate how these men became interested in botany. No doubt their interest in wild plants grew out of their interest in cottage garden herbal remedies and growing flowers, vegetables and fruit for themselves. For example Joseph Evans (1803–74), a Tyldesley handloom weaver, and William Kent (1789–1850) of Chadderton were herbalists. The cultivation of a variety of flowers and fruit including auriculas, pinks and especially giant gooseberries followed by competitive shows is recorded. No doubt the publication of Linnaeus' *Species Plantarum* and subsequent English publications provided an enormous impetus to the study of wild plants.

It has been suggested that one of the reasons why these early artisan naturalists flourished is that handloom weavers and those in other occupations two hundred years ago were able to organise their own time. Some, e.g. John Horsefield, who pinned details of the classes and orders of the Linnean system to the post of his loom, were able to study whilst pursuing their job. However by the mid nineteenth century the factory system was fully established and cotton operatives and others were largely employees of mill owners. Now in addition to concepts of self-help there was a growing movement for providing education for artisans. Perhaps the short life of one of the last artisan natural history societies illustrates this change. The Banksian Society of Manchester, named after Sir Joseph Banks, was founded in 1829 but only survived until 1836. It was then reincarnated as a natural history society within the Manchester Mechanics Institution, one of a number of similar institutions providing evening classes established at that time. Many survived for several years but the Manchester Mechanics Institution folded in 1843.

The rising middle classes

Some of the working men's naturalist societies survived well into the twentieth century, but from the early nineteenth century literary, scientific and philosophical societies catering for a mainly middle class clientele were established in several towns and cities. Later, other societies covering a wide range of natural history interests,

Box 2.3 *The rising middle classes – a case study*

Once the industrial revolution had arrived a rising middle class of entrepreneurs developed the factory system employing thousands of workers. Two Lancashire botanists illustrate the importance of these people in natural history.

Samuel Simpson (1802–81) was descended from yeomen farmers of Furness and Bowland but his immediate antecedents were Lancaster merchants. He trained as a solicitor in Liverpool and there (presumably) met Henry Borron Fielding (1805–51), who was also training to be a solicitor. Simpson's brother Richard Salisbury (1810–88) was an Indian army officer and his sister Mary Maria (1804–95) was an artist who married Fielding. All were botanists. Samuel Simpson was prominent in botanical circles around 1840 but marriage and becoming a cleric marked an abrupt end to his botanical interests. His brother, however, made a number of collections in India. Meanwhile, Mary Maria supported her husband by painting the plants in the substantial collections he acquired. Until recently little was known of their botanical explorations in this country, but a collection of six volumes of paintings of British plants collected in the 1830s was acquired by the Bodleian Library, Oxford in 2000. Most of these illustrate Lancashire plants often found in the vicinity of their home near Lancaster. Their accuracy and accompanying text bear testimony to the diligence of two accomplished field botanists. Like Lord Derby and Anna Blackburne, Fielding purchased collections, but he also hired an assistant for a short time to help publish a work of his own (*Sertum Plantarum*, 1844). Fielding had always suffered from ill health and died in Lancaster in his mid forties. His will was brief: he left everything to his wife, who in accordance with his wishes gave his herbarium to the University of Oxford. This formed the foundation of the Fielding–Druce Herbarium, one of the most important collections in the British Isles. Later Mrs Fielding, who survived her husband until 1895, left a further legacy of money to Oxford University, some of which was to be invested to provide part of the stipend of a curator for ever.

The Fieldings never worked and spent the whole of their lives studying natural history. They were a quiet couple with a few but influential friends, including Professor William Hooker (1785–1865), later to become Sir William, Director of the Royal Botanic Gardens, Kew, with whom they stayed when he was at Glasgow University. Ill health is said to have precluded Fielding from working, but he had private means from his father, Henry Fielding (1757–1816) who was a self-made, wealthy calico printer at Catterall. His ancestors are difficult to trace but his wife's ancestors were wealthy Manchester cotton merchants and before that were landowners in the Warrington area. In the developing industrial revolution fortunes were lost as well as made and it is perhaps ironic that ill health prevented H. B. Fielding from taking any part in the family business. In 1831 this failed spectacularly leaving the rest of the family financially ruined but left H. B. Fielding free to enjoy the wealth his father had left him years earlier when he died in 1816.

admitting women (although women were present at some of the early societies' meetings they do not seem to have taken an active part) and more broadly based socially were established. Good examples of these were the Manchester Field Naturalists Society founded in 1860 and the Liverpool Naturalists Field Club founded at about the same time. These changes heralded an upsurge in natural history that, with ups and downs and changing fashions of interest, continues to the present day.

The evolution of the study of Lancashire natural history is a fascinating branch of both natural and social history in this country but the story from the middle of the nineteenth century to the present day has still to be researched.

Chapter 3

Sea Life

Jon Hickling and Pete Liptrot

Marine environments, by Jon Hickling

Most of the Lancashire coastline comprises soft sandy sediments; rocky outcrops or cliffs only occur at Heysham Head near Morecambe and Jenny Brown's Point at Silverdale, while there are also glacial boulder 'skears' off Morecambe. Most coastal land is built up and heavily developed including the industrial, holiday and residential areas of Liverpool, Southport, Lytham St Annes, Blackpool, Fleetwood and Morecambe. Inter-tidal areas of foreshore consist largely of the soft sediments of 5 major inter-linking estuarine systems, the Mersey, Ribble and Alt in the south within Liverpool Bay, and the Wyre and Lune in the north, which combine with the Kent and Leven in Cumbria to form the shallow enclosed embayment of Morecambe Bay.

Glacial cobbles ('skears') off Morecambe provide a hard substrate for seaweeds and marine animals.
(Jon Hickling)

Wildlife of Lancashire

Tidal ranges on the Lancashire coast are nearly 10 metres, and are only exceeded in Britain by the Severn estuary. As a consequence these estuaries support vast expanses of inter-tidal mud and sand flats, backed by areas of salt marsh, sand dune, especially along the Sefton coast, and vegetated shingle, mainly round Morecambe Bay. These large estuaries are of international importance for thousands of wildfowl and wading birds that arrive from their arctic breeding grounds for the winter months of the year. Others pass through during autumn and spring migrations to over-winter in Africa.

The tide and current regimes of both Liverpool Bay and Morecambe Bay result in both accreting and eroding shorelines, while the relatively warm shallow waters that are caressed by the Gulf Stream extend some 10 kilometres out to sea for much of the coast. These conditions have given rise to extensive areas of sandy foreshore and sea bed with low species diversity but with a high biomass of marine invertebrates. This forms a nursery area for flatfish, which in turn provides a rich source of food for thousands of wintering sea duck, notably Common Scoter off Blackpool and also diving birds, such as Cormorant, Red-breasted Merganser and Great Crested Grebe. Small numbers of Harbour Porpoises and Bottle-nosed Dolphins feast on this rich food source at certain times of the year, whilst Grey Seals are occasionally seen along the coast which supports a number of fisheries including cockles, mussels and shrimps.

23

Sea Life:
Marine environments

The Mersey Estuary

Due to the extensive modification of the Mersey, as a result of past industrial and port activities, the estuary supports a limited range of marine invertebrate communities. The greatest variety of communities occurs on the extensive sandy shores at its mouth. Here wave exposure and strong tidal streams and currents have lead to the development of mobile banks of inter-tidal sediments, the Mersey Narrows.

The uppermost shores of these Narrows are sands and gravels with populations of highly mobile burrowing shrimp-like amphipods and Common Lugworm (*Arenicola marina*). These sands grade into muddy mid to lower shore communities dominated by Baltic Tellin (*Macoma balthica*) and Lugworm. Areas where there are locally accelerated

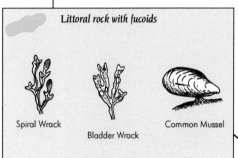

Littoral rock with fucoids

Spiral Wrack

Bladder Wrack

Common Mussel

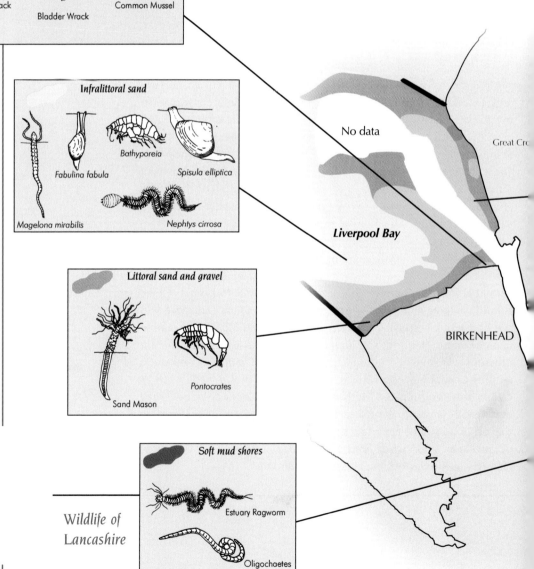

Infralittoral sand

Fabulina fabula

Bathyporeia

Spisula elliptica

Magelona mirabilis

Nephtys cirrosa

Littoral sand and gravel

Sand Mason

Pontocrates

Soft mud shores

Estuary Ragworm

Oligochaetes

No data

Great Cro

Liverpool Bay

BIRKENHEAD

Wildlife of Lancashire

tidal streams have dense aggregations of the Sand Mason worm (*Lanice conchilega*).

Upstream of Liverpool the estuary broadens out into extensive inter-tidal mudflats dominated by the Estuary Ragworm (*Hediste diversicolor*) and oligochaete worms, with abundant Baltic Tellin and the mud snail *Hydrobia ulvae* that provide an important source of food for thousands of wildfowl and wading birds, notably Pintail, Teal, Shelduck, Dunlin, Curlew and Redshank.

Away from the mouth of the estuary, into Liverpool Bay, shallow mobile sands support communities dominated by the polychaete worms *Nephtys cirrosa* and *Magelona mirabilis*, as well as bivalves including Venus shells (*Venus* spp.), trough shells (*Spisula elliptica*) and *Fabulina fabula*.

The Sand Mason builds its tube with spidery projections from grains of sand.
(Mark Woombs)

Diagram 1.
Marine sediments of the Mersey Estuary and Liverpool Bay, with key species in each habitat.
(Malcolm Edmunds and Lucy Day)

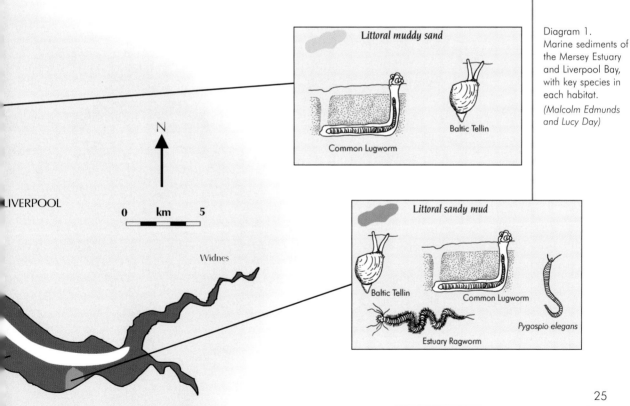

Sea Life:
The Mersey Estuary

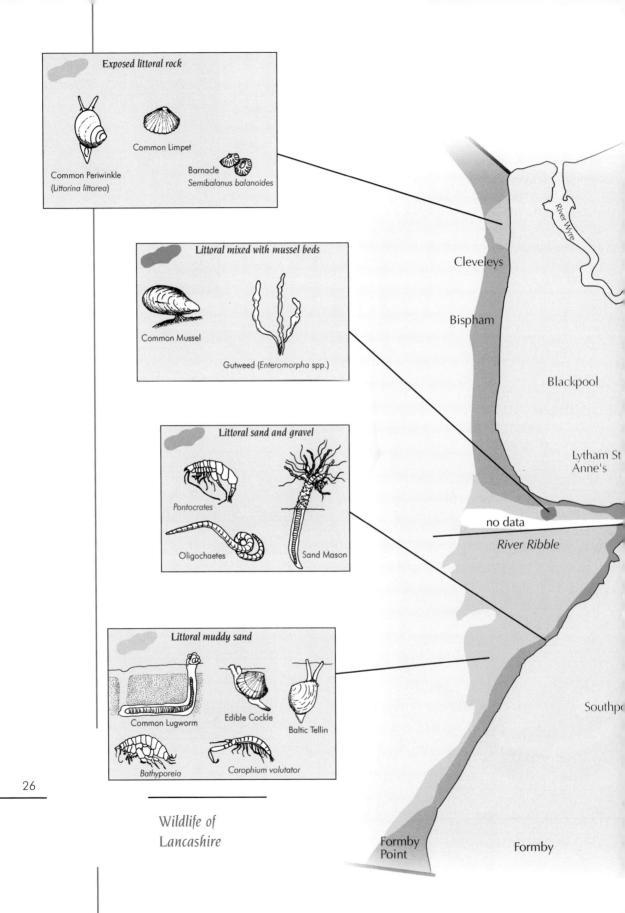

Exposed littoral rock

Common Periwinkle
(*Littorina littorea*)

Common Limpet

Barnacle
Semibalanus balanoides

Littoral mixed with mussel beds

Common Mussel

Gutweed (*Enteromorpha* spp.)

Littoral sand and gravel

Pontocrates

Oligochaetes

Sand Mason

Littoral muddy sand

Common Lugworm

Edible Cockle

Baltic Tellin

Bathyporeia

Corophium volutator

Cleveleys

Bispham

Blackpool

Lytham St
Anne's

no data

River Ribble

Southpo

River Wyre

Formby
Point

Formby

Wildlife of
Lancashire

The Ribble Estuary

The Ribble estuary, with its extensive sand flats and mudflats, is long and narrow, broadening out into a bay at its mouth where it is bounded by Salter's Bank in the north (beyond Lytham St Annes) and Formby Point in the south along the Sefton coast. Its sediments are characterised by fine silty sands at the mouth of the estuary, grading into a narrow zone of soft mud flats towards Preston. These are backed by some of the most extensive grazed salt marshes in the country.

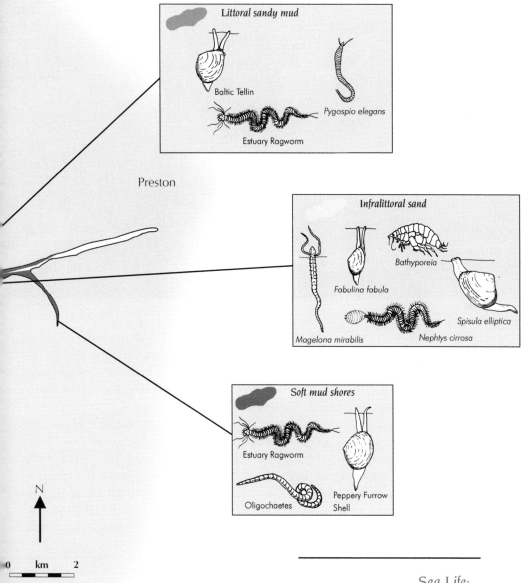

Diagram 2.
Marine sediments of the Ribble Estuary and Fylde coast with key species in each habitat.
(Malcolm Edmunds and Lucy Day)

27

Bed of Common Mussels.
(Mark Woombs)

Offshore from the mouth of the estuary, shallow sandy sediments are kept mobile by wave exposure and strong currents, so they only support a sparse invertebrate fauna. At the mouth of the estuary wave action and strong tides also keep the inter-tidal sediments mobile so that invertebrate communities in the upper to mid shore zone are dominated by burrowing amphipods and polychaetes, especially the Common Lugworm. Increased sediment stability on the lower shore allows the settlement of Edible Cockles (*Cerastoderma edule*), whilst dense beds of Sand Mason occur on the lowest part of the foreshore where it enters the main river channel. A very small glacial boulder scar just south of Lytham St Annes also supports a mixed community of Common Mussels (*Mytilus edulis*) and the barnacle *Semibalanus*

*Wildlife of
Lancashire*

balanoides. This habitat is rare on the Lancashire coast but is similar to the glacial boulder skears at Heysham and Morecambe further north where such features are commoner.

Further up the estuary sediment stability increases and the deposition of fine grained silts has led to the formation of mudflats supporting vast numbers of Estuary Ragworms, Baltic Tellin and the burrowing worm *Pygospio elegans*. These provide an important food for large numbers of wading birds including Oystercatcher, Sanderling, Dunlin, Black-tailed Godwit, Lapwing, Grey Plover, and Golden Plover. These also feed upon the extensive beds of cockles, while the abundant Baltic Tellin is the main food of wintering Knot, for which the Ribble and Alt are amongst the most important estuaries in North West England.

The Fylde Coast

The Fylde coast is one of the most extensively built up areas of the Lancashire coastline and is protected by hard coastal defences, except for areas of sand dune between the holiday centres of Lytham and Blackpool. As a consequence the inter-tidal sand is highly mobile due to scour and wave action caused by the reflective wave energy of the sea defences. Few marine invertebrates are able to colonise these mobile sediments except for burrowing shrimp-like amphipods and polychaete (bristle) worms such as *Scololepis squamata*. With increasing stability, however, a range of amphipods, bivalves and polychaetes are able to colonise the mid to lower foreshore, with the Rayed Trough Shell (*Mactra stultorum*) especially numerous towards Fleetwood where the shore is influenced by the waters of Morecambe Bay.

To the south, where the shore is influenced by the Ribble estuary, large numbers of Common Lugworm occur on the lowest part of the silty sand foreshore. These provide an important food for wintering Black-tailed Godwits for which the Ribble is one of the most important estuaries in Britain. Further north, on the glacial boulder scars off Cleveleys, there are sparse communities of barnacles, mussels and periwinkles (*Littorina* spp.).

Offshore communities are dominated by species associated with mobile sands, although richer invertebrate communities also occur in waters more than 5 metres deep with the polychaete catworm *Nephtys cirrosa* and burrowing amphipods. Sediments more than 10 metres deep off Fleetwood close to the Lune Deep are more sheltered from wave action and support sea anemones and several other burrowing polychaetes.

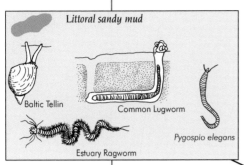

Morecambe Bay

Morecambe Bay is one of the largest areas of inter-tidal flats in Great Britain, second only to the Wash, at over 34,000 hectares. It is a large embayment, extending from Rossall Point near Fleetwood, in the south, to Walney Island in the north, and includes estuaries of the rivers Wyre, Keer and Lune in Lancashire, and the Kent and Leven as well as the southern part of the Walney Channel in Cumbria. The vast expanses of shallow inter-tidal sand and mudflat are backed by

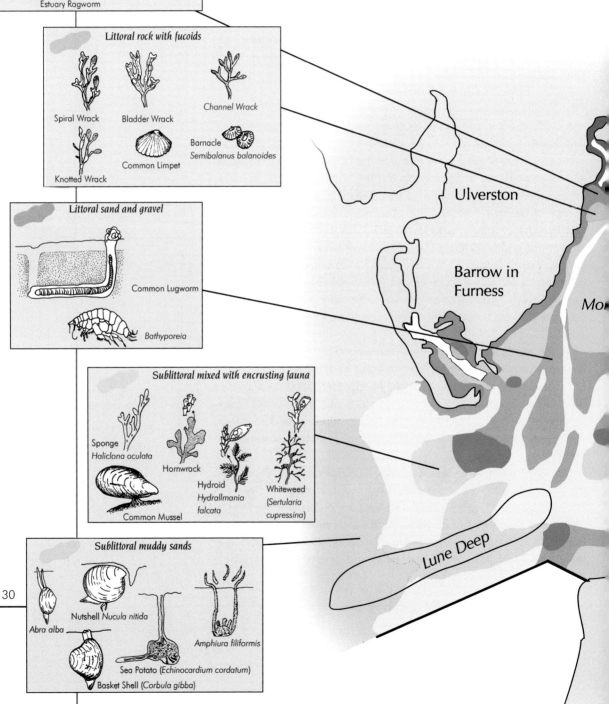

30

extensive areas of salt marsh, especially within the Wyre and Lune estuaries, in addition to areas of foreshore at Carnforth, Silverdale and Meathop. These features are of European importance. Small stretches of limestone cliffs also occur at Jenny Brown's Point in Silverdale, and Humphrey Head, in Cumbria, whilst the sandstone cliffs at Heysham Head also provide a rocky foreshore habitat not found elsewhere along the Lancashire coast.

Brown Shrimps are an important fishery in Morecambe Bay. *(Mark Woombs)*

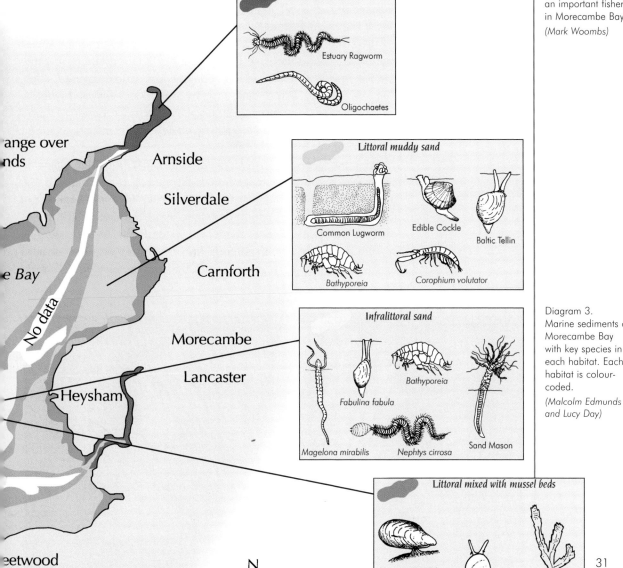

Diagram 3. Marine sediments of Morecambe Bay with key species in each habitat. Each habitat is colour-coded. *(Malcolm Edmunds and Lucy Day)*

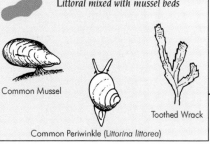

31

Burrowing brittle stars (this is probably *Amphiura brachiata*) project their five arms above the sand to collect food and oxygen.
(Mark Woombs)

The sponge *Haliclona oculata* with fan-worms lives offshore on rocks and firm sand.
(Mark Woombs)

The Bay is an important fishery for Brown Shrimp (*Crangon crangon*), Edible Cockle and Common Mussel, which occurs on extensive areas of glacial cobbles off Fleetwood, Heysham and Morecambe. These cobbles were deposited during the last Ice Age and are known locally as 'scars' or 'skears'. Off Morecambe there are also extensive reefs of the nationally scarce Honeycomb Worm (*Sabellaria alveolata*) colonising the scars.

At the entrance to Morecambe Bay, near Rossall Point, the extensive shallow sand flats are cut by an 80 metre deep channel known as the Lune Deep. This extends south westwards and is the main channel into which all of the Morecambe Bay rivers drain into the Irish Sea. It is a glacial feature (a kettle hole) believed to have been formed by the scouring action of water draining from beneath an ice sheet that once covered the Lake District and North Lancashire during the last Ice Age. It has steep glacial boulder and cobble covered sides that are heavily silted and support dense growths of hydroids (notably Seabeard, *Nemertesia antennina*) and bryozoan 'turves' of Hornwrack (*Flustra foliacea*) down to a maximum depth of 35 metres, together with a wealth of other invertebrates.

The Lune Deep contrasts markedly with the surrounding plains of sandy sediments, which range from highly mobile coarse sands at the mouth of the Bay to muds at the heads of the Wyre and Lune estuaries. On the upper parts of the shore along the open coast, wave exposed medium grained sands are extensively rippled. Here a sparse community of amphipods and the woodlouse-like isopod *Eurydice pulchra* may be present, with the polychaete worm *Scololepis*

Peacock Fan-worm (*Sabella pavonina*) collecting plankton that stick to its crown of tentacles.
(Mark Woombs)

squamata in areas where the sediments are more stable and retain water. With further decreases in wave exposure a wider range of polychaete worms may also be present often with high densities of Common Lugworm.

More stable sediments within the central part of the Bay are colonised by bivalve molluscs including the Banded Wedge Shell (*Donax vittatus*), Thin Tellin (*Angulus tenuis*) and Rayed Trough Shell, but much of the central area of the Bay is dominated by polychaete worms and Edible Cockles, and this supports an extensive cockle fishery.

The lower reaches of the estuaries and the shores of the Bay have reduced salinities and large numbers of Estuary Ragworm. Here the sandy mud supports communities characterised by Baltic Tellin, while in more muddy areas these are replaced by the Peppery Furrow Shell (*Scrobicularia plana*), and, within estuaries of lower salinity, by the mud shrimp *Corophium volutator*.

The small areas of rocky upper and mid shore at Heysham and Humphrey Head support 'splash zone' communities of yellow and grey lichens, with a sparse fringe of Channel Wrack (*Pelvetia canaliculata*) below a zone of the black lichen *Verrucaria manura* on the uppermost part of the foreshore. Below this a narrow band of Spiral Wrack (*Fucus spiralis*) may also be present followed by zones of barnacles (*Balanus* spp.) and Common Limpets (*Patella vulgata*) in exposed situations, or Bladder Wrack (*Fucus vesiculosus*) and Knotted Wrack (*Ascophyllum nodosum*) where it is sheltered.

Sea Life:
Morecambe Bay

Glacial boulder scars are more widespread in the intertidal zone of the Bay than are bedrock outcrops. These support substantial mid-shore growths of mussels that are harvested commercially. Such areas also provide a habitat for other species of marine invertebrates including Bread Crumb Sponge (*Halichondria panicea*), Common Shore Crab (*Carcinus maenus*) and sea anemones, as well as red seaweeds and Toothed Wrack (*Fucus serratus*) with their associated faunas.

At low water the extensive mussel beds and the surrounding inter-tidal sand and mud flats provide an important source of food for up to a quarter of a million wintering wildfowl and wading birds, including internationally important populations of Oystercatcher, Dunlin, Knot, Curlew, Redshank, Turnstone, Bar-tailed Godwit, and Grey Plover, as well as passage migrant Ringed Plover and Sanderling.

Sub-tidal communities of Morecambe Bay are rather uniform but they vary in response to depth and sediment mobility. Wave action in shallow water (<5 m), particularly during winter storms, prevents the development of stable invertebrate communities, and where fine sand is present communities tend to be dominated by Common Shore Crab, the swimming crab *Liocarcinus depurator* and the Common Hermit Crab (*Pagurus bernhardus*). In some areas Common Lugworms are also able to settle. In the outermost parts of the Bay, where sediments at depths greater than 5 m are more stable though still moved by tidal currents, sand amphipods, such as *Bathyporeia pelagica*, polychaete worms including *Magelona mirabilis* and *Nephtys* spp. and bivalves such as the Baltic Tellin and the Banded Wedge Shell are common. Deeper, more stable, sediments may support a rich invertebrate community dominated by brittlestars.

Swimming crab *Liocarcinus depurator* in defensive posture.
(Mark Woombs)

Wildlife of Lancashire

Box 3.4 *Plankton off the Lancashire coast*

There have been very few detailed studies of plankton off the coasts of Lancashire and Merseyside, but the species present are much the same as those found throughout the Irish Sea. The phytoplankton (microscopic plants) peak in abundance in April–May (the 'spring bloom'), but the typical summer decline is not as pronounced as in more open seas due to more regular mixing and enrichment of the shallow waters with nutrients. The spring bloom is dominated by diatoms, especially species of *Asterionella*, *Skeletonema* and *Navicula*, all of which require silica for their skeletons. In Morecambe Bay they often use up all the silicates in the water so that the summer plankton is dominated by other algae. *Phaeocystis pouchetii* is often dominant in May–June, but more serious are the occasional swarms of two dinoflagellates, *Gyrodinium aureolum* and the giant *Noctiluca scintillans*, both of which may colour the sea red ('red tides'). *Gyrodinium* can produce toxic chemicals causing mass mortalities of lugworms and other animals, but *Noctiluca* blooms appear not to be so toxic. The even more abundant ultra-microscopic nanoplankton have hardly been studied in our area.

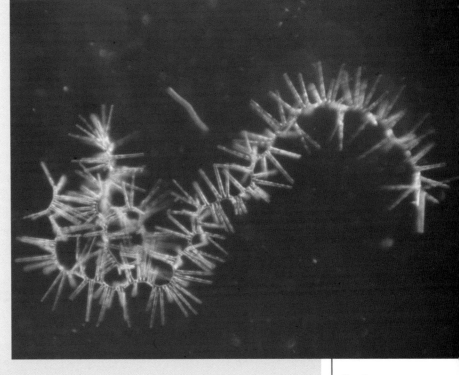

The diatom *Asterionella* forms chains of cells in the plankton.
(© OSF/ Photolibrary.com)

The planktonic animals (zooplankton) are mostly just visible to the naked eye (as is the dinoflagellate *Noctiluca*), but they are usually as transparent as glass so are easily overlooked by the casual observer. Almost every phylum of animals is represented in the zooplankton from single celled Protozoa to larval fish, and some of the most weird and wonderful animals in the world occur here including bizarrely shaped arrow-worms (*Sagitta*), elaborately lobed larvae of marine snails, and spiky larvae of crabs. All you need to study this fascinating world is a good microscope for the phytoplankton and a binocular microscope for the zooplankton, together with suitable mesh tow nets. These can be dragged through shallow water by hand or towed in a rowing boat to collect a rich sample.

Malcolm Edmunds

Fish from coastal waters, by Pete Liptrot

The eastern Irish Sea is an important spawning and nursery ground for commercially valuable species of fish, particularly flatfish. Often the spawning grounds are in a different location from the nursery areas, the inshore areas being particularly important for post-larval fish. Any visitor to a sandy shore during summer who takes time to investigate the shallow pools is likely to see postage-stamp sized young flatfish darting away from their feet. These are most likely to be Flounder (*Platichthys flesus*), although Sole (*Solea solea*), Plaice (*Pleuronectes platessa*) and others may also be encountered.

The fish fauna shows considerable variation depending on whether the sediment is hard or soft. In the sandy areas are large numbers of young flatfish and sand-eels (*Ammodytes* spp.), with seasonal influxes of Sprat (*Sprattus sprattus*), Herring (*Clupea harengus*), juvenile gadoids (cod family), Grey Mullet (*Mugil cephalus*) and Sea Bass (*Dicentrarchus labrax*). The infamous Greater and Lesser Weevers (*Trachinus draco* and *Echiichthys vipera*) can also be found here, partly buried in sand. In the shallow waters of Morecambe Bay the barefoot shrimper can easily tread on Lesser Weevers and receive a painful jab from their venomous spines. Muddy areas will be inhabited by various gobies, and particularly Sole (although these are suffering from overfishing). With Morecambe Bay being the second largest area of intertidal sand and mudflats in British waters, its extremely high density of invertebrates represents a huge foraging resource for both young and adult fish of many different species. Several species of pipefish (Syngnathidae) occur over sandy and muddy sediments, including the

Flounder resting among fan-worms.
(Mark Woombs)

Grey Mullet.
(Steve Colclough)

Wildlife of Lancashire

largest of the commoner species, the Greater Pipefish (*Syngnathus acus*). At least four of the gurnards (family Triglidae) may be found, usually over sand and gravel but also over intermediate habitats with rocky zones.

Rocky shores are scarce in our area, and the fish fauna here is dominated by small species such as wrasses (*Labrus* spp.), gobies (*Gobius* and *Pomatoschistus* spp.) and blennies (e.g. the Shanny, *Lipophrys pholis*), as well as young Pollack (*Pollachius pollachus*) and Saithe (or Coalfish, *Pollachius virens*). Rocky intertidal areas also support gobies and blennies adapted to surviving periods of low oxygen levels and high temperatures. During winter, the diversity of fish species on the shore is dramatically reduced, although the Butterfish (*Pholis gunnellus*) may still be encountered. Unusually for a littoral species, this fish spawns during January and February. The eggs are laid in a clump between stones or under discarded shells, and the clutch is then guarded by one or both parents until hatching.

The northern Irish Sea represents the most southerly area in the western UK for the Viviparous Blenny (*Zoarces viviparus*), which is found in rocky areas inshore but also over sediments in deeper water. Several species of pipefish may occasionally be found on rocky shores, particularly the Worm Pipefish (*Nerophis lumbriciformis*).

The majority of marine fish species found in the area produce planktonic eggs (but Herring, sandeels and many littoral species have benthic eggs), and the larvae also frequently have a long planktonic stage during the first few months of early life prior to metamorphosis. Spawning occurs during the first half of the year for many species, the most notable exception being the Irish Sea Herring stocks which spawn in the autumn on gravelly sediments where the higher oxygenation meets with their requirements. Morecambe Bay is important for Salmon and Sea Trout, which spawn in all rivers draining into the Bay.

top Shanny, Morecambe Bay.
(Mark Woombs)

above Fifteen-spined Stickleback (*Spinachia spinachia*) resting in seaweeds, Morecambe Bay.
(Mark Woombs)

37

Sea Life:
Fish from coastal waters

River estuaries are valuable habitats for young fish including Sprat, juvenile Herring and Flounder, the predators that feed on them such as Sea Bass, and also detritivores such as mullet. Estuarine fish are further discussed in Chapter 10.

Schooling pelagic fish such as Mackerel (*Scomber scombrus*) and Herring range widely within the region, migrating between summer feeding grounds, spawning grounds and over-wintering grounds, and occur more or less anywhere.

Among elasmobranchs both Dogfish and Nursehound (*Scyliorhinus canicula* and *S. stellaris*) are commonly seen by anglers. Smooth-hound (*Mustelus mustelus*) and Starry Smooth-hound (*M. asterias*) are caught occasionally, with the Starry being the commoner. The Spurdog (*Squalus acanthias*) has been intensively exploited, and is now rarely found. However, Tope (*Galeorhinus galeus*) numbers are increasing, and small- to medium-sized fish enter Morecambe Bay in early summer following the small schooling fish on which they feed. The absence of Common Skate (*Dipturus batis*) in the Irish Sea is due to extreme over-fishing (and the paucity of its preferred deep water habitats), while populations of Thornback Ray or Roker (*Raja clavata*) have declined steeply in recent decades through over-exploitation. Other species of ray, such as Blonde Ray and Spotted Ray (*Raja brachyura* and *R. montagui*), occur less frequently.

*Wildlife of
Lancashire*

Among our primitive jawless fish, the Hagfish (*Myxine glutinosa*) is usually found only over muddy sediment in deeper water. The Sea Lamprey (*Petromyzon marinus*) and the Lampern (*Lampetra fluviatilis*) are not uncommon in Morecambe Bay (see also Box 10.9). There is also an intriguing record of our third native lamprey, the normally freshwater Brook Lamprey (*Lampetra planeri*), where isotope analysis indicated that some time at least had been spent in the sea.

Further reading

Barnes, J. H., Robson, C. F., Kazonowska, S. S., Doody, J. P. and Davidson, N. C. (eds) (1996). *Coasts and seas of the United Kingdom. Region 13 Northern Irish Sea: Colwyn Bay to Stranraer, including the Isle of Man*. Joint Nature Conservation Committee, Peterborough.

Covey, R. (1998). *Marine Nature Conservation Review. Sector 11 Liverpool Bay and the Solway Firth: area summaries*. Joint Nature Conservation Committee (Coasts and seas of the United Kingdom, MNCR series), Peterborough.

Hayward, P., Nelson-Smith, A. and Shields, C. (1996). *Collins Pocket Guide to the Sea Shore of Britain and Europe*. Harper-Collins, London.

Mackie, A. S. Y. (1990). Offshore benthic communities of the Irish Sea. *The Irish Sea: an environmental Review. Part 1: nature conservation* (Ed. the Irish Sea Study Group), pp. 169–218. Liverpool University Press for Irish Sea Study Group, Liverpool.

Taylor, P. M., and Parker, J. G. (eds) (1993). *The coast of north Wales and north west England: an environmental appraisal*. Hamilton Oil Company, London.

Shoal of Bib
(*Trisopterus luscus*),
Morecambe Bay.
(*Mark Woombs*)

Chapter 4

Flowers and Ferns

Eric Greenwood

Wood on limestone pavement, Challan Hall Allotment.
(Peter Wakely, English Nature)

Introduction

The Lancashire village of Dunsop Bridge claims to be at the centre of the British Isles, and plants representative of most geographical regions in the British Isles can be found in Lancashire. Our islands have an oceanic climate dominated by the Atlantic Ocean and the North Atlantic Drift, but the influence of the enormous Eurasian land-mass on Lancashire is minimal so that it has hardly any plants typical of a continental climate. Similarly the county is neither far enough north nor has high enough mountains to have many arctic or arctic-alpine species.

The landscape is profoundly altered by human interference. Most of the lowland mosses (raised bogs) were drained in the nineteenth century and the remaining fragments are small and much modified. Grasslands are almost all rye-grass monocultures, but here and there fragments of traditionally managed neutral grasslands survive. Similarly many much modified ancient woodlands survive in the river valleys (cloughs), whilst in the Silverdale area a mosaic of woodland and limestone pavement provides a series of special habitats in that region.

The 'big' rivers of the county, the Mersey, Ribble, Lune and to a lesser extent the Wyre, have their own interesting plants, although little is left of the Mersey's natural flora. Other wetland habitats are extensive but apart from Hawes Water are almost all man-made. The large numbers of marl pits on the boulder clay

regions of the county are the oldest, followed by the canals. The huge
reed beds of Leighton Moss developed following the failure of the
pumping engine. Reservoirs and gravel pits were also built or dug and
now support their own interesting plant life.

This chapter covers both flowering plants and ferns. However many
people forget that flowering plants include grasses, sedges and
rushes; plants with small flowers lacking the showy parts typical of
garden plants. Similarly many trees lack showy flowers and are often
not thought of as flowering plants.

Ferns lack flowers altogether but the large leafy spore-bearing
plants are familiar. Amongst the ferns and related plants are the
horsetails and clubmosses. Whilst many horsetails are common and
one, Field Horsetail (*Equisetum arvense*) is a difficult garden weed to
eradicate once it is established, the clubmosses are less well known,
yet have particular associations with Lancashire (Box 4.1).

41

Flowers and Ferns:
Introduction

Box 4.1 *Clubmosses in Lancashire*

Looking superficially like large, sturdy mosses, clubmosses are actually more closely related to ferns. Generally with rather stiff stems and leaves, they are distinguished by their erect cone-bearing shoots up to 25 cm tall that are quite unlike those of mosses. They are the only surviving descendants of an ancient group of plants without flowers, the Lycopsida, which, 200 million years ago, included some of the major trees of the swamp forests of the Upper Carboniferous (Coal Measures) Period. Fossil remains of these trees have been found in rocks of this age in the south Lancashire coalfield.

Today there are only 7 species of clubmoss in Britain, of which 4 (formerly 5) grow in Lancashire. Whilst never very common, at one time they were widespread, with various species in the uplands, on the lowland mosslands, and the coastal dune slacks. A combination of habitat loss, moor-burning, air pollution, over-grazing and possibly over-collecting by botanists, brought about a sharp decline in Victorian times. With the exception of Lesser Clubmoss (*Selaginella selaginoides*), they were extinct in south Lancashire by about 1880, although Stag's-horn

Fir Clubmoss.
(Peter Jepson)

Clubmoss (*Lycopodium clavatum*) and Fir Clubmoss (*Huperzia selago*) survived in a decreasing number of places north of the Ribble. Marsh Clubmoss (*Lycopodiella inundatum*) and Alpine Clubmoss (*Diphasiastrum alpinum*), were always rare in our area, and appear to have been completely lost at about the same time.

Since the 1970s, however, the fortunes of some of these forgotten little plants have reversed, probably as a result of cleaner air. First, Stag's-horn Clubmoss, and in the last few years, both Alpine and Fir Clubmoss have returned to a few scattered locations across Lancashire and Greater Manchester. They have been found mostly in the environs of old quarries or on spoil, and could well turn up elsewhere on similar sites in the future.

Geoff Morries

Plant identification

Superficially flowering plants and ferns are easy to identify. For one thing they stay still and let you look at them in detail, and there are guides, most with coloured illustrations, to help with identification. Unfortunately whilst this will satisfy most people a more critical approach may result in the plant in front of you not quite fitting the description in the book.

Such an approach can lead to a fascinating exploration of the differences between closely similar species, discovering how these differences have arisen and perhaps finding out if these slightly different plants require different habitats. There is also the problem of introduced plants. Old introductions are usually described well but there are so many new ones that it is quite likely that the plant you discovered has not yet found its way into the popular guides. To identify plants critically you need specialist guides, e.g. Stace's *New Flora of the British Isles*, and specialist monographs, e.g. those published by the Botanical Society of the British Isles.

There are two major plant-breeding mechanisms that cause problems with plant identification.

(a) Some plants produce seed without fertilization of an egg by a process called apomixis. As a consequence slight changes in the genetic make-up of a plant tend to be perpetuated in subsequent generations giving rise to a number of different but similar micro-species. Lancashire has a number of these. The most important are dandelions (*Taraxacum* spp.), hawkweeds (*Hieracium* spp.) brambles (*Rubus* spp.), whitebeams (*Sorbus* spp.) and scaly male-ferns (*Dryopteris affinis* complex) (see Box 4.2).

Box 4.2 *Dandelions and whitebeams*

The dandelion, so colourful in waste places in late April and early May, is a most attractive plant and grows as well in North West England as perhaps anywhere in the world. However, it is not just one species: there are nearly 200 micro-species recognised from Lancashire including one named after the county where it was first found in the lanes bordering the Bowland fells, *Taraxacum lancastriense*. Many are localised and characteristic of particular habitats, e.g. small plants of Section *Erythrosperma* are characteristic of well-drained sandy soils of the sand dunes or limestone.

The 'interesting' whitebeams are mostly found on the limestones of Morecambe Bay. Some micro-species comprise a few scattered individuals, including another plant named after the county, *Sorbus lancastriensis*, the Lancashire Whitebeam, which is nationally rare (Wigginton 1999). *Sorbus rupicola* is a similar species but is more widespread on the limestones of northern England.

Flowers and Ferns:
Identification

(b) Hybrids are the offspring of two dissimilar individuals, usually different species or sub-species. These offspring may be fertile or sterile; indeed sterility is often a sign of hybridity.

Until quite recently, hybrids were not given any prominence in identification manuals, yet they are extremely common occurring in many groups. Where a hybrid is sterile and is clearly intermediate between the parents then it is easily spotted. Unfortunately if a sterile or fertile hybrid is rather similar to one of its parents, it is often wrongly identified (see Box 4.3).

Box 4.3 *Three examples of hybrids*

The oak is a tree familiar to most people. The Pedunculate Oak (*Quercus robur*) is the characteristic oak of lowland Britain whilst the Sessile Oak (*Q. petraea*) is found in the uplands of the north and west. Local floras indicate that both species are present in Lancashire. However the hybrid between the two (*Q. x rosacea*) is fertile, and the recording of the parents has been based on plants more or less like one or other of them. In reality most oaks are probably hybrids and evidence for this is clearly seen on careful examination of individual trees.

Other fertile hybrids are found with roses and willows. Roses have proved exceptionally difficult to identify, and it was not until publication of Graham and Primavesi's handbook in 1993 that the characteristics and limits of the species were defined.

The publication in 1984 of Meikle's *Willows and Poplars* provided a detailed account of numerous willow species and hybrids. In Lancashire hybrids involving Goat Willow (*Salix caprea*), Grey Willow (*Salix cinerea*) and Osier (*Salix viminalis*) can usually be found on any excursion. However some hybrids are particularly associated with Lancashire sand dunes. Some of these were pointed out in *Travis's Flora of South Lancashire* (Savidge *et al*. 1963) but more recently the rare *Salix x friesiana*, the hybrid between Creeping Willow (*Salix repens*) and Osier, has proved to be widespread, even frequent, both north and south of the Ribble. The rarer triple hybrid *Salix x angusensis*, involving Creeping Willow, Osier and Grey Willow, has also been found on both the Merseyside and Lytham St Annes dunes. The Lancashire coast is particularly noteworthy for these and other hybrids with Creeping Willow.

In town and city streets, waste ground, weedy gardens etc a few inconspicuous willowherbs can usually be found. They are not particularly attractive especially when they start shedding their seed. But look closely particularly if you can check them in your own garden. Over a number of years it is likely that the commonest species will be Broad-leaved Willowherb (*Epilobium montanum*) followed by the alien American Willowherb (*Epilobium ciliatum*). This latter species spread rapidly in Lancashire from the 1960s onwards. However these two species readily hybridise and the relative numbers of parents and hybrids varies greatly from year to year. Of course there may be other species that will make the situation more complex. The hybrids are largely sterile but even with a good hand lens it may be difficult to see that the small seeds are malformed.

Wildlife of Lancashire

The places plants grow

There are very few species that grow everywhere. As you tend your garden it may seem that the Daisy (*Bellis perennis*) in your lawn or Common Couch (*Elytrigia repens*) in the border must be able to thrive anywhere. Far from it. The weeds in your garden grow there because that is the habitat they like best. They thrive in the conditions you provide for them – if you let them. With this in mind the sorts of places and the kind of plants that grow in them will be described.

Flowers of the coast

Salt marshes

Lancashire has a long coastline with major estuaries extending inland for up to twenty miles. The estuaries of the Mersey, Ribble, Wyre and Lune together with the shores of Morecambe Bay form one of the largest salt marsh systems in Britain if not in Europe. Many of them have been extensively grazed for centuries giving rise to a short turf of Red Fescue (*Festuca rubra* ssp. *littoralis*). However closer examination of the marshes reveals a much more complex system, and where there is no grazing a rich and diverse flora develops.

Salt marshes are not static but change. Over the centuries the position of the coast has changed, but salt marshes have always been somewhere though not necessarily where they are today. On almost any marsh former levels can be seen above existing developing marshes, whilst on Morecambe Bay there seems to be a 70–100 year oscillation of erosion on one side of the Bay and accretion on the other. At the moment there is erosion on the Silverdale side after a long period of accretion.

Salt marshes typically start on mudflats with the growth of eelgrasses (*Zostera* spp.). The native Eelgrass, *Zostera marina*, became extinct in Lancashire about 150 years ago, but it is still found on the Furness shores of Morecambe Bay, and perhaps long-term pollution or too muddy waters has caused its extinction elsewhere.

Next come the glassworts (*Salicornia* spp.), a culinary delicacy for which Lancashire is famous. The glassworts comprise a puzzling range of species that can be identified best in late September and October when they turn into a variety of colours.

Slightly higher up, but still part of the lower marsh, Common Cordgrass (*Spartina anglica*) usually covers large areas. It arose by a spontaneous doubling of the number of chromosomes in the sterile hybrid between European Small Cord-grass (*Spartina maritima*) and

left A typical Lancashire hybrid oak: the stalkless acorns are typical of the Sessile Oak, but the leaf shape shows characters of the Pedunculate Oak.
(Peter Jepson)

Salt marsh creek at Barnaby Sands, with Sea-purslane lining the banks.
(Jon Hickling)

Glasswort colonising mud at Marshside.
(Phil Smith)

North American Smooth Cord-grass (*Spartina alterniflora*) to form a new vigorous and highly fertile species. It was first recorded in Lancashire from the Ribble estuary where it was planted in 1932 (Hubbard and Stebbings 1967).

In ungrazed marshes the middle zones are a riot of colour from early summer (Box 4.4), but lining the creeks there is often a zone of the greyish Sea-purslane (*Atriplex portulacoides*).

Common Cord-
grass growing at
Marshside.
(Phil Smith)

Common Sea-
lavender is often
abundant on salt
marshes.
(Phil Smith)

47

Higher up the marsh, where inundation by the tide does not occur every day, other communities develop. Some may be dominated by Saltmarsh Rush (*Juncus gerardii*), Sea Rush (*Juncus maritimus*) and occasionally in the north, by a northern species, Saltmarsh Flat-sedge (*Blysmus rufus*). Some parts of the marsh may be dominated by couch grasses, but these are often difficult to identify. Both Common Couch and its hybrid with Sea Couch (*Elytrigia atherica*) are common, but Sea Couch is very rare and in Lancashire is probably a plant of coastal cliffs and sandy ground near the sea although it has not been seen recently.

Another plant at the top of some Lancashire salt marshes is the pleasantly aromatic Sea Wormwood (*Serephidium maritimum*), which forms conspicuous silver-grey patches, especially on parts of the Wyre estuary.

Where fresh water stands for a time, reed beds develop forming fens, with Common Reed (*Phragmites australis*) dominant and Grey Club-rush (*Schoenoplectus tabernaemontani*) and Blunt-flowered Rush (*Juncus subnodulosus*) sometimes present. Recently, with improved management of the salt marshes on the north bank of the Ribble estuary at Warton, plant communities dominated by Reed Sweet-grass (*Glyceria maxima*) and Divided Sedge (*Carex divisa*) have developed. Reed Sweet-grass is common in fens and by canals in South Lancashire but rare further north. The discovery of Divided Sedge in 2003 is not only an extension of its range northwards but the re-discovery of a species thought to be extinct in Lancashire. It was last seen on the south bank of the Ribble estuary at Marshside in 1954 (Box 4.5).

Box 4.5 *Typical plants of freshwater irrigated salt marshes*

Wherever fresh water percolates through the marsh there are flush communities with Brookweed (*Samolus valerandi*), Few-flowered Spike-rush and Slender Spike-rush (*Eleocharis quiqueflora* and *E. uniglumis*), scarce Lesser Centaury and Seaside Centaury (*Centaurium pulchellum* and *C. littorale*), Parsley Water-dropwort (*Oenanthe lachenalii*), Strawberry Clover (*Trifolium fragiferum*), Marsh Arrowgrass (*Triglochin palustre*) and forget-me-nots (*Myosotis* spp.).

*Wildlife of
Lancashire*

Spear-leaved
Orache.
(Phil Smith)

A feature of the topmost zones of Lancashire salt marshes is an abundance of oraches. Spear-leaved Orache (A*triplex prostrata*) is the most frequent, but where the highest zones merge into fen the scarce Northern Long-stalked Orache (A*triplex longipes*) is found, although its hybrid with *A. prostrata* is much commoner. The attractive pink and white flowered subspecies of Hedge Bindweed (*Calystegia sepium* ssp. *roseata*) also occurs occasionally at these highest levels in the reed swamp or lining brackish ditches and banks. This plant has only been found on the western side of the British Isles and should not be confused with the closely similar garden escape *Calystegia sepium* ssp. *sepium* f. *colorata*. Common Meadow-rue (*Thalictrum flavum*) and Wild Celery (A*pium graveolens*) also favour brackish conditions.

All Lancashire salt marshes are truncated because for centuries humans have erected embankments to cut off the top zones and reclaim them for agriculture; this process continues today. If this had not happened the topmost zones dominated by Common Reed would have formed extensive fens merging into inland raised bogs. In places the salt marsh would have developed directly into bog. Unfortunately there are no records of the plants that grew in these places before they were reclaimed.

49

Sand dune and salt marsh transition zones

Extensive sand dunes once stretched from Liverpool to beyond Southport and from Lytham to Blackpool, with further fragments at Fleetwood, round the estuary of the Lune and into Morecambe Bay. Today, although much reduced, the sand dunes form a substantial area in Sefton whilst large fragments occur at Lytham St Annes. Smaller fragments occur elsewhere including some fine fore dunes at Fleetwood.

Like the salt marshes the extent and position of the dunes has shifted over the centuries. Currently erosion occurs at Formby Point but elsewhere, where allowed by humans, accretion occurs. In places the shore is becoming increasingly muddy with the development of salt marsh rather than sand dune, and interesting transition zones develop, especially if they are irrigated by fresh water. Transition zones are found both north and south of the Ribble estuary but there is an exceptionally fine example at Birkdale. Plants typical of sand dunes and salt marshes are found, but some interesting species seem to favour these habitats including Grass-leaved Orache (*Atriplex littoralis*), Reflexed Saltmarsh-grass (*Puccinellia distans*), Hard-grass (*Parapholis strigosa*), Long-bracted Sedge (*Carex extensa*) and Lesser Centaury.

Yellow Horned-poppy spreading on shingle at Morecambe Bay.
(Jon Hickling)

Mobile dunes at Ravenmeols covered in Marram.
(Phil Smith)

Shingle beaches

Formerly the only well-developed shingle beaches in Lancashire were found between the clay cliffs at North Shore, Blackpool and the sand dunes at Fleetwood. These were lost to sea defences so that today only transitional zones to salt marshes or sand dunes occur, although at Hightown coastal erosion of tipped material has produced a shingle zone of water worn house bricks and other builder's rubble. In these rather stable situations some striking plants are found. Perhaps the most attractive is Yellow Horned-poppy (*Glaucium flavum*) with its large bright-yellow flowers, grey-green foliage and strikingly long seed pods. Almost as striking is Sea-kale (*Crambe maritima*) with its large fleshy grey-green leaves and large inflorescences of white flowers. Other plants include Rock Samphire (*Crithmum maritimum*), more usually found on sea walls and cliffs, Sea Beet (*Beta vulgaris* ssp. *maritima*), Spear-leaved Orache and its close relative Babington's Orache (*Atriplex glabriuscula*). Perhaps the commonest plant of all is the diminutive yellow-green Sea Sandwort (*Honckenya peploides*) that often covers extensive areas in a zone at the top of a shingle foreshore.

Sand dunes

The calcareous sand dunes of the Lancashire coast provide a wide range of habitats, which enables a large number of species of plants and animals to survive on them. Smith (2000) in his studies of the dunes south of the Ribble recorded about 850 species, subspecies and hybrids of flowering plants and ferns, although this total includes

Sea-holly colonising
mobile dunes.
(Phil Smith)

a large number of plants either accidentally or deliberately introduced by humans.

Debris left by the highest spring tides traps wind blown sand and here the first colonizers take hold, most noticeably the mauve flowers of Sea Rocket (*Cakile maritimum*). Less showy species include the spiny Prickly Saltwort (*Salsola kali*), various oraches including the local Frosted Orache (*Atriplex laciniata*) and Babington's Orache, and occasionally the northern Ray's Knotgrass (*Polygonum oxyspermum* ssp. *raii*).

Usually the strand line is colonized by Sand Couch (*Elytrigia juncea*), which, together with the other plants, is important for trapping and binding more sand to form low fore or embryo dunes. Another vigorous and tougher grass that can grow in this harsh environment is Lyme-grass (*Leymus arenarius*).

Once the dunes have been colonized by Marram (*Ammophila arenaria*) they grow in height, as this plant likes nothing more than to be buried in sand through which it then grows vigorously. These larger mobile dunes are covered by Marram but with plenty of bare sand showing between the tussocks. They provide a habitat for a few other plants that can survive the extreme conditions. 'Weedy' species including Groundsel (*Senecio vulgaris*), Creeping Thistle (*Cirsium arvense*) and Common Ragwort (*Senecio jacobaea*) are more familiar as weeds in gardens, farms and on waste ground, but are also especially characteristic of this habitat (see also Box 4.6).

Box 4.6 *Plants of mobile dunes*

Characteristic species include blue-green Sea Spurge (*Euphorbia paralias*), its close relative Portland Spurge (*Euphorbia portlandica*), which generally prefers older dunes, and Sea-holly (*Eryngium maritimum*) with its blue-grey foliage and blue flowers. As the dunes get older and less mobile a host of other species appear including Sea Bindweed (*Calystegia soldanella*), now confined to only a few sites having suffered badly through the building of sea walls and the development of coastal towns. Still abundant in places is Sea Radish (*Raphanus maritimus* ssp. *maritimus*) and much more locally Isle of Man Cabbage (*Coincya monensis* ssp. *monensis*) – a speciality of the Lancashire coast. This subspecies is confined to Britain. In Lancashire it grows in a few sites on both sides of the Ribble but can appear in large numbers, especially at Lytham St Annes, and individual plants can reach up to 2m across. It is an annual or short-lived perennial, but unless conditions are just right a large colony can quickly disappear.

Sea Bindweed.
(Phil Smith)

*Wildlife of
Lancashire*

Older dunes become more stable and grasses such as Red Fescue and Spreading Meadow-grass (*Poa humilis*) take hold whilst Marram becomes less robust and less frequent. These more stable conditions provide a suitable habitat for a range of both common and uncommon species, and they are full of colour during spring and summer (Box 4.7).

The dune subspecies of Creeping Willow (*Salix repens* ssp. *argentea*) often clothes the dunes and the damper slacks and wet hollows. With it grow the exceptionally rare greenish flowered dune variety of the Narrow-lipped Helleborine (*Epipactis leptochila* var. *dunensis*) and its close relative the Green-flowered Helleborine (*Epipactis phyllanthes*). Other plants of older dunes include Burnet Rose (*Rosa pimpinellifolia*), Polypody (*Polypodium vulgare*) and Common Milkwort (*Polygala vulgare*), which north of the Ribble occurs in a white flowered subspecies (*P. vulgare* ssp. *collina*).

Bare areas in the older dunes form inhospitable habitats for plants, especially in the summer when the surface becomes very hot and dry. However during the wet winter months there is sufficient warmth and moisture for a range of winter annuals to grow (Box 4.8). These flower

left The dune variety of the Narrow-lipped Helleborine. *(Phil Smith)*

right Green-flowered Helleborine. *(Malcolm Edmunds)*

Flowers and Ferns:
Sand dunes

Box 4.7 Plants of older dunes

a. Yellow flowers

Common yellow flowers include species of dandelion in spring, followed by Cat's-ear (*Hypochaeris radicata*), Smooth Hawk's-beard (*Crepis capillaris*), Lesser Hawkbit (*Leontodon saxatilis*), Common Bird's-foot-trefoil (*Lotus corniculatus*), Lady's Bedstraw (*Galium verum*), Hop Trefoil (*Trifolium campestre*), Lesser Trefoil (*Trifolium dubium*), Biting Stonecrop (*Sedum acre*) and Kidney Vetch (*Anthyllis vulneraria*). Yellow-wort (*Blackstonia perfoliata*), a blue-grey plant with yellow flowers, is a southern species and apart from casual occurrences reaches its northernmost limits in western England on the Lancashire coast.

b. Blue flowers

Early in the year Heath Dog-violet (*Viola canina*) flowers, and whilst it may be plentiful, in Lancashire it is now confined to the sand dunes. Other blue flowers include Viper's-bugloss (*Echium vulgare*), Hound's-tongue (*Cynoglossum officinale*) and Wild Pansy (*Viola tricolor*) with its subspecies *curtisii* that is confined to the sand dunes and often has yellow or yellow and blue flowers. Also found occasionally on older dunes are Field and Autumn Gentians (*Gentianella campestre* and *G. amarella*). Especially characteristic of older dunes is the Dewberry (*Rubus caesius*), which has white flowers like other brambles, but is perhaps best known for its bluish waxy looking fruits.

c. Pink flowers

Pink flowers are represented by Common Restharrow (*Ononis repens*) with its characteristically sticky leaves, Common Centaury (*Centaurium erythraea*), Hare's-foot Clover (*Trifolium arvense*), Stork's-bill (*Erodium cicutarium*) and the much rarer Sticky Stork's-bill (*Erodium lebelii*). At the base of fixed dunes Common Spotted-orchid (*Dactylorhiza fuchsii*), Pyramidal Orchid (*Anacamptis pyramidalis*) and Bee Orchid (*Ophrys apifera*) can be found.

above
Wild Pansy.
(Phil Smith)

top right
Kidney Vetch on mature dunes.
(Phil Smith)

centre right
Common Restharrow.
(Phil Smith)

below right
Dewberry showing the characteristic bluish or waxy bloom to the ripe fruits.
(Phil Smith)

Wildlife of Lancashire

early in the year and survive the summer as seeds before germinating in the autumn. Early Sand-grass (*Mibora minima*) was recently added to the list of Sefton coast dune annuals. It is a tiny plant flowering in February and March so although it was only found in one locality it may occur elsewhere, and searching for it in the winter may be rewarding. It is a nationally rare species of Western and South Western Europe.

Box 4.8 *Dune annuals*

These include Early Hair-grass (*Aira praecox*), Thyme-leaved Sandwort (*Arenaria serpyllifolia*), Hairy Bitter-cress (*Cardamine hirsuta*), Sea Mouse-ear and Little Mouse-ear (*Cerastium diffusum and C. semidecandrum*), Lesser Chickweed (*Stellaria pallida*), Common Whitlowgrass and Glabrous Whitlowgrass (*Erophila verna and E. glabrescens*), Early Forget-me-not (*Myosotis ramosissima*), Sand Cat's-tail (*Phleum arenarium*), Rue-leaved Saxifrage (*Saxifraga tridactylites*), Common Cornsalad (*Valerianella locusta*), Spring Vetch (*Vicia lathyroides*) and Dune Fescue (*Vulpia fasciculata*).

Common
Whitlowgrass.
(Phil Smith)

The oldest fixed dunes are not as floristically rich as the younger ones because rain has washed away many nutrients, especially lime, making the sandy soil more acidic. Nevertheless these conditions are suitable for grasses, e.g. Common Bent (*Agrostis capillaris*), Sheep's Fescue (*Festuca ovina*), Sweet Vernal-grass (*Anthoxanthum odoratum*) (that when crushed smells of new-mown hay) and occasionally Crested Hair-grass (*Koeleria macrantha*). South of the Ribble Grey Hair-grass (*Corynephorus canescens*), another nationally rare species more typical of East Anglia, is found. Other plants on these older dunes include Hare-bell (*Campanula rotundifolia*) and Wild Thyme (*Thymus polytrichus*).

In between the hills of the dunes are hollows or dune slacks. The wettest of these retain water throughout the year whilst others are always dry. Slacks provide fertile habitats and support the greatest number of species on the dune systems including some that are especially noteworthy.

Flowers and Ferns:
Sand dunes

Some of the slacks closest to the sea are brackish and contain plants more usually associated with salt marshes, e.g. Sea Aster, Sea-milkwort (*Glaux maritima*), Saltmarsh Rush, Sea Rush, Sea Plantain, Sea Club-rush and Sea Arrowgrass. Usually, however, the flora is typical of freshwater communities with Yellow Iris (*Iris pseudacorus*), Bulrush (*Typha latifolia*) and Grey Club-rush.

Many plants are much more localised with Lesser Water-plantain (*Baldellia ranunculoides*), Shoreweed (*Littorella uniflora*) and Various-leaved Pondweed (*Potamogeton gramineus*), none of which occur on the Fylde coast dunes. Unless conditions are just right these species soon disappear but south of the Ribble they responded well to the excavation of ponds and scrapes formed over the last 20–30 years.

The rare and inconspicuous northern Baltic Rush (*Juncus balticus*) colonizes slacks near the sea and has hybridised with both Soft-rush (*Juncus effusus*) and Hard Rush (*Juncus inflexus*). These rushes have had mixed fortunes. Baltic Rush has fluctuated in abundance south of the Ribble but with developing dunes at Birkdale it is currently flourishing. North of the Ribble it became extinct in the 1950s with the building of a tennis court on its only known site. The hybrids were discovered in the 1960s but that with Soft-rush was lost in the wild (it remains in cultivation) whilst the hybrid with Hard Rush flourishes on both sides of the river. Both hybrids are vigorous and favour the wettest slacks.

Many of the slacks are carpeted with Creeping Willow. Associated with it is Yellow Bird's-nest (*Monotropa hypopitys*), which is often hidden under the willow. This biscuit coloured plant with scale-like leaves contains no chlorophyll so does not require sunlight; it obtains all its nutrients from the breakdown of organic matter in the soil with the help of a fungus in its roots. Also associated with Creeping Willow is Round-leaved Wintergreen (*Pyrola rotundifolia* ssp. *maritima*), a coastal subspecies particularly associated with sand dunes from Devon to Cumbria.

top Dune slack at Birkdale.
(*Phil Smith*)

above Hybrid between Baltic Rush and Hard Rush at Lytham St Annes Local Nature Reserve.
(*Phil Smith*)

Yellow Bird's-nest.
(*Phil Smith*)

Wildlife of Lancashire

far left Round-leaved Wintergreen.
(Phil Smith)

left Northern Marsh-orchid.
(Malcolm Edmunds)

Where the slack vegetation is not dominated by Creeping Willow a range of interesting plants may be found (see Box 4.9), perhaps the most memorable being the abundance of orchids. The brick-red flowers of Early Marsh-orchid (*Dactylorhiza incarnata* ssp. *coccinea*) and the near white flowers of Marsh Helleborine (*Epipactis palustris*) are characteristic of dune slacks. Both the Southern and Northern Marsh-orchids (*Dactylorhiza praetermissa* and *Dactylorhiza purpurella*) occur more rarely, whilst the Fragrant Orchid (*Gymnadenia conopsea*) is found in only one locality.

Landward of the main dune system sand was blown inland forming an interesting area of dune heath and shallow lakes before the raised bogs or mosses of lowland Lancashire were reached. Today the lakes have long since been drained and no record was kept of their flora, while many of the dune heaths were converted into golf courses. Fragments survive within the golf courses but the largest occurs in and around Woodvale Aerodrome at Formby. The heaths are dominated by Heather (*Calluna vulgaris*) and Gorse (*Ulex europaeus*), whilst grasses typical of these areas include Sheep's-fescue and its close relative, Fine-leaved Sheep's-fescue (*Festuca filiformis*), Yorkshire-fog (*Holcus lanatus*), Wavy Hair-grass (*Deschampsia flexuosa*), Heath-grass (*Danthonia decumbens*) and Mat-grass (*Nardus stricta*). Other plants found here include woodrushes (*Luzula* spp.), Sheep's Sorrel (*Rumex acetosella*), Heath Rush (*Juncus squarrosus*), and much more rarely Bird's-foot (*Ornithopus perpusillus*), Crowberry (*Empetrum nigrum*) and Royal Fern (*Osmunda regalis*) often in a diminutive form.

Early Marsh-orchid.
(Phil Smith)

57

Flowers and Ferns:
Sand dunes

Royal Fern.
(Malcolm Edmunds)

Bog Pimpernel.
(Phil Smith)

Box 4.9 *Some dune slack plants*

Low growing plants include Few-flowered Spike-rush, creeping Variegated Horsetail (*Equisetum variegatum*), pink flowered Bog Pimpernel (*Anagallis tenella*), the nationally scarce pink flowered Seaside Centaury and its close relative, Lesser Centaury, which has become especially abundant on the newly formed slack on Birkdale beach. Other interesting plants are the delicate white flowered Knotted Pearlwort (*Sagina nodosa*), Small-fruited Yellow-sedge (*Carex viridula* ssp. *viridula*) and Strawberry Clover, so named because its fruits are reminiscent of strawberries. A rare summer flowering plant is the southern Yellow Bartsia (*Parentucellia viscosa*). Like so many plants conditions have to be just right for it to flourish.

Late in the summer the white flowers of Grass-of-Parnassus (*Parnassia palustris*) in its coastal rather compact form (var. *condensata*) are a conspicuous feature.

Coastal cliffs

Unfortunately Lancashire has few rocky coastal cliffs or shores, but it does have clay cliffs. In the north rocky limestone cliffs occur at Silverdale where the most notable species are the whitebeams. These include the distinctive palmate leaved Wild Service-tree (*Sorbus torminalis*), which reaches its northern limit at Morecambe Bay and occurs as a low growing tree on the exposed cliffs at Silverdale. Strong winds cause considerable damage to the plants and they frequently lose their leaves by August; this may be the reason why they remained unnoticed until 1984.

At Heysham a small exposure of sandstone supports a cliff flora with Royal Fern, Orpine (*Sedum telephium*) and Sea Spleenwort (*Asplenium marinum*). This last was one of the earliest records of a Lancashire plant having been seen at Heysham by Thomas Lawson, the Cumbrian Quaker botanist, in 1685.

Much more extensive are the 'soft' clay banks that occur at intervals from the shores of the Mersey estuary to Morecambe Bay. The habitats they provide are amongst the most natural in the county having never been deliberately managed by humans and perhaps infrequently grazed by large mammals. They are often very unstable

Coastal cliffs at Heysham and the nuclear power station.
(Jon Hickling)

above Wild Cherry or
Gean.
(Malcolm Edmunds)

and subject to erosion and landslips. The unstable slopes support little or no vegetation. At the other extreme stable cliffs support scrubby woodland with Hawthorn (*Crataegus monogyna*), Blackthorn (*Prunus spinosa*), Gorse, roses (*Rosa* spp.) and small trees of oak (*Quercus* spp.), Ash (*Fraxinus excelsior*) and Sycamore (*Acer pseudoplatanus*). In between these two extremes tall herb grassland develops with False Oat-grass (*Arrhenatherum elatius*) and Cock's-foot (*Dactylis glomerata*) abundant. Few unusual or rare species occur but Wood Small-reed (*Calamagrostis epigejos*) is sometimes abundant, e.g. at Conder Green south of Lancaster, and the more southern species, Wild Teasel (*Dipsacus fullonum*) and Bristly Oxtongue (*Picris echioides*), are noteworthy on the Ribble and Mersey estuaries. This is also one of the habitats to look for Spiny Restharrow (*Ononis spinosa*). Very often springs provide wet patches where Round-fruited Rush (*Juncus compressus*) occurs, and as the Saltmarsh Rush can also grow nearby, identifying which is which can be problematic. Common Couch is often abundant and the cliffs should be searched for Sea Couch with which it has hybridised to form extensive colonies on the adjacent salt marshes, but Sea Couch has not been recorded in recent years.

Inland habitats

It is generally supposed that without human intervention in the last few thousand years Lancashire would have had a wooded landscape, but this is a great over simplification. Lowland Lancashire would most likely be a mosaic of bog (mosses), fens, and lakes with woodland only on the drier and better drained land and extending up into the hills before giving way to further bogs in less well-drained areas and on the hill tops. Even here some scrubby woodland might have persisted.

By 1800 this idealised landscape had been profoundly altered by humans. Large areas were cleared of forest and most wetlands drained, whilst common grazing created many heaths that even then

Bird Cherry.
(Malcolm Edmunds)

Boilton Wood, one of our
many fine bluebell woods.
(Jon Hickling)

Woodland floor in the Ribble valley carpeted with Ramsons.
(Peter Jepson)

below Hybrid between 'native' and Spanish Bluebell.
(Malcolm Edmunds)

were being enclosed, drained and cultivated. Lancashire became largely treeless, yet natural woodland, albeit more or less managed, survived in steep-sided river valleys especially in the eastern fells. Many of these woods survive today.

Woodland

Native Lancashire woodlands are a mixture of deciduous trees with oak and Ash. Wych Elm (*Ulmus glabra*) was also common, especially on the clay of the Ribble valley woods, notably Tun Brook and Red Scar, near Preston. This was often the most important tree but suffered badly from Dutch Elm Disease.

Common under storey trees are Wild Cherry (*Prunus avium*) and Bird Cherry (*Prunus padus*), the former particularly conspicuous in the Ribble valley woods whilst the latter, a northern species, becomes more abundant towards the north and east of the county. Higher up the valleys the woodlands thin, and Downy Birch (*Betula pubescens*), Rowan (*Sorbus aucuparia*) and Holly (*Ilex aquifolium*) are the main trees. Much rarer, and perhaps mostly associated with rocky outcrops or in river valleys, is Small-leaved Lime (*Tilia cordata*). This southern species reached the head of Morecambe Bay, but since the warmer Atlantic period ended six thousand years ago it has only been able to survive rather than spread. The warm summers necessary for seed development occur only occasionally now.

The woodland ground flora is rich, and many of the drier woodlands are carpeted with a magnificent blue haze of Bluebells (*Hyacinthoides*

Flowers and Ferns:
Woodland

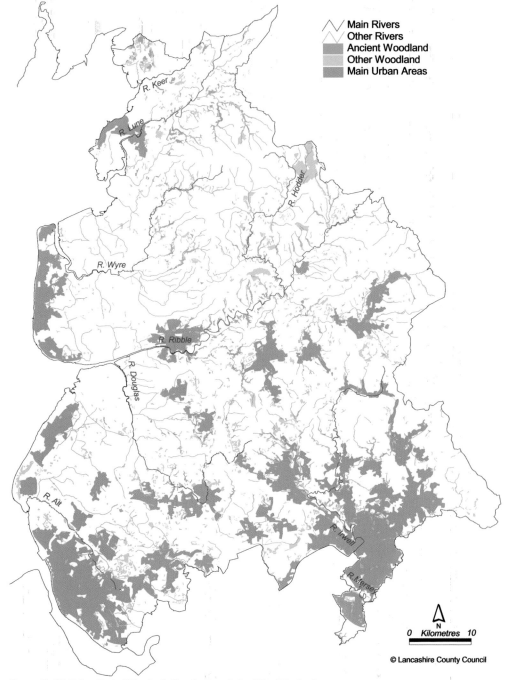

Map 5
Woodland within the Wildlife Trust Area.
The map shows how very little woodland there is in our area; most of our woods are of no great age and so lack the flora typical of ancient woods.
(Nik Bruce)

Main Rivers
Other Rivers
Ancient Woodland
Other Woodland
Main Urban Areas

R. Keer
R. Lune
R. Hodder
R. Wyre
R. Ribble
R. Douglas
R. Alt
R. Irwell
R. Mersey

N
0   Kilometres   10

© Lancashire County Council

Source: English Nature (Ancient Woodland); Forestry Commission (Other Woodland)
© Crown copyright. All rights reserved (2004).

Wildlife of Lancashire

non-scripta) in the May sunshine. But we should not too readily take this common plant for granted. Whilst this species is found elsewhere in Europe, only in Britain does it form such a feature and Lancashire is as good a county as any to see it. But it is under threat. It has been picked for centuries and occasionally uprooted, though this does not pose a real problem unless undertaken on a large scale. Destruction of woodland is a problem, as it does not readily colonize new woods although it will persist for many years in cleared areas. The real threat has only been appreciated recently. For a long time nurseries and garden centres have sold bluebells but instead of selling native Bluebells they sell a related species, the Spanish Bluebell (*Hyacinthoides hispanica*), or more frequently the hybrid between the British and Spanish species. This hybrid is fertile, is extensively naturalized and backcrosses with the native Bluebell to form hybrid swarms. As a rule of thumb most bluebells west of the M6 south of Lancaster are hybrids whilst in woodlands north of Lancaster and to the east of the M6 they are native Bluebells, but extensive overlap occurs. Surprisingly the non-native hybrid is not too difficult to identify but until recently it was often overlooked.

Another attractive woodland plant, but this time on the wetter clay soils, is Ramsons (*Allium ursinum*). It too can carpet the woodland floor

63

with its white flowers, but for many its strong onion smell detracts from its appeal. Yet another carpet forming plant is Dog's Mercury (*Mercurialis perennis*), which is also characteristic of heavy clay soils. Its green male and female flowers are borne on different plants and are inconspicuous. Red woodland flowers are Herb Robert (*Geranium robertianum*) and Red Campion (*Silene dioica*), whilst one of the last plants to flower is the green flowered Sanicle (*Sanicula europaea*). The pink flowered Bistort (*Persicaria bistorta*) is often found on the edge of woods or in woodland clearings. Another name for this plant is Passion Dock and Mabey (1996) gives a number of recipes for dock pudding from the north of England.

The flora of Lancashire woodlands is typical of northern woodlands in Britain and some species are especially characteristic. These include the delicate white flowered Wood Stitchwort (*Stellaria nemorum*), the white or sometimes pink flowered Large Bitter-cress (*Cardamine amara*) and the small Alternate-leaved Golden-saxifrage (*Chrysosplenium alternifolium*), which is not to be confused with the much commoner Opposite-leaved Golden-saxifrage (*Chrysosplenium oppositifolium*). Another typical plant is the yellow flowered Marsh Hawk's-beard (*Crepis paludosa*). All these plants are found in wet, base-rich areas or by the side of streams and springs. Another curious early flowering plant is Moschatel or Town-hall Clock (*Adoxa moschatellina*), so called because the inflorescence is cube shaped and reminiscent of a Victorian town hall clock. Other species found mostly in the north and east of the county, especially as woodland edge or meadow species, are Wood Crane's-bill (*Geranium sylvaticum*) and, particularly in the Slaidburn area, Melancholy Thistle (*Cirsium heterophyllum*).

top Wood Stitchwort.
(*Eric Greenwood*)

above Large Bitter-
cress.
(*Malcolm Edmunds*)

Alternate-leaved Golden-
saxifrage.
(*Malcolm Edmunds*)

64

Additional colour is provided early in the year by the white flowers of Wood-sorrel (*Oxalis acetosella*), the blue of Common Dog-violet (*Viola riviniana*) and the brilliant yellow of Lesser Celandine (*Ranunculus ficaria*). There are two easily distinguished subspecies of Lesser Celandine: in late April and May as the leaves die down ssp. *bulbifer* develops conspicuous bulbils at the bases of the leaves whilst these are absent in ssp. *ficaria*. Both subspecies occur widely and are probably native but it is possible that at least some populations of ssp. *bulbifer* are garden escapes, especially west of the M6 where there are few natural woodlands. Much more work is needed to plot the occurrence of these subspecies and to attempt to explain their distribution.

Some plants that are common further south reach their northern limits in Lancashire. Yellow Archangel (*Lamiastrum galeobdolon* ssp. *montanum*) is found in a very restricted band about 1m wide above the flood level of the river Ribble (e.g. in the Trust's Red Scar Wood Nature Reserve), but as a native plant does not occur further north. It is not to be confused with its close relative with variegated leaves, ssp. *argentatum*, which is a garden escape and is spreading rapidly. Another much more localised southern plant found in the Hodder valley is the nationally scarce grass Wood Barley (*Hordelymus europaeus*).

Amongst the rushes and sedges some are particularly attractive. On the wet clay soils of the Ribble valley, Pendulous Sedge (*Carex pendula*) makes a fine show in June whilst on drier more acid soils Great Wood-rush (*Luzula sylvatica*), a close relative of the early flowering woodland Hairy Wood-rush (*Luzula pilosa*), can be found. Superficially similar is Wood Club-rush (*Scirpus sylvaticus*), which may be more frequent than records suggest.

Enchanter's-nightshade (*Circaea lutetiana*) is common throughout Lancashire woodlands but in some places a sterile hybrid (*Circaea x intermedia*) with Alpine Enchanter's-nightshade (*Circaea alpina*) is frequent. However Alpine Enchanter's-nightshade is an arctic alpine confined to the higher mountains of Wales, the Lake District and Scotland, and is long extinct in Lancashire. It is amazing that a sterile hybrid can survive and indeed thrive possibly for thousands of years in the absence of one of its parents.

The highly oceanic climate of Lancashire favours the growth of many ferns (Box 4.10). The commonest are Lady-fern (*Athyrium filix-femina*), Broad Buckler-fern (*Dryopteris dilatata*) and Male-fern (*Dryopteris filix-mas*). However the woodlands of the eastern and northern fells, especially at higher levels, also contain an abundance of Scaly Male-fern (*Dryopteris affinis*) in its many different forms.

top Pendulous Sedge. (Malcolm Edmunds)

above Limestone Fern. (Phil Smith)

Flowers and Ferns:
Woodland

Some Lancashire woodland ferns

Many other ferns occur in Lancashire woodlands. The strap like fronds of Hart's-tongue (*Phyllitis scolopendrium*) are characteristic of calcareous soils or walls. In more acidic places banks of Beech Fern (*Phegopteris connectilis*) occur, while in rocky places the delicate fronds of Oak Fern (*Gymnocarpium dryopteris*) can be found particularly in the north of the county. Until recently Soft Shield-fern (*Polystichum setiferum*) was very much under recorded, possibly in error for its relative Hard Shield-fern (*Polystichum aculeatum*) that favours more calcareous soils and rocks. However, Soft Shield-fern may have become much commoner in the last 100 years.

Where the swift flowing rivers cut through banks of shale there are sometimes calcareous springs or layers of calcareous shale. Here the flora changes and is more diverse. Very rarely these habitats are the site for Green Spleenwort (*Asplenium viride*), Limestone Fern (*Gymnocarpium robertianum*) and Brittle Bladder-fern (*Cystopteris fragilis*). All are more characteristic of limestone and European mountains. They are probably relicts of the late glacial flora and have persisted at these sites for thousands of years, yet they are highly vulnerable to erosion by floods or river and woodland management schemes.

One of the most conspicuous features of Lancashire woodlands is the abundance of horsetails – close relatives of plants that dominated the carboniferous landscape about 300 million years ago and whose remains are preserved in the coal measures. In the Ribble valley the large pale green to white stems of Great Horsetail (*Equisetum telmateia*) cover large areas of wet clay. Often close by is the much more delicate Wood Horsetail (*Equisetum sylvaticum*). A third species, Rough Horsetail (*Equisetum hyemale*), is sometimes difficult to see when other vegetation tends to swamp it in summer, but its simple dark green stems up to a metre long are conspicuous in winter. It is a perennial and grows in several woods, but it may have been introduced by humans as it was used in the textile industry.

Until comparatively recently woodland extended to over 1000ft in steep-sided river valleys and on crags. There is evidence that burning by humans several thousand years ago removed trees on the moor tops but more recently grazing sheep have further reduced tree cover.

Great Horsetail with the large leaves of Butterbur (*Petasites hybridus*) behind. (*Malcolm Edmunds*)

Wildlife of Lancashire

However, at least in some places in Bowland, it appears that trees can re-establish themselves as occasional Rowan seedlings can be found on the fell tops. The remains of these upland woods are home to some of the county's rarest plants. An example is Chickweed Wintergreen (*Trientalis europaea*) known from only one site. The removal of trees has left many crags very exposed and sheep grazing probably continues to take its toll. Nevertheless these crags still support Fir Clubmoss, Wilson's Filmy-fern (*Hymenophyllum wilsonii*), Parsley Fern (*Cryptogramma crispa*), Hay-scented Buckler-fern (*Dryopteris aemula*) and Mountain Male-fern (*Dryopteris oreades*). All are now found in very small quantity – sometimes only as single plants – yet 100 to 200 years ago some of them were common. The most striking feature of this assemblage of plants is that they are relicts of an extreme oceanic climate only well developed on the western edge of the British Isles. This kind of climate is rare on a world scale being confined to the western shores of land bordering the largest oceans.

Chickweed Wintergreen. *(Peter Jepson)*

Parsley Fern. *(Phil Smith)*

Limestone Pavement

The north of the county is characterised by carboniferous limestone forming a variety of crags and pavements. This karst limestone landscape is as well represented in England at the head of Morecambe Bay and in the northern Pennines as anywhere in the world. In Lancashire much of the area is well wooded but this is a recent phenomenon and it presents a problem for the survival of many of the specialities that require plenty of light.

The natural vegetation is indeed woodland except where the ice of the last glaciation removed all the soil leaving a smooth rock surface. Apart from small areas of Gait Barrows, thick woodland was once established, but even here there were clearings or open areas created by large grazing animals. As humans became more numerous they gradually killed these animals replacing them with their own grazing cattle, goats and sheep. For thousands of years woodland was in retreat with the only pockets remaining on the deeper soils of the Leighton Hall Estate and as mini woods in the grikes of the limestone.

By 1800 it was largely a treeless landscape. However during the nineteenth century new woods were established on the deeper soils and, particularly in the twentieth century as grazing decreased, many woods regenerated.

The result of this changing land use, the more recent establishment of gardens and the slightly warmer climate is that the Silverdale area is home to the largest number of flowering plants and ferns in the county. Many of these are confined to this part of Lancashire and are nationally rare or scarce (see Box 4.11).

Amongst the shrubs Common Juniper (*Juniperus communis*) and Yew (*Taxus baccata*) are frequent or abundant. Common Juniper formerly occurred throughout upland Lancashire but now only a few old bushes remain in northern Bowland. However on the limestone it regenerates freely in the absence of domesticated grazing animals. Similarly Yew is widespread in Lancashire but it is usually planted in association with churches. In the Silverdale area it is especially abundant and at Cringlebarrow forms a yew wood.

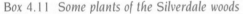

Box 4.11 *Some plants of the Silverdale woods*

Among the first flowers to appear in spring are Fingered Sedge (*Carex digitata*), which favours the sides of woodland tracks, and Early Dog-violet (*Viola reichenbachiana*). Much rarer early flowering plants include Yellow Star-of-Bethlehem (*Gagea lutea*) that also occurs in the valleys of the Ribble and its tributaries, and Mezereon (*Daphne mezereum*), which may or may not be native and regrettably has suffered from people uprooting the few bushes that can be found for their gardens. Much more common is its evergreen relative, Spurge-laurel (*Daphne laureola*). Other shrubs flowering later include Spindle (*Euonymus europaeus*) and Buckthorn (*Rhamnus catharticus*) – both southern species. One of the most attractive of the early flowers is the Daffodil (*Narcissus pseudonarcissus*), which sometimes appears in profusion. Whilst it is still common in the limestone woods, it used to be more widespread in the north and east of the county, but it seems to have become rarer here in recent years. Often confused with the native Daffodil, yet readily seen as distinct from it, are a variety of cultivated forms that are found, mostly in waste places, throughout Lancashire.

above right Daffodil, or Lent Lily, grows in limestone woods and in many of the Ribble Valley woods. *(Malcolm Edmunds)*

right Horseshoe Vetch. *(Phil Smith)*

69

Flowers and Ferns:
Limestone pavement

Green-winged
Orchid.
(Phil Smith)

Even when forest cover was greatest some cliffs and nearby areas were kept free of trees with the help of grazing animals. Here some characteristic plants have survived including the yellow flowered Common Rock-rose (*Helianthemum nummularium*), Horseshoe Vetch (*Hippocrepis comosa*) and Spring Cinquefoil (*Potentilla neumanniana*). The last two are southern species reaching their northernmost limits in Britain at the head of Morecambe Bay. So too are two orchids, Green-winged Orchid (*Orchis morio*) once found more widely in meadows mostly in the west of the county, and Autumn Lady's-tresses (*Spiranthes spiralis*) also formerly found on link sand dunes. Green-winged Orchid has prominent green veins on the wings of an otherwise pink flower and appears at the end of April or early May, whilst the twisted spike of tiny whitish flowers of Autumn Lady's-tresses appear at the end of August. Another unusual plant of this habitat is Rare Spring-sedge (*Carex ericetorum*), which is closely similar to and often grows with the more widespread Spring-sedge (*Carex caryophyllea*). Probably because of its similarity, this continental species was not discovered in Lancashire until 1948. Elsewhere in Britain it is found in the Derbyshire Pennines and in East Anglia. Also in this habitat and nearby grasslands are Autumn and Field Gentians, both now very rare in Lancashire. Formerly Mountain Everlasting (*Antennaria dioica*) grew in pastures at Silverdale as well as on sand dunes and in pastures in the east of the county. It is therefore gratifying that it has recently been refound at one of its old sites in the Ribble valley.

The thinly wooded or bare limestone pavements are home to a host of semi-woodland plants requiring some shade and moisture. The deep grikes provide an ideal place for them. Amongst the ferns two are noteworthy: Limestone Fern and Rigid Buckler-fern (*Dryopteris submontana*). Fine populations of both are found in the Silverdale area and on the limestone crags fringing Leck Beck. These species are fairly plentiful elsewhere on the limestones of northern England but are very rare or absent in the rest of the British Isles (Box 4.12).

Rigid Buckler-fern in
limestone pavement.
(Phil Smith)

*Wildlife of
Lancashire*

A fern that is especially frequent on limestone is Intermediate Polypody (*Polypodium interjectum*). It occurs thinly distributed throughout the county and often hybridises with the commoner Polypody. Much rarer on the Morecambe Bay limestones is its close relative and oceanic species Southern Polypody (*Polypodium cambricum*). Spring Sandwort (*Minuartia verna*), Limestone Bedstraw (*Galium sterneri*) and the very rare Northern Bedstraw (*Galium boreale*), reaching its southernmost limit here, are characteristic of this area. Several orchids are found in the limestone pavements, cliffs and woodlands but two are of particular interest. Dark-red Helleborine (*Epipactis atrorubens*) is especially characteristic but although nationally scarce it is found elsewhere from North Wales and Derbyshire to the north coast of Scotland. On the other hand the Fly Orchid (*Ophrys insectifera*) is found more commonly on the chalk of southern England but just manages to survive on the limestone around Morecambe Bay. It is a beautiful but well camouflaged orchid that favours woodland clearings. It may be present in one place for a number of years but its survival depends on new clearings becoming available. Once these would have been created by grazing animals and woodland coppicing but more recently abandoned copper mine waste and old quarries have proved suitable.

Rare and localised plants that favour deeper shade in limestone woods include Angular Solomon's-seal (*Polygonatum odoratum*), not to be confused with Solomon's-seal (*Polygonatum multiflorum*) as well as hybrids between them found as garden outcasts. In some places the increasingly rare yellowish brown saprophytic Bird's-nest Orchid (*Neottia nidus-avis*) occurs, but it is not confined to the limestone woodlands.

Dark-red
Helleborine.
(Malcolm Edmunds)

Angular Solomon's-
seal in limestone
pavement.
(Malcolm Edmunds)

71

Blue Moor-grass.
(Eric Greenwood)

In many limestone woods and especially in the grikes of pavements Lily-of-the-valley (*Convallaria majalis*) is often abundant, a beautiful scented spring flowering plant found only rarely as an indigenous species elsewhere in Lancashire. Throughout the limestone area of northern England, where the woodland canopy does not provide too much shade as well as in open areas on cliffs etc., Blue Moor-grass (*Sesleria caerulea*) often forms a dominant sward with its characteristic bluish flowers in April and May. Despite its abundance in northern England it is very rare elsewhere in the British Isles except on the similar limestones of Western Ireland. These limestone woods also have one of our rarest British plants, the Lady's-slipper (Box 4.13).

Box 4.13 *Lady's-slipper* (Cypripedium calceolus)

This is arguably the most beautiful British orchid and a relative of tropical species so prized by gardeners. It is a plant of well-drained calcareous soils derived from limestone, in herb-rich grassland or, formerly, in open woodland. It is native in Yorkshire, but its status in Lancashire is uncertain.

The first British record, in the early seventeenth century, is attributed to a London apothecary John Parkinson, but his description of its locality (quoted by Peter Marren, 1999) introduces the idea that this might be a Lancashire plant:

'It groweth . . . neare upon the border of Yorkshire in a wood or place called the Helkes, which is three miles from Ingleton as I am enformed by a courteous Gentlewomen, a great lover of these delights, called Mistress Thomasin Tunstall, who dwelleth at Bull-banke, neare Hornby Castle in those parts, and who hath often sent mee up the rootes to London, which have borne faire flowers in my garden'.

Hornby Castle is in Lancashire and so is Bull Bank, at Wrayton, but Helkes to the north of Ingleton is a few miles away in Yorkshire.

This account also shows that Lady's-slipper was even then taken into cultivation and its extinction at Helkes by the 1790s is attributed to uprooting for gardens. Yet it must have been quite plentiful as there are accounts

Wildlife of Lancashire

of it being sold in Settle market in the 1780s. However every landowner wanted a row of 'golden slippers' in his garden. One such row, taken from Helkes, survived at Hipping Hall, near Cowan Bridge, Leck until 1835, whilst a border of the orchid was maintained at Hornby Castle until about the late 1970s. Plants from this border remain in cultivation elsewhere.

Apart from this record, there are few claims for the Lady's-slipper being a Lancashire plant in the eighteenth and nineteenth centuries. James Jenkinson (1775), who lived at Yealand Conyers, only knew of the Helkes site belonging to 'Mr Foxcroft Esq'. Similarly Wheldon and Wilson (1907) did not know of a Lancashire site. Yet there is a nineteenth-century specimen at the Natural History Museum, London collected from 'Nr Lancaster' by Mrs Humble. C. J. Ashfield (1864) mentions that 'A gentleman living near Preston showed me a few weeks since some specimens of this scarce plant in blossom the plants of which he found growing wild near Milnthorpe not far from Silverdale a few years since'. Another record attributed to a Lancashire fern enthusiast suggests that the Lady's-slipper grew in Gait Barrows Wood and in a field not far from there in about 1890.

From the middle of the nineteenth century secrecy surrounded the locations of both wild and cultivated plants. To some this offered a challenge to track them down, but at the same time rumours started to circulate that some plants were re-introduced into the wild. Then, in 1938 the orchid was found on Arnside Knott although it was never seen there again. However, the rumours persisted that it grew near Silverdale until in 1975 it was found flowering wild in the area. This was reported in *The Lapwing* (No. 5, Oct. 1975). Coincidentally Eric Hardy wrote an article in the *Manchester Evening News* (6 June 1975) referring to the Lady's-slipper flowering in Reginald Kay's nursery at Silverdale. The discovery of the wild Silverdale plant raised questions as to its status. Was it planted or was it genuinely native? This debate continues and perhaps even with modern technology this question may never be answered. Sadly, in spite of thriving with eight flowers in 2003 and being carefully guarded every year whilst in flower, in July 2004 someone dug up the plant and removed it.

The single native colony in Yorkshire is also closely guarded and a recovery programme is under way including introduction of the species to new and former sites (Preston, Pearman and Dines, 2002). Details of the sites are not available. It is hoped that these measures will enable the public at some future date to enjoy the sight of a woodland glade filled with the flowers of this magnificent but internationally endangered orchid.

In compiling this account I am grateful for the help of Peter Corkhill, Jennifer Newton and Geoff Morries.

Flowers and Ferns:
Limestone pavement

Indian or Himalayan
Balsam.
(Phil Smith)

Giant Hogweed with
Japanese Knotweed
in the foreground.
(Phil Smith)

Before leaving woodlands a note is needed on those introduced species that have become established, some of which are conspicuous and even attractive. Sycamore is found in most if not all woodlands. Its history in Lancashire is not known but it was probably planted from the fifteenth century onwards. Beech (*Fagus sylvatica*), native further south, has also been planted from time to time. On many riverbanks one of the most invasive yet attractive plants is Indian Balsam (*Impatiens glandulifera*), commonly called Himalayan Balsam. It was introduced over a hundred years ago as a garden plant and seemed to favour polluted rivers. In the Ribble valley Broad-leaved Ragwort (*Senecio fluviatilis*) has been known for over 150 years. It can form large colonies but the closely related Wood Ragwort (*Senecio ovatus*) can also be found, especially on the south bank of the river. By far the largest of these large flowering plants is Giant Hogweed (*Heracleum mantegazzianum*). It is a handsome plant but because its sap can cause nasty blisters on human skin in the presence of sunlight, it is also a plant where active measures are taken to eradicate it. Nevertheless it seems to be spreading and is not confined to the Ribble valley where it was particularly conspicuous. Finally in the tributaries of the River Ribble (and elsewhere) the much smaller and attractive Pink Purslane (*Claytonia sibirica*) has become established. Like the other species mentioned it is also invasive.

*Wildlife of
Lancashire*

Hay meadow at
Clearbeck, near
Wray, Forest of
Bowland.
(Jon Hickling)

Grasslands

On the deeper soils derived from boulder clay woodland clearance for
farming and settlement started thousands of years ago. Before this
large grazing animals maintained clearings where grassland and
woodland edge communities developed. Humans made larger and
larger clearings until by the end of the eighteenth century, apart from
steep sided river valleys, the landscape was largely treeless. Until
recently farming was mixed with arable, pastures and meadows but
productivity was low and mainly at subsistence level. Towards the
west of the county farms tended to have more land under arable cultivation whilst towards the hills pastures and meadows predominated.

Until the late eighteenth century farming was relatively primitive
and fertilizers were largely confined to marl and sometimes lime and
farmyard manure. Weeding was by hand. Over the centuries this practice gave rise to grasslands on neutral soils that were floristically rich
with several species of grass and numerous flowering plants.

From about 1800 there was a continuous drive to improve productivity, with increasing mechanisation, drainage and the use of lime,
manure, clean seed and, more recently, the use of manufactured
fertilizers and pesticides. As a result the grasslands of 200 or so years
ago have almost disappeared with just occasional fragments
surviving. Many of the exceptionally attractive woodland edge plants
typical of these grasslands are on the verge of extinction in Lancashire
(Box 4.14).

Greater Butterfly-
orchid.
(Phil Smith)

Characteristic species are: lady's mantles (*Alchemilla filicaulis, A. glabra, A. xanthochlora* and the 'Red Data Book' species *A. acutiloba*), Melancholy Thistle, Globeflower (*Trollius europaeus*), Greater and Lesser Butterfly-orchids (*Platanthera chlorantha* and *Platanthera bifolia*), Common Twayblade (*Listera ovata*), Adder's-tongue (*Ophioglossum vulgatum*), Yellow-rattle (*Rhinanthus minor*) and eyebrights (*Euphrasia arctica ssp. borealis,* and *Euphrasia rostkoviana* are among the more interesting). In damp pastures and flushed areas Common Butterwort (*Pinguicula vulgaris*), Grass-of-Parnassus, Fragrant Orchid, Bird's-eye Primrose (*Primula farinosa*), Saw-wort (*Serratula tinctoria*) and Marsh Lousewort (*Pedicularis palustris*) may also occur.

below left
Common Butterwort.
(Phil Smith)

below right
Globeflower.
(Peter Jepson)

right
Bird's-eye Primrose.
(Phil Smith)

Wildlife of
Lancashire

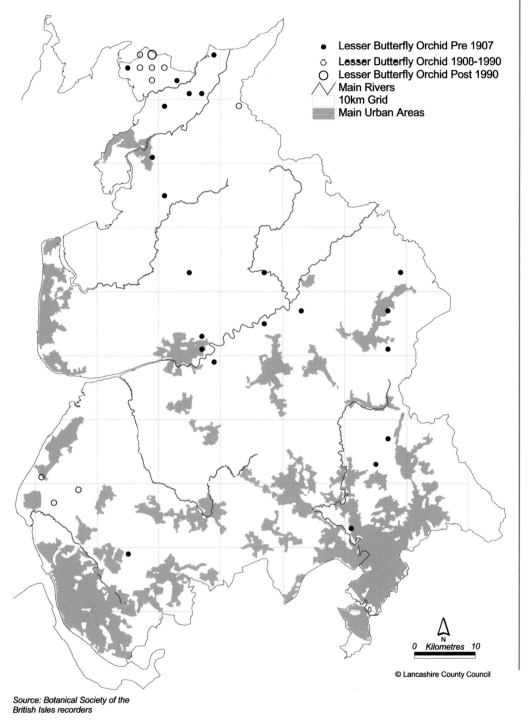

Legend:
- • Lesser Butterfly Orchid Pre 1907
- ○ Lesser Butterfly Orchid 1900-1990
- ○ Lesser Butterfly Orchid Post 1990
- Main Rivers
- 10km Grid
- Main Urban Areas

Map 6.
Distribution of Lesser Butterfly-orchid in the Wildlife Trust Area. This orchid was never common in Lancashire but old records show it was thinly distributed in heathy grassland throughout the county. Some populations persisted until the 1960s, especially in the Formby and Silverdale areas. The last known colony at Yealand Redmayne dwindled slowly during the 1980s and 1990s to a single spike in 1999. It has not been recorded since.
(Nik Bruce)

0 Kilometres 10

© Lancashire County Council

Source: Botanical Society of the British Isles recorders

Flowers and Ferns: Grasslands

Tormentil on
Haskayne cutting,
near Formby.
(Phil Smith)

The grass species too have changed. Meadow Fescue (*Festuca pratensis*) and Meadow Foxtail (*Alopecurus pratensis*) were often the dominant species with an abundance of others including the attractive Quaking-grass (*Briza media*), Crested Dog's-tail (*Cynosurus cristatus*), Yellow Oat-grass (*Trisetum flavescens*) and Downy Oat-grass (*Helictotrichon pubescens*). On more acid soils bents (*Agrostis* spp.), Sweet Vernal-grass and Heath-grass were more prominent. Red Fescue was common on coastal grasslands but not elsewhere whilst Perennial Rye-grass (*Lolium perenne*) and Timothy (*Phleum pratense*) were almost unknown. Similarly although not a grass, White Clover (*Trifolium repens*) was not a common grassland plant. Today, through extensive plantings, the relative abundance of these two groups is more or less reversed and in the more intensively farmed areas monocultures of rye-grass species are usual. Another grass regarded perhaps more as a weed in neutral grasslands, both historically and today, is Soft-brome (*Bromus hordeaceus*). Its recently described and probably recently evolved subspecies *longipedicellatus* is also probably common, but the closely related Meadow and Smooth Bromes (*Bromus commutatus* and B. *racemosus*) are much rarer.

In between the extremes of herb (i.e. wildflower) rich grassland and grassland monocultures, weedy grasslands still occur, most commonly when there is a lapse in the intensive husbandry necessary to maintain the most productive sward. Then they may become colourful with Meadow and Creeping Buttercups (*Ranunculus acris* and R. *repens*), while the coarse grasses Cock's-foot and False Oat-grass are often more prominent. In wetter places Soft-rush and Hard Rush may be present. Sometimes where intensive farming has never been fully developed but perhaps where some lime and fertilizers were used (especially the use of basic slag in the first half of the twentieth century) a relatively herb rich pasture or meadow may survive. Here the characteristic meadow grasses, a number of sedges and more especially some of the more colourful herbs can still be found.

In more upland areas acid grasslands are common, and as conditions get wetter they merge into bogs with the development of *Sphagnum* moss. Mat-grass often with Heath rush and bents cover large areas. There are few other species but these may include Heath Bedstraw (*Galium saxatile*), Heath Milkwort (*Polygala serpyllifolia*), Tormentil (*Potentilla erecta*), Heath-grass and Wavy Hair-grass. On drier soils in the east and north of the county acid grasslands may merge into heath with dwarf shrubs covering huge areas (Box 4.15).

Box 4.15 *More flowers of neutral grasslands*

Colourful grassland flowers are still found in a few places, especially in the east of the county, but these are often on roadsides rather than in fields. They include buttercups but especially Bulbous Buttercup (*Ranunculus bulbosus*), Dyer's Greenweed (*Genista tinctoria*) on shrubby banks, the semi-parasitic eyebrights (usually *Euphrasia nemorosa* and *Euphrasia confusa* and hybrids) and Yellow-rattle. There are also a number of white flowered members of the carrot family including Burnet-saxifrage (*Pimpinella saxifraga*), Greater Burnet-saxifrage (*Pimpinella major*) characteristic of the Ribble valley, and in hedges adjoining fields Upright Hedge-parsley (*Torilis japonica*), Rough Chervil (*Chaerophyllum temulum*) and the very abundant Cow Parsley (*Anthriscus sylvestris*), which makes a fine show in May. Hogweed (*Heracleum sphondylium*) appears later in the summer and is also very common. Great Burnet (*Sanguisorba officinalis*) and Meadow Crane's-bill (*Geranium pratense*) may also be found.

Wesham Marsh is one of the very few damp semi-natural grasslands surviving on the Fylde.
(Geoff Morries)

Common Spotted-orchid.
(Phil Smith)

Roadside verges and railway banks

Several studies have shown that the larger the number of shrubs and trees in a hedge the greater its age, but few have attempted to study the range of habitats between the field side of the hedge and the adjacent roadway. Typically there is also a ditch and a metre or more wide grass verge. The hedge and the ditch usually contain species characteristic of woodland scrub (especially roses) and of marshy places respectively. The verge, however, sometimes contains a number of interesting species. These include lady's-mantles, Common Spotted-orchid, Twayblade, Adder's-tongue and a variety of grasses, rushes, sedges and other flowering plants typical of herb rich grasslands or meadows. In recent years the number of floristically interesting verges seems to have decreased. However, motorway verges have created new grasslands of considerable interest although as they can usually only be observed from a distance the extent of their floristic diversity is not known. Nevertheless Common Spotted-orchid, Northern Marsh-orchid, Twayblade, Bee Orchid, Common Broomrape (*Orobanche minor*) and Danish Scurvygrass have been seen (Box 4.16).

Flowers and Ferns:
Roads and railways

Bee Orchid.
(Phil Smith)

Danish Scurvygrass.
(Peter Jepson)

The building of railways in the middle of the nineteenth century created extensive grasslands on their banks. These were kept free of shrubs and trees as sparks from steam locomotives often set fire to them in spring. Primroses found these habitats ideal and sometimes appeared in huge quantity. Since steam trains were replaced by diesel and electric locomotives the regular springtime fires have ceased, scrub has encroached on many railway banks and coarse vegetation has developed dominated by False Oat-grass and Cock's-foot. Nevertheless from time to time rare plants are recorded including Royal Fern, while the best colonies of Wood Crane's-bill and Pepper-saxifrage (*Silaum silaus*) are found on a railway bank.

Box 4.16 *Danish Scurvygrass* (Cochlearia danica)

One of the most remarkable changes that has taken place in recent years is the spread of Danish Scurvygrass. This attractive white or mauve flowered plant was usually found on sandy and gravely ground on the coast in April and May. Then about fifty years ago a few inland populations were seen on waste cindery ground, but it was not until about twenty years ago that it started to invade the motorway verges of Lancashire. Its spread here and on some A class roads has been spectacular causing speculation as to the cause of the invasion. The winter use of de-icing salt and possibly some weed killers, both of which it tolerates, may produce a vacant niche to which it is well suited.

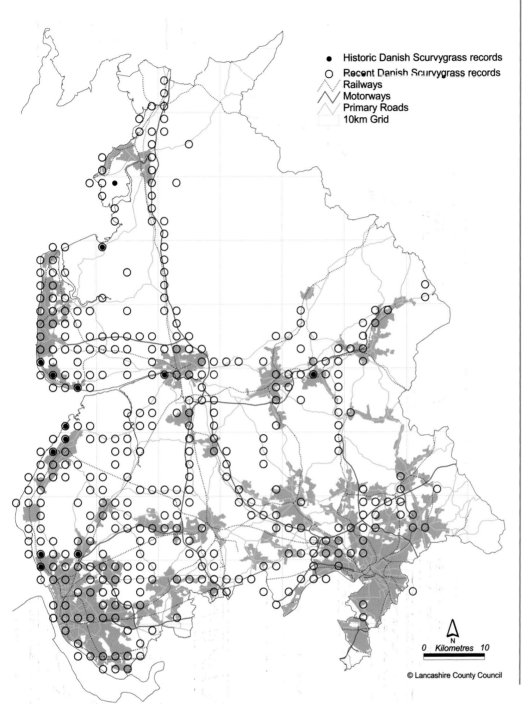

Legend:
- ● Historic Danish Scurvygrass records
- ○ Recent Danish Scurvygrass records
- Railways
- Motorways
- Primary Roads
- 10km Grid

Map 7.
Distribution of Danish Scurvygrass in the Wildlife Trust Area.
One hundred years ago Danish Scurvygrass was a rare coastal plant with occasional inland records, notably at Accrington. By 1962 it had become more frequent on the coast near Liverpool, but recent records show a strong association with motorways and primary roads reflecting the situation nationally. (Data reproduced by permission of Chris Preston and Henry Arnold of the Biological Records Centre, Centre for Ecology and Hydrology.)
(Nik Bruce)

0 Kilometres 10

© Lancashire County Council

Source: Botanical Society of the British Isles recorders

*Flowers and Ferns:
Roads and railways*

Heaths

These areas are dominated by dwarf shrubs, usually Heather and heaths (E*rica* spp.)

Historically lowland heaths were derived from sparse woodland and were used as common grazing. They survived well into the eighteenth century when most were enclosed, drained and converted into farmland. Even their names have often disappeared but the first edition of the Ordnance Survey maps show that the name 'moor' was used frequently, e.g. Warbreck Moor (Liverpool) and Ribbleton Moor (Preston). These 'moors', consisting of a mixture of dry and wet heath and maintained by grazing, had a characteristic vegetation comprising species that have mostly gone with the habitat. The best fragments of dry heath are found behind the sand dunes (see p. 57) where, apart from Bracken (P*teridium aquilinum*), Common Bent and occasional flowers of Heath Milkwort and Tormentil, there is little else. Nevertheless, there is one wet heath species that survives in a single locality in the Mersey basin, the beautiful blue flowered Marsh Gentian (*Gentiana pneumonanthe*) (see p. 276).

In the uplands heather moors are generally managed for Red Grouse and merge into bogs wherever drainage is impeded or rainfall is sufficiently high. Both in the lowlands and uplands overgrazing may produce acid grassland, or in the uplands a Bilberry (*Vaccinium myrtillus*) heath, e.g. at Clougha near Lancaster. On the drier soils in the east and north of the county dwarf shrub communities cover large areas with Heather and Bilberry often being especially abundant. However Bell Heather (E*rica cinerea*) and Cowberry (*Vaccinium vitis-idaea*) can also be common.

Wetlands (lakes, reservoirs, fens, bogs and rivers)

Historically wetlands probably covered at least half the county. Where they survive today, they are with one exception profoundly altered by humans, yet human intervention has also created some of the most interesting wetlands of the region.

The most natural surviving wetland is Hawes Water, Silverdale, but even here the water level was lowered at some stage in the fairly recent past. It is a highly calcareous lake with an abundance of shell marl at its northern end where a stream enters from nearby Little Hawes Water. At the outlet end a fen that developed into a bog probably partially blocked the outflow from the lake. However attempts were made to drain this and a main drainage channel, Myer's Dike, with side drains was constructed possibly in the 1760s. Prior to this

the area was probably cut for peat. Fortunately drainage attempts were not particularly successful and after at least 100 years a fen or fen carr has re-formed. The whole complex is unique in Lancashire and amongst the most fascinating places supporting a number of rare and localised species. In the lake itself the insectivorous Greater Bladder-wort (*Utricularia vulgaris*) grows and occasionally sends up its yellow flowers above water level. Also submerged are the beautifully veined leaves of Shining Pondweed (*Potamogeton lucens*). Occasionally round the edge the floating leaves of Least Bur-reed (*Sparganium natans*) appear along with the large leaves of White Water-lily (*Nymphaea alba*), whilst in the reeds in its only Lancashire locality (together with Little Hawes Water), Great Fen-sedge (*Cladium mariscus*) is sometimes abundant.

In the fen, primarily composed of Common Reed, the large leaves of Water Dock (*Rumex hydrolapathum*) can be seen. Shrubs here include Alder Buckthorn (*Frangula alnus*) and willows, and the latter repay critical examination. Grey Willow is one of Lancashire's commonest willows but usually as ssp. *oleifolia*. However, ssp. *cinerea* survives in the Hawes Water fens together with many intermediates with ssp. *oleifolia*.

Subspecies *cinerea* is more characteristic of East Anglia, but it is found elsewhere where fens were once extensive, so it may be an indicator plant and should be looked for in other places. So far it has been found scattered in the west of the county including Marton Mere – another ancient lake but now nothing like its original form.

Fens and fen carr were once more extensive features of the Lancashire landscape. The most extensive was at Martin Mere behind Southport but today the largest is the reed bed, mostly composed of Common Reed, at Leighton Moss, which is less than 100 years old. This was formerly Warton and Storrs Moss – a large peat bog used for fuel. By the end of the nineteenth century it was almost all cultivated but depended on a steam pump for drainage. When this failed in 1917 the present wetland was created. Other large reed beds are found near Wigan and at the top of ungrazed salt marshes, e.g. on the Wyre estuary.

Marshy areas occur in numerous places throughout the county, and a variety of attractive plants grow in them (Box 4.17).

Raised bogs – mosses

There is a natural succession from fen to raised bog. In Lancashire most of the lowland areas were covered in bog commonly known as mosses. Chat Moss was probably the largest but in addition to the large bogs there were many small ones of which all trace has gone. Here and there fragments of much modified mosses survive. Some have a flora reminiscent of an unmodified raised bog. At Cockerham,

The strongly aromatic Bog-myrtle dominating Formby Moss.
(Phil Smith)

Winmarleigh and on the Trust's new reserve at Heysham some characteristic species survive including Bog-myrtle (*Myrica gale*), Bog-rosemary (*Andromeda polifolia*) typical of bogs in northern England and Ireland, Cranberry (*Vaccinium oxycoccus*), White Beak-sedge (*Rhynchospora alba*) and the insectivorous Round-leaved Sundew (*Drosera rotundifolia*). Elsewhere bog fragments are usually dominated by Purple Moor-grass (*Molinia caerulea*) with few associated species.

These bogs are maintained by high rainfall. Similar bogs are found in the foothills of the eastern and northern hills on flat areas where drainage is impeded, but nearly all of these were drained, many in recent years.

Blanket bogs

A layer of deep peat forming blanket bog covers the tops of most fells. As with other bogs its development is due to the growth of *Sphagnum* spp. and depends on high rainfall or impeded drainage or both. The bogs are thousands of years old and possibly originated following human interference of the woodland (burning and grazing) and/or a deterioration of the climate (wetter and colder). None are now in a completely natural state, all having been to some extent modified by human interference. Often they show evidence of huge erosion episodes some of which are active today. In some places only islands of peat are left in a surrounding stony area of thin grassland or upland heath.

above Bog-myrtle. *(Phil Smith)*

below Purple Moor-grass growing in peat pool, Risley Moss. *(Phil Smith)*

Cloudberry.
(Geoff Morries)

In some areas, especially in the north of the county, there is a hummock – hollow system of bog vegetation with a mixture of species including Cranberry, Bog-rosemary and *Sphagnum* spp. In other places, especially further south, the moors are more often covered by Common Cottongrass (*Eriophorum angustifolium*) in the wetter places and Hare's-tail Cottongrass (*Eriophorum vaginatum*) in the drier parts. Together these plants make a striking picture in June, e.g. on Waddington Fell, with their nodding white fruiting heads.

In the north the moors are usually managed for Red Grouse and the regular patchwork of springtime burning favours the growth of Heather. Other plants that grow here include Cowberry, Bilberry, Cranberry and Cross-leaved Heath (*Erica tetralix*). On the very tops relicts of an arctic flora can be found including Cloudberry (*Rubus chamaemorus*), that rarely fruits, the hybrid Deergrass (*Trichophorum cespitosum* ssp. *cespitosum* x ssp. *germanicum*), and Stiff Sedge (*Carex bigelowii*), the latter two are both found on Leck Fell. Cloudberry was first recorded from Pendle Hill in 1597 making it one of the first records for the county (Savidge *et al.* 1963).

Moving waters, e.g. flushes, streams, rivers and canals

Below the summits of the hills springs arise and these often form flushed areas. With so much of the Lancashire uplands formed on acid, nutrient poor millstone grits many of these springs and flushes have a very poor flora: sometimes nothing more than Soft-rush can thrive. However, every spring, flush and rill is different and all deserve close scrutiny.

As the flushes and hill rills merge to form streams, the fast flowing water cuts into the rocks and clay with more springs appearing in these open situations. In the marshy and unstable clay banks a rich assemblage of marsh plants may be seen. In the more acid conditions Marsh Violet (*Viola palustris*) and Lousewort (*Pedicularis sylvatica*) occur, together with Round-leaved Crowfoot (*Ranunculus omiophyllus*) higher

Round-leaved
Crowfoot.
(Malcolm Edmunds)

up and Ivy-leaved Crowfoot (*Ranunculus hederaceus*) lower down. In more base rich situations species such as Marsh Ragwort (*Senecio aquaticus*), Ragged-robin (*Lychnis flos-cuculi*), Sneezewort (*Achillea ptarmica*) and Common Spotted-orchid can be seen along with Soft-rush, Hard Rush, Sharp-flowered Rush (*Juncus acutiflorus*), Common Marsh-bedstraw (*Galium palustre*) and more rarely Fen Bedstraw (*Galium uliginosum*) (see Box 4.18).

Eventually the streams or brooks, having travelled through woodlands, emerge on to the Lancashire plain and merge to form the 'big' rivers: Lune, Wyre, Ribble and Mersey. Some of these have a special flora of their own.

Box 4.18 *Plants of upland springs and rills*

In slightly less nutrient poor conditions the flushes may be covered with Blinks (*Montia fontana*). Other common species include Star Sedge (*Carex echinata*), Bog Pondweed (*Potamogeton polygonifolius*) and Yellow Sedge (*Carex viridula ssp. oedocarpa*), while the tiny eyebright *Euphrasia scottica*, with small white or pinkish flowers, Dioecious Sedge (*Carex dioica*), Flea Sedge (*Carex pulicaris*) and Few-flowered Spike-rush are seen occasionally. In more acid flushes Round-leaved Sundew, Cranberry and the yellow Bog Asphodel (*Narthecium ossifragum*), sometimes called Lancashire Asphodel because it was once so abundant in the county, are frequent. Another insectivorous plant, Common Butterwort, with its pale yellowish green leaves and blue flowers, was also common, but in recent years it has declined markedly and today is found in very few places.

Grass-of-Parnassus, Bog Pimpernel and Lesser Skullcap (*Scutellaria minor*) are much rarer although still plentiful in some localities. In highly calcareous flushes the tiny yellowish Lesser Clubmoss may occur. More interestingly the small 'Red Data Book' lady's-mantle *Alchemilla minima*, only known from a few localities in Yorkshire, was found recently in Leck. The beautiful pink flowered Bird's-eye Primrose was found in flushes from near the coast at Lancaster to several places in the eastern fells, but in the last thirty years or so it has become extinct in almost all its sites. The first British record was from Great Harwood in 1597 (Savidge *et al.* 1963). Perhaps the most interesting plant of the upland flushes is Pale Forget-me-not (*Myosotis stolonifera*), only found in northern England and southern Scotland and in alpine areas elsewhere in Europe.

top Star Sedge. *(Peter Jepson)*
centre Grass-of-Parnassus. *(Phil Smith)*
bottom Bog Asphodel. *(Phil Smith)*

Pale Forget-me-not growing in an upland flush.
(Peter Jepson)

The flora of the river Lune may be changing as it becomes more eutrophic (nutrient rich). As a less nutrient rich (mesotrophic) river it was characterised by the presence of Opposite-leaved Pondweed (*Groenlandia densa*), Alternate Water-milfoil (*Myriophyllum alterniflorum*), Pond Water-crowfoot (*Ranunculus peltatus*) and the nationally scarce Flat-sedge (*Blysmus compressus*). Small populations of these species survive in ponds and marshy areas of old meanders but they are now much scarcer.

As Lancaster is approached a fringe of tall sedges lines the banks. These are a mixture of Slender Tufted-sedge (*Carex acuta*) and Lesser Pond-sedge (*Carex acutiformis*) together, more surprisingly, with an abundance of the partially fertile hybrid between them, *Carex* x *subgracilis*.

Of the other rivers the Ribble is the most interesting botanically. From time to time there are extensive mats of the large flowered Stream Water-crowfoot (*Ranunculus penicillatus* ssp. *pseudofluitans*), but River Water-crowfoot (*Ranunculus fluitans*) and the highly sterile hybrid *Ranunculus* x *bachii* have also been found. Large flowered water-crowfoots occur in the river Wyre, but the absence of old records suggests that they are recent immigrants. Just after the Ribble leaves Yorkshire and enters Lancashire one of the country's rarest plants is found. This is the inconspicuous Northern Spike-rush (*Eleocharis austriaca*). It is a relatively recent addition to the Lancashire flora having only been recognised as a British plant since 1960 although an herbarium specimen was first gathered in 1947.

Stream Water-crowfoot in the River Ribble.
(Eric Greenwood)

Man-made aquatic habitats

Most of Lancashire's open still waters are man-made. They are today more widespread and extensive than they have been for thousands of years. The oldest of these water bodies are the marl pits. They were dug from Roman times onwards but many thousands were dug in the eighteenth century in order to extract the calcareous clay to use as fertilizer or for reclaiming peat mosses. Once dug they soon filled with water and were abandoned.

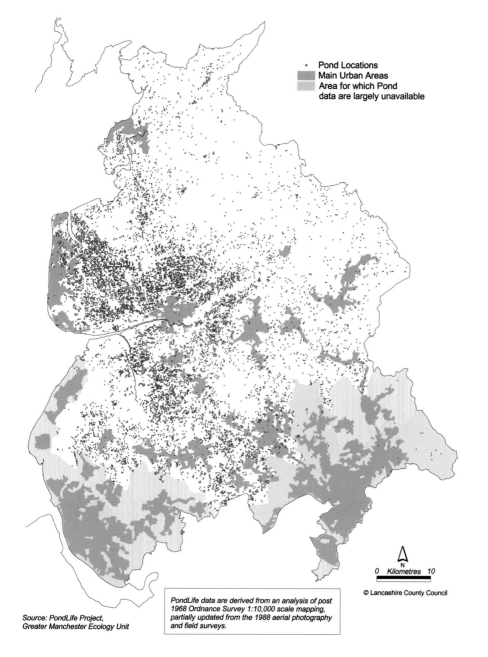

Legend:
- Pond Locations
- Main Urban Areas
- Area for which Pond data are largely unavailable

Map 8.
Locations of Ponds in the Wildlife Trust Area.
(Based on map prepared by John Boothby at Liverpool John Moores University using UKBORDERS™ data supplied under the CHEST Licence. The work is based on data provided with the support of the ESRC and JISC and uses boundary material which is copyright of the Crown and the ED-LINE Consortium.)
(Nik Bruce)

PondLife data are derived from an analysis of post 1968 Ordnance Survey 1:10,000 scale mapping, partially updated from the 1988 aerial photography and field surveys.

Source: PondLife Project, Greater Manchester Ecology Unit

© Lancashire County Council

0 Kilometres 10

Pits and ponds

Marl pits are found in all the clay areas of the county (see Map 8). Each marl pit or pond is different depending on the degree of shading and silting. Typically an unshaded pond with open water will have the odd Hawthorn or Grey Willow bush on its bank, with a marshy area round the edges containing a number of common species (see Box 4.19).

89

Box 4.19 *Plants of pond margins*

Typical plants include Water, Creeping and Tufted Forget-me-nots (*Myosotis scorpioides*, *M. secunda* and *M. laxa*), Various-leaved and Common Water-starworts (*Callitriche platycarpa* and *C. stagnalis*), Water Plantain (*Alisma plantago-aquatica*) that is almost always present if only as a single plant, Brooklime (*Veronica beccabunga*), Blue Water-speedwell (*Veronica anagallis-aquatica*), Bog Stitchwort (*Stellaria uliginosa*), Clustered Dock (*Rumex conglomeratus*), Water Mint, Unbranched and Branched Bur-reeds (*Sparganium emersum* and *S. erectum*) and various sweet-grasses (*Glyceria fluitans*, *G. x pedicellata*, *G. declinata* and *G. notata*). Sometimes a denser fringe of one species, e.g. Common Spike-rush (*Eleocharis palustris*), may occur. Much rarer are Lesser Marshwort (*Apium inundatum*), and Tubular and Fine-leaved Water-dropworts (*Oenanthe fistulosa* and *O. aquatica*).

Broad-leaved Pondweed with pair of Common Blue Damselflies, the female laying eggs. (Geoff Morries)

Towards the centre of the pond floating leaved plants such as Broad-leaved Pondweed (*Potamogeton natans*) and Amphibious Bistort (*Persicaria amphibia*) occur whilst free floating plants include species of duckweed (*Spirodela polyrhiza*, *Lemna minor* and *Lemna gibba*). In the centre of the pond submerged aquatics include Canadian Waterweed (*Elodea canadensis*), not yet replaced by its North American relative Nuttall's Waterweed (*Elodea nuttallii*), Common and Thread-leaved Water-crowfoots (*Ranunculus aquatilis* and *R. trichophyllus*), Least Duckweed (*Lemna trisulca*) and Small Pondweed (*Potamogeton berchtoldii*).

Flowering-rush.
(Peter Jepson)

Canals

The next oldest group of man-made water bodies are the canals dating from the late eighteenth century. Some, like the Lancaster Canal, are more like slow moving rivers. However, canals have their own characteristic flora. Typical species include Arrowhead (*Sagittaria sagittifolia*), Sweet-flag (*Acorus calamus*), especially common on the Lancaster Canal, Flowering-rush (*Butomus umbellatus*) and Reed Sweet-grass in canals south of the Ribble.

For a number of years in the 1960s and 70s the 'Red Data Book' species Water Soldier (*Stratiotes aloides*) became abundant in the Lancaster Canal but then disappeared as suddenly as it had arrived. It is still found in ponds. Similarly Floating Water-plantain (*Luronium natans*) colonised canals and first appeared in Lancashire in the Ashton Canal, Manchester in 1939 (Savidge *et al.* 1963). Subsequently it spread to the Rochdale Canal where it is still found. Although in the British Isles it is found in several localities and diverse habitats (Preston and Croft 1997), it is an endangered species enjoying protection under international legislation (Wigginton 1999). Many other aquatics and moisture loving species occur in and along the banks of the canals making them one of the richest habitats for these species in the county (Box 4.20).

91

Not seen so easily are submerged plants some of which are nationally scarce. These include hornworts (*Ceratophyllum spp.*) and Autumn Water-starwort (*Callitriche hermaphroditica*) together with a number of submerged pondweeds e.g. *Potamogeton crispus, P. pusillus, P. trichoides, P. pectinatus* and *P. perfoliatus*). Red Pondweed (*Potamogeton alpinus*) seems to have gone from the Lancaster Canal very recently as did Opposite-leaved Pondweed about twenty years ago. Similarly pondweeds have gone from many places in the Leeds and Liverpool Canal. The hybrid Linton's Pondweed (*Potamogeton crispus x P. friesii = P. x lintonii*) was also found in the Lancaster Canal but has not been seen recently. Interestingly one of its parents, Flat-stalked Pondweed (*P. friesii*), does not grow in the county although it was recorded erroneously from time to time. In the mid nineteenth century Canadian Waterweed became a major problem in British canals and remained common until 20–30 years ago when it was largely replaced by Nuttall's Waterweed. It remains a mystery why this should have happened.

Quarries, gravel pits, reservoirs, mill lodges, flashes and clay pits

Where stone was quarried, ponds were often left behind some of which are very deep. They may be alkaline or acid depending upon the type of rock quarried, but they do not seem to have any special characteristics. Exceptions occur and one old limestone quarry near Longridge contains a number of very rare Lancashire plants including Lesser Tussock-sedge (*Carex diandra*) and Large Yellow-sedge (*Carex viridula* ssp. *brachyrrhyncha*).

Much richer is the flora associated with gravel pits, many of which were dug to extract gravel for building motorways from the 1960s onwards. They include the Wildlife Trust's nature reserve at Mere Sands Wood, and others are still being formed, e.g. east of the M6 by the river Ribble at Preston. Even more interesting is the flora associated with the fluctuating water levels of reservoirs. These were often built in the east of the county about 100 years ago and filled with acidic water giving rise to nutrient poor (oligotrophic to mesotrophic) conditions. Today they provide suitable habitats for a number of rare and localised species that have colonized the gravel banks. Typical of this group are Shoreweed, Small Water-pepper (*Persicaria minor*), Water-purslane (*Lythrum portula*), Mudwort (*Limosella aquatica*), Thread Rush (*Juncus filiformis*) and, recently discovered in Lancashire, Northern Yellow-cress (*Rorippa islandica*). This last species was only distinguished from its much commoner relative Marsh Yellow-cress (*Rorippa palustris*) in 1968 and may be more frequent than records suggest, or it may be spreading. In years when water levels remain high these species are rare or often overlooked, but as the water level drops they can occur in great abundance.

In coal mining areas, especially near Wigan, subsidence has occurred creating large wetland areas called flashes. The best known of these are the Wigan Flashes and here a variety of wetland habitats were created. There are large reed beds with Common Reed, and a mosaic of marshy areas with marsh orchids, Marsh Helleborine and other commoner species.

Brick or clay pits were dug in many places and when these were abandoned they often left ponds and marshy areas. Typically they contain a variety of common marshy plants and, as so often when the opportunity arises, marsh orchids colonize them e.g. at Longton south of Preston.

Arable fields, gardens and waste places

When humans started to clear the woodlands they encouraged the growth of annual plants and introduced others. Many of the annual plants such as Common Chickweed (*Stellaria media*) and Groundsel occur naturally on sand dunes and in other disturbed places. However, much has been written about the disappearance of colourful 'cornfield' weeds such as Corncockle (*Agrostemma githago*), Cornflower (*Centaurea cyanus*) and poppies (*Papaver* spp.) Much of this discussion is based on research carried out in the English midlands and further south. Furthermore many of these species were ancient introductions.

In Lancashire arable farming was established as long ago as anywhere else in the country but the county's weed flora has been little studied. It is important, therefore to appreciate that many characteristic weeds of the south are southern species and have only grown as far north as Lancashire as casual introductions, e.g. fluellens (*Kickxia* spp.). Also the location of arable farming within the county has changed. For thousands of years Lancashire's arable farming was confined to fields on clay soils, especially those with a southerly aspect, but as the peat mosses were drained in the eighteenth and nineteenth centuries more crops were grown on the reclaimed peat leaving the clay soils for meadows and pasture. Today there seems to have been a return to arable farming on clay soils, but in addition to cereals the peat soils are especially good for growing root crops, particularly potatoes, salad crops and vegetables. Modern crop husbandry has largely eliminated weeds from the actively growing cereal crop but field margins and crops such as potatoes, which are

Marsh Helleborine thrives both in 'natural' dune slacks and in similar marshy areas of the Wigan Flashes and elsewhere.
(Phil Smith)

Flowers and Ferns:
Arable fields

sometimes left after their main growth has ceased before harvesting, allow the growth of a profusion of weeds (see Box 4.21).

Nevertheless some plants, e.g. Corncockle and Cornflower that were once abundant elsewhere, always seem to have been rare in Lancashire. Today they are occasionally found in waste places. Similarly poppies that were once abundant as cornfield weeds on clay soils are rarely found in crops today, yet they are common enough in waste sites. Their seeds can remain dormant for a long time and sometimes if old grassland is cultivated they germinate in profusion.

Only a few of Lancashire's common weeds have large attractive flowers but the county has a few specialities. On the mossland soils Corn Marigold (*Chrysanthemum segetum*) (see p.273) and Large-flowered Hemp-nettle (*Galeopsis speciosa*) can make a colourful show, but as they are susceptible to weed killers they are not often seen in cereal crops – both are ancient introductions. A number of fumitories are found as arable weeds and Lancashire, with a few other areas, might be considered the headquarters of the nationally rare British endemic Purple Ramping-fumitory (*Fumaria purpurea*). It is found throughout lowland Lancashire but is especially frequent to the south and west of Lancaster where it turns up in builder's rubble and waste ground as

---

Box 4.21 *Typical Lancashire weeds*

Today many arable field weeds are low growing annuals. Some of the commonest are Common Chickweed, Annual Meadow-grass (*Poa annua*), Redshank (*Persicaria maculosa*), Pale Persicaria (*Persicaria lapathifolia*), Knotgrass and Equal-leaved Knotgrass (*Polygonum aviculare* and *P. arenastrum*), Scentless Mayweed (*Tripleurospermum inodorum*), Scented Mayweed (*Matricaria recutita*) and Pineappleweed (*Matricaria discoidea*) only introduced from North America about 100 years ago. Also frequently found are the ancient introductions, Green Field-speedwell (*Veronica agrestis*) and Grey Field-speedwell (*Veronica polita*), both much less frequent than formerly, and the more recently introduced Common Field-speedwell (*Veronica persica*), first recorded in Lancashire in the 1830s only a few years after its first British record in 1825. It is a native of S.W. Asia. Scarlet Pimpernel (*Anagallis arvensis*), Wild Pansy (*Viola tricolor*) and Field Pansy (*Viola arvensis*) can also be found but possibly more rarely than formerly. Wild-oat (*Avena fatua*) is becoming increasingly common and can be a problem in cereal crops. In potato fields especially, Common Orache (*Atriplex patula*) and Fat-hen (*Chenopodium album*) can be abundant. Some perennial weeds can be a problem to farmers and amongst the commonest are Greater Plantain (*Plantago major*), Common Couch, Creeping Buttercup, particularly on wet soils and dandelions.

Wildlife of Lancashire

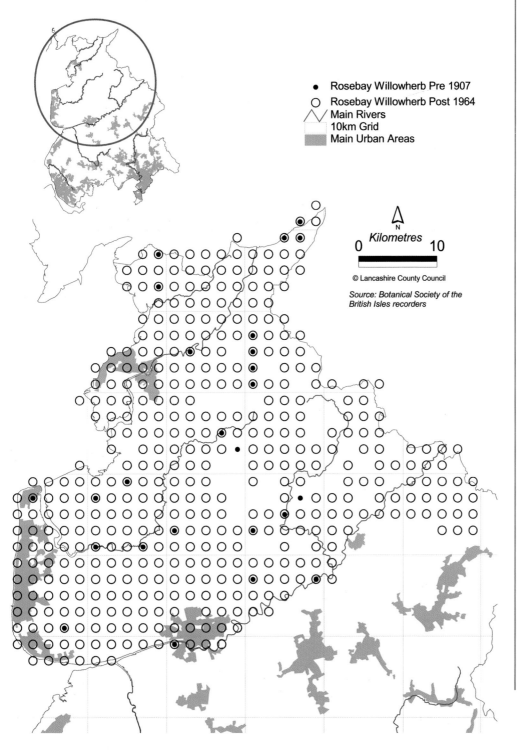

Rosebay Willowherb Pre 1907

○ Rosebay Willowherb Post 1964

/\/\ Main Rivers

□ 10km Grid

▨ Main Urban Areas

N

Kilometres

0   10

© Lancashire County Council

Source: Botanical Society of the British Isles recorders

Map 9.
Distribution of Rosebay Willowherb in Northern Lancashire.
One hundred years ago Rosebay Willowherb was beginning to spread away from its natural rocky habitats in the hills to become a species of railway banks and waste places. In this map only the records in Leck and Roeburndale reflect its natural distribution whilst most if not all the other records reflect natural spread or introductions. Today it is found throughout the county although it is still absent from parts of Bowland.
(Nik Bruce)

Flowers and Ferns:
Arable fields

Rosebay Willowherb.
(Phil Smith)

well as farmland. It is a handsome, large flowered dark pink species, but its conservation is difficult, as often it does not appear in its wasteland habitats in consecutive years.

Many plants found in waste places are often simply ignored, but the diversity of species in these open habitats is possibly greater than anywhere else. The flora at any one site is transient lasting for at best a few years, and the species composition varies from site to site. Tall grasses such as False Oat-grass and Cock's-foot are often abundant along with a number of common annual and short-lived perennial species. In some places Great Willowherb (*Epilobium hirsutum*) and Rosebay Willowherb (*Chamerion angustifolium*), a rare plant of mountains until the late nineteenth century when it spread on to railway banks and waste land, make fine displays in July and August, yet the small but ubiquitous Broad-leaved Willowherb and its North American relative, American Willowherb, with which it readily hybridises are hardly noticed. Another conspicuous plant is the introduced Japanese Knotweed (*Fallopia japonica*), which can be a particularly nasty weed only eradicated with great difficulty. Waste ground is also a likely place to find garden outcasts: plants that are grown in gardens or used

Wildlife of Lancashire

in landscaping schemes. Two groups, the michaelmas-daisies (*Aster* spp.) and goldenrods (*Solidago* spp.), are amongst the most colourful and make fine late summer and autumn displays. In recent years the Butterfly-bush (*Buddleja davidii*) has become a colourful addition to the urban flora, with the added benefit of being particularly attractive to insects. Despite the difficulties and their transient nature, urban sites provide a challenging opportunity for naturalists to discover much that is new about their flora.

In addition to holes left in the ground by extractive industries Lancashire's industry also left behind a variety of waste heaps. The less poisonous heaps were colonised by plants and a rich flora developed on the more alkaline ones. Hilary Ash (1999) reviewed those in the Mersey Basin but they were found throughout the county from Carnforth southwards (see Box 4.22).

Box 4.22 *Lancashire's industrial past*

A feature of these waste heaps, along with clay pits, other industrial wastelands and some motorways, was the large number of orchids that colonised them, in particular Southern Marsh-orchid, Northern Marsh-orchid, Early Marsh-orchid and Common Spotted-orchid with which the other species formed a bewildering array of hybrids. Often these orchids were found in thousands providing a mass of colour in early summer. More rarely Marsh Helleborine was also found. Other orchids in these places include Pyramidal Orchid (*Anacamptis pyramidalis*), Fragrant Orchid and Bee Orchid. One of the best sites where these interesting plants continue to thrive is Nob End, Bolton where the plants grow on Leblanc waste. The site has been known for many years and because of its importance it is a Site of Special Scientific Interest.

Hybrid between Southern Marsh and Common Spotted-orchids, growing at Astley Moss. *(Geoff Morries)*

97

Conclusion

The Lancashire flora is both varied and diverse. In Britain about 4100 species and hybrids have been recorded (excluding micro-species) of which something like 1600 are known from Lancashire, North Merseyside and Greater Manchester. About 40% of these were accidentally or deliberately introduced by humans. However, some 60% of these are casual having been recorded on only a few occasions, or if more frequent seem to be repeatedly introduced. Of the naturalized introduced species by far the largest number historically and recently are garden escapes. This means that at any one time many fewer than 1600 species are growing in the county – perhaps as few as 1000.

The impact of humans has been profound yet such is the adaptability of plants that probably less than 10% of native species are truly extinct. It must be remembered that simply because a species has not been recorded for a few years does not necessarily mean it is extinct. The annual Bur Chervil (*Anthriscus caucalis*) was recorded in 1904 at St Annes and then disappeared before reappearing again in 1999. Presumably its seeds remained dormant until the exacting open conditions required for its growth returned. Unfortunately suitable conditions for species such as Great Sundew (*Drosera anglica*) and Dwarf Cornel (*Cornus suecica*) may never return, but even if they do there may be no seed source available. Furthermore many more species are found in just one or two sites and may be critically endangered especially as some are not subject to any conservation measures.

The richest areas of the County appear to be around Silverdale, Lytham St Annes and the Sefton coast but this may reflect more intensive recording than elsewhere. These are areas where the large number of native plants is increased by a large number of introduced species. In these areas 1000 or more species have been recorded in the appropriate 10 x 10 km squares. This compares with similar totals for parts of North Wales but is well short of the 1300 species recorded in parts of London where most species recorded are introduced.

The composition of the Lancashire flora has never been static. It has responded to changing climate and to the changes caused by humans. During the late eighteenth century and later the pace of change accelerated with the agricultural and industrial revolutions. Today that rate of change appears to be accelerating still further.

Further reading

Fitter, R., Fitter, A, and Blamey, M. (2003). *Wild Flowers and Ferns of Britain and Ireland.* A. & C. Black, London.

Stace, C. (1997). *New Flora of the British Isles*, 2nd edn, Cambridge University Press, Cambridge.

The first is a popular well-illustrated guide, the second is comprehensive with no colour illustrations. For specialist guides to individual groups the Handbooks (all illustrated) and other publications of the Botanical Society of the British Isles are indispensable.

Flowers and Ferns:
Conclusion

Chapter 5

Lower Plants

John Lowell and Mark Seaward

Introduction, by Malcolm Edmunds

When the proverbial man in the street thinks of plants it is probably the flowering plants, conifers and ferns that he has in mind. These so-called 'higher plants' are reviewed in Chapter 4. In contrast the 'lower plants' are much less well known, partly because they are all relatively small and inconspicuous, but also because some of them are difficult to identify without a microscope. Marine and freshwater algae are mentioned in Chapters 3 and 10, and there are also a few that grow on land, notably species of *Pleurococcus* which can be found on damp, shady tree trunks. In this chapter we concentrate on two groups of rather larger plants, first the bryophytes comprising mosses and liver-worts, and second the lichens which are intimate associations between green (or blue-green) algae and fungi. The association is said to be 'symbiotic', meaning that both the alga and the fungus benefit from living together, the alga gets a watery medium in which to live while the fungus acquires some of the sugars synthesised by the alga.

Bryophytes, by John Lowell

Bryophytes (see Box 5.1) are surely the Cinderellas of the plant world; they are there in the background but they don't get seen. Look under the next patch of Nettles and you will very likely find masses of the big moss *Brachythecium rutabulum*. There will be more moss plants than nettles and quite possibly the moss will have the greater biomass: but to many people, there are just nettles. And yet bryophytes are often of ecological importance as colonisers. The sand dunes of the Sefton and Fylde coast are justly famous for their flowering plants; but how does vegetation get established in shifting, wind-blown sand? Look in the loose sand around the Marram grass and you will find clumps of the beautiful gold-green moss *Tortula ruraliformis* binding the sand and providing a foothold for bigger plants.

The moist slacks on the landward side of the Sefton dunes are the home to a number of rare bryophytes of National and even European

The moss *Leucobryum glaucum* forms compact colonies in woodland and sometimes moorland that occasionally develop into large swollen cushions detached from the substrate. As they are moved around by the wind or animals, they can shed viable plants, an efficient method of propagation. The characteristically pale green or whitish colour is due to large numbers of dead, empty cells which, as in *Sphagnum* spp., can store water and enable the plant to continue growing during dry weather. *(Tim Mitcham)*

Lower Plants:
Mosses and Liverworts

Box 5.1 Mosses and Liverworts

right The moss *Polytrichum commune* will be familiar to everyone – it is ubiquitous in moorland bogs and also common on drier ground so long as it is acidic. Its stems may reach 20 cm or more, and being so large it is not always recognised as a moss. Another somewhat smaller species, *P. formosum*, prefers less open situations. *(Jason Smalley)*

Bryophytes, the mosses and liverworts, have no flowers but, like ferns, reproduce by means of spores and/or vegetatively. They range in size from species just visible to the naked eye to those, like *Polytrichum commune*, whose stems may be 20 cm or more long.

It is not a simple matter to distinguish mosses from liverworts, but liverworts split naturally into two kinds. *Thallose* liverworts are just a ribbon or plate of tissue (they do not have stems or leaves) and are very easily recognised – they are familiar weeds on plant pots and in greenhouses. (Some lichens share this thallose habit; if the thallus is white below or anything but green on top it is not a liverwort.) Species of the other kind of liverwort, *leafy liverworts*, are often confused with mosses There is one easy distinction: if the leaves are deeply divided into two or more lobes, then it is a liverwort. Other distinguishing features between the more confusing liverworts and mosses are given by Watson (1981).

Metzgeria species (this one is *M. furcata*) differ from most thallose liverworts in that the thallus is thin and translucent rather than thick and opaque. The combination of a frequently forked translucent thallus and a very prominent midrib makes the genus instantly recognised. *Metzgeria* spp. are most often found on the bark of trees but they also occur on rock as in this photograph. *(Jason Smalley)*

Lophocolea bidentata is a typical leafy liverwort. The flattened shoots and the leaves deeply divided into two finely pointed lobes distinguish it from a moss. *(Jason Smalley)*

The nationally scarce thallose liverwort *Petalophyllum ralfsii* grows on the Fylde coast dune slacks. It is tiny, but easily recognised by its overlapping laminae of tissue. These are male plants – the yellowish spheres are the male sex organs.
(Dan Wrench)

importance. Several of these are species of *Bryum*, superficially resembling *Bryum capillare* which is common on many wall tops and conspicuous for its large drooping capsules, but it is difficult to distinguish the different species. However, there is no mistaking our prize liverwort of the dune slacks, *Petalophyllum ralfsii*; the problem is finding it! Although spectacular it is *tiny*, and best searched for on hands and knees. This species and some of the *Bryum* species are protected by law and must not be interfered with in any way.

The Trough of Bowland, and the South and West Pennines provide a range of bryophyte habitats and a remarkable diversity of species; this has been quantified in recent surveys by counting species numbers in 2 km square areas (tetrads). Among the richest areas are deep rocky cloughs with fast-flowing streams, especially those with woodland. Many tetrads in Bowland have well over 100 species and around Leck Beck there are a couple of tetrads with well over 200 species. Even the Pennine fringes adjoining industrial areas are remarkably rich, with around 100 species in the tetrads containing Lead Mines Clough (east of Chorley) and Gorpley Clough near

Lower Plants:
Mosses and Liverworts

Todmorden. In such habitats one finds some spectacular large mosses such as *Dicranum majus* and *Rhytidiadelphus loreus* and the streams will have big green cushions of the liverwort *Scapania undulata* and perhaps *Nardia compressa* which is nationally rather scarce but quite frequent in Lancashire.

The moorland around these rocky cloughs is generally less species rich but there is still much of interest. In particular, the springs and flushes have beautiful and colourful bryophyte communities. Patches of glaucous-green *Philonotis fontana* (often with spherical capsules above the stick-like shoots) mingle with patches of bright green *Dicranella palustris*, and it is likely there will be *Bryum pseudotriquetrum*, darkish green touched with red. If there is wet rock, perhaps around a little water-fall, it may be draped with coppery-brown *Sphagnum denticulatum*. Many bryophytes are, like lichens, sensitive to air pollution (Box 5.2). Any naturalist who learns to recognise these interesting mosses can make useful records of their recolonisation of our county.

The long, curving, finely pointed leaves of *Dicranum majus* make this moss instantly recognisable. It can be found in open woodland, especially on old walls, and also in heathy areas growing among heather or Bilberry. It is widespread in the hills, and rare in lowland areas. *Dicranum scoparium* has shorter and less curved leaves, but is much more frequent than *D. majus*. (Dan Wrench)

Box 5.2 *Recolonisation by clean-air bryophytes*

A cheering feature of the bryophyte flora of the industrial areas of South Lancashire is the gradual recolonisation by pollution sensitive species – presumably as a result of cleaner air.

This recolonisation is most apparent in moss species growing as tufts or cushions on the smaller branches and twigs of trees, especially willow (*Salix* spp.) and Elder (*Sambucus nigra*). While big branches and tree trunks have a diverse flora, relatively few species grow on twigs, but all of them should be identifiable with the help of Watson (1981). *Ulota phyllantha* and *Orthotrichum pulchellum* were both unknown south of the Ribble until the mid-nineties and rare in the north, but have increased spectacularly and are now frequent. *Orthotrichum affine* and the *Ulota crispa* aggregate (including *U. crispa* and *U. bruchii*) have been present in Lancashire for many years, but have also become much commoner recently. Finally, *Orthotrichum stramineum* has very recently been reported from South Lancashire and may be colonising this area.

Lichens, by Mark Seaward

Lichens are well known for their ability to monitor air pollution, which has clearly had a dramatic impact on the Lancashire lichen flora over the past two centuries (see Box 5.3), but the different species and assemblages of lichens reflect a wide range of environmental factors. Leo Grindon (1859), through his work on the Manchester flora, has been widely quoted as one of the first to recognize the impact of air pollution on lichens, but William Borrer had made a similar observation four decades earlier. As a result of the Industrial Revolution, which gained momentum after the end of the eighteenth century, the county's lichen flora became impoverished, with large areas of South Lancashire losing many species over the next hundred or so years; indeed, in some highly industrial and urban areas none at all survived. Unfortunately for much of the county this scenario is only conjecture since Lancashire was (and continues to be) surprisingly short of lichenologists. Nevertheless, it has been possible to piece together a reasonable picture of the past glory from published papers and herbarium material (Box 5.4).

The current status of our lichen flora can be assessed from field-work undertaken over the past 30 years in support of the British Lichen Society's national mapping programme, including, more

The lichen *Flavoparmelia caperata* is widely distributed in England and Wales, mainly on well-lit broad-leaved trees. It suffered from air pollution, particularly in Lancashire, but is now returning as air quality improves. (Mark Seaward)

opposite Orthotrichum affine.
(Dan Wrench)

opposite lower Ulota bruchii.
(Dan Wrench)

Lower Plants:
Lichens

Melanistic and
typical forms of the
Peppered Moth.
*(Inigo Everson/
Woodfall Wild
Images)*

The impact of air pollution on ecosystems is clearly demonstrated by the long-term studies of the Peppered Moth (*Biston betularia*) and lichens on trees centred on Manchester. The first black-coloured melanic (*carbonaria*) form of the moth in England was collected in Manchester in 1848, and it became progressively more numerous until by 1952 98% of Manchester moths were melanic. At the same time soot and smoke killed lichens so that lichen diversity on trees declined dramatically. The light-coloured peppered form of the moth (*typica*) was beautifully camouflaged on the mosaic of lichens which formerly clothed tree branches and trunks, but as the lichens died these moths became conspicuous to predatory birds on the blackened trunks while the black moths were now better camouflaged. The ratio of these two forms of Peppered Moth proved valuable in pollution monitoring studies along a 125 km transect from the centre of Manchester to North Wales (Bishop *et al.* 1975). However, following the Clean Air Acts of 1956 and 1968, air quality in Manchester has improved dramatically and the frequency of melanic moths has declined. At first lichens were slow to recover and their relationship to melanic moth frequency was less pronounced (Cook *et al.* 1990), but the effects of striking increases in lichen diversity in more recent years have yet to be evaluated.

recently, a survey of some of the county's churchyards. However, lichens are notoriously difficult to identify, and considerable work still needs to be done to document lichen diversity and the current status of species, especially those on the Red Data list. This is particularly important following pollution changes as a result of implementation of the Clean Air Acts, and changes in energy requirements, transportation needs and agricultural practices.

As well as air pollution, many other environmental disturbances have also been responsible for the decline in the county's lichen flora. Due to their sensitivity to change, lichens have proved effective for monitoring habitat stability and measuring ecological continuity. Lichen-rich habitats still occur in the north of the county, and some central and southern areas have seen the return of a few pollution sensitive species following a dramatic reduction in sulphur dioxide pollution. However, lichen assemblages are now under threat from increases in other atmospheric pollutants such as nitrogen oxides, ammonia and agrochemicals.

*Wildlife of
Lancashire*

The Lancashire lichen flora up to 2002 can be summarized as follows:

* 487 taxa (i.e. species or distinctive varieties) have been recorded from the north of the county, of which 37 have not been seen for a century or more;

* 354 taxa have been recorded from the south, of which only 224 have been recorded in recent years; of the remainder, 50 have not been recorded since the early nineteenth century but probably still survive, and 70, not seen for a century, are either extinct or difficult to confirm in the absence of herbarium material.

Xanthoria polycarpa is a lichen of nutrient-rich bark, particularly twigs. Its dramatic spread in recent years has been due to nutrient enrichment, mainly caused by agricultural practices. *(Mark Seaward)*

Lecanora muralis is a widespread lichen on rocks and building materials, especially those rich in nitrates. In air polluted areas it prefers calcareous substrates, then as pollution levels fall it spreads to other surfaces including dusty bark and timber.
(Mark Seaward)

These figures emphasize not only the considerable scope for lichenological studies in Lancashire, but also the county's north – south biodiversity gradient.

Further reading

Watson, E. V. (1981). *British Mosses and Liverworts.* Cambridge University Press, 3rd edn, Cambridge.

Wigginton, M. J. (1995). *Mosses and Liverworts of North Lancashire.* Lancaster University, Lancaster.

A new Flora of South Lancashire, to include bryophytes, is in preparation and is expected to appear in about 2005.

Those wishing to study lichens are strongly recommended to join the British Lichen Society (website: www.theBLS.org.uk) and to attend field meetings, courses and taxonomic workshops. The first three books give excellent introductions while the last gives useful ideas for projects.

Baron, G. (1999). *Understanding lichens.* Richmond Publishing, Slough.

Laundon, J. R. (1986). *Lichens.* Shire Publications, Aylesbury.

Purvis, O. W. (2000) *Lichens.* The Natural History Museum, London.

Richardson, D. H. S. (1992). *Pollution monitoring with lichens.* Naturalists' Handbooks 19. Richmond Publishing, Slough.

Lichen lists for particular 10 km x 10 km squares can be obtained from the British Lichen Society's Mapping Recorder (e-mail: m.r.d.seaward@bradford.ac.uk).

Wildlife of Lancashire

Fungi

Chapter 6

Richard Thompson

What are fungi?

Fungi are not plants but belong in a Kingdom of their own. Their cell walls are made of chitin (like insects) and instead of photosynthesising they obtain energy by digesting organic matter. They can be divided into three nutritional groups:

* Saprophytes are probably the most numerous, performing a vital role in breaking down dead organic matter such as wood and leaf litter, e.g. waxcaps and stinkhorns.

* Parasites attack a living host. A plant parasite commonly seen locally is the honey fungus *Armillaria mellea* (see Box 6.1). Animal parasites include the Scarlet Caterpillar Fungus (*Cordyceps militaris*) whose orange to scarlet fruit-bodies sprouting from buried caterpillar corpses are a common autumnal sight in grassland throughout Lancashire.

Scarlet Caterpillar Fungus.
(Pat Livermore)

Box 6.1 The Bad Guys? Honey Fungus in Lancashire

The honey fungus is often seen as a scourge of our trees and shrubs, however we now know that Lancashire is home to at least three

The honey fungus *Armillaria mellea*. (Pat Livermore)

different species. *Armillaria ostoyae* and *A. mellea sensu stricto* are aggressive pathogens, the former in native woodlands and the latter in conifer plantations. The third species, *A. gallica*, is largely benign, playing an important role in the recycling of nutrients from dead wood. It is also the most commonly seen species in our native woodlands and is beneficial to the trees.

Research in the USA suggests *A. ostoyae* could be among the world's largest and oldest living organisms. One individual is estimated to be at least 2400 years old, with an

underground network of hyphae occupying 890 hectares (3 km across) and weighing perhaps over 600 tons. Other honey fungi also ramify through soil, though it seems they do not usually exceed 10 hectares.

Honey fungi (and a few other fungi) are also responsible for one of the eeriest sights in the natural world. Their digestive processes result in luminescence, sometimes causing entire logs, stumps and leaves to glow. So pick a warm, moonless night far away from street-lights and step into their twilight world.

So are these fungi the bad guys? In truth, most fungi found in and around living wood are benign or even beneficial to their hosts. Most species attack only the dead heartwood of trees, returning trapped nutrients to the soil, thereby feeding their hosts. They also reduce the weight of old trees, increasing their stability and longevity, whilst providing an essential, but increasingly rare, habitat for thousands of invertebrates and dozens of bats and birds. Moreover, their presence may prevent the establishment of pathogens such as *A. mellea*. In other words, since fungicides are indiscriminate, their illiberal use may actually be disastrous for the trees we are trying to protect by allowing the pathogens to run rife. But where would our woodlands be without pathogens anyway? Pathogens thrive in monocultures, hence they help promote woodland biodiversity by diversifying woodland structure and allowing a whole suite of plants and animals to establish and survive. So perhaps the honey fungi are the good guys after all!

* Symbionts live in close association with another organism to their mutual benefit, for example lichens which are associations between algae and fungi (see chapter 5), and mycorrhizal fungi which infect plant roots. The fungus benefits by receiving sugars from the plant and the plant obtains phosphates and other

nutrients from the fungus. Mycorrhizal fungi in our woodlands are usually macro-fungi, such as the Fly Agaric (*Amanita muscaria*) and Death Cap (*Amanita phalloides*), which is why such species only occur in association with certain species of tree. In grasslands, this role is generally performed by micro-fungi, which lack visible fruiting bodies so their presence is not obvious. Mycorrhizal associations probably occur in 85% of plant species. They play a crucial role in determining plant survival and plant community structure, while plants such as orchids cannot germinate without their mycorrhizal fungi.

The vast Fungal Kingdom dominates almost every habitat, yet it is shrouded in mystery. In Britain 12,000 species are known, not including lichens, but this figure is far from complete. 120 new species are being found every year and it is likely that the true figure far exceeds 20,000.

Fungi have reclusive habits; they are composed of microscopic filaments or 'hyphae', hidden away in the substrates on which they feed, offering little or no impression of how profoundly they shape the world about them. Clues to their presence are fleeting and usually related to reproduction, for many species are extroverts – sprouting an extraordinary variety of spore-producing structures that are clearly visible to the naked eye. These so-called 'macro-fungi' offer the naturalist a ready portal into the mysteries of the Kingdom and our knowledge of the fungi of Lancashire is largely confined to them.

top left Death Cap.
(*Pat Livermore*)

above Fly Agaric.
(*Peter Smith*)

111

Fungi:
What are fungi?

Box 6.2 Fungi in Cuerden Valley Park

This site adjacent to the Lancashire Wildlife Trust's headquarters has habitats ranging from broadleaf and coniferous woodland to grassland and wet flushes. An interesting species recorded from the grass lawn near the buildings is the Woolly Milk Cap (*Lactarius torminosus*). It is very shaggy or woolly with pinkish salmon colours and darker concentric bands on the cap. When broken it exudes a white milk. Also near the buildings an unusual polypore, the Split Gill (*Schizophyllum commune*), has been recorded on an old fallen beech. It is fan shaped and covered in whitish down sometimes with a purple tint. Cock Cabin Wood is another area of interest with records of the Sulphur Tuft (*Hypholoma fasciculare*) and the Red Cracked Boletus (*Xerocomus chrysenteron*). Other fungi in the park include Fairies Bonnets (*Coprinus disseminatus*), Oak Milk Cap (*Lactarius quietus*), Rufous Milk Cap (*Lactarius rufus*) and St George's Mushroom (*Calocybe gambosum*) which is well known for culinary purposes.

Lancashire fungi

Macro-fungi occur in every terrestrial habitat in Lancashire, but are most diverse in old woodlands, grasslands and dunes. The county is blessed with many prime examples of these habitats, and the climate and the broad spectrum of soils and geology add further to the diversity.

The richest known site in the county is Gait Barrows National Nature Reserve, near Silverdale, with nearly 1,200 species recorded within its woodland, grassland and wetland habitats, including the rare wet woodland species Amanita friabilis. Associated with alder, it produces a small greyish toadstool. Better known, and much more widely distributed in old woodlands throughout the county, are two closely related species: the Fly Agaric, associated with birch, and the Death Cap, associated with oak. The Death Cap is well named, for even a fragment of the fruit body can kill. It has a pale, yellow-green colour, with a bag-like base and a ring around its mid-riff. The Fly Agaric, with white flecks on a brilliant red cap, is the archetypal toadstool of northern mythology, particularly associated with pixies (unsurprising, when one considers the fruit body's hallucinogenic properties!). Experimentation is dangerous, however, since it also contains many of the same toxins as the Death Cap. Fungi from two other well-studied sites are described in Boxes 6.2 and 6.3).

Grassland fungi are most diverse on un-improved pastures, particularly around Silverdale and the fringes of the West Pennines and Bowland Fells. Most striking are the brightly coloured 'waxcaps' and, with white, yellow, orange, green, scarlet and pink species, few flowers can rival the sheer exuberance of their colours. At up to 15 cm across, the largest of these is the Crimson Waxcap (Hygrocybe punicea). It favours calcareous pastures, though not exclusively, and is at home in the Silverdale area on such sites as Jack Scout. By contrast, the Ballerina Waxcap (H. calyptriformis) favours the neutral to acid soils of the upland fringes. With a pink conical cap like a tutu, and a stalk or 'stipe' of pure white, it is an extraordinary sight. These waxcaps, and many other grassland fungi, have become rare in the UK as a result of intensive farming methods, but many sites in Lancashire

Ballerina Waxcap.
(Pat Livermore)

opposite top Woolly Milk Cap.
(Pat Livermore)

opposite middle Red Cracked Boletus.
(Pat Livermore)

opposite bottom Fairies Bonnets.
(Peter Smith)

113

remain a stronghold. for them. In a four hectares area of grassland near Whalley, for instance, nearly 600 macro-fungi have been recorded, including a remarkable 35 species of waxcap (over half of all known northern European species). Doubtless, more such sites await discovery.

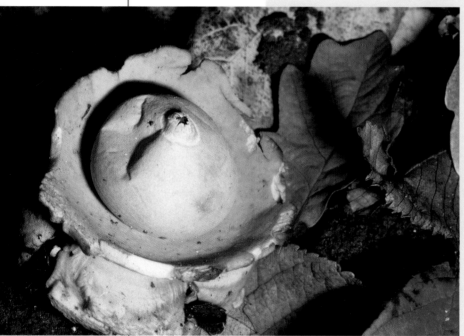

Earthstar *Geastrum triplex*.
(Eddie Campion)

Box 6.3 *Fungi of Ainsdale National Nature Reserve*

This site is well known for its flowering plants, but is also excellent for fungi. This unique dune system supports several distinct habitats, of which the grey dune scrub beneath pine (*Pinus* spp.), Creeping Willow, Sea Buckthorn (*Hippophae rhamnoides*) and birch (*Betula* spp.) is particularly rich.

Interesting fungi at Ainsdale include the strange earthstars (*Geastrum* spp.) which belong to a group known as puffball fungi. As the fruiting body develops the outer casing splits open exposing the spore bearing tissue and curves outwards forming a star like shape, hence the name. The Fly Agaric also frequents the dunes as do several of the morels (*Morchella* spp.). The spore bearing surface on these fungi produce ridges and folds and within these are shallow depressions where the actual spores mature and are then dispersed. Morels appear early, in April and May and are very attractive. False morels, *Gyromitra* spp., also occur on the dunes but are darker coloured and have a more chubby appearance. A dune specialist is the Dune Stinkhorn (*Phallus hadriani*), which is similar in appearance to the more widespread Common Stinkhorn, but the stalk quickly turns pink or red. The insects attracted to it must have a more delicate sense of smell, for its fragrance is faint and relatively pleasant. In total, over 600 species of fungi are known from Ainsdale, including a number of rarities, and more are being discovered each year.

Wildlife of Lancashire

Common Stinkhorn.
(Peter Smith)

Finally, a tour of Lancashire's fungi would be incomplete without mention of the Common Stinkhorn (*Phallus impudicus*), a peculiar, 20 cm high phallus sprouting from a gelatinous ball which, it is said, so offended the sensibilities of some Victorian ladies that they resolved to purge it from our countryside. They failed, for it remains extremely common in woodlands, easily located by the vile stench it produces which attracts spore-dispersing flies.

Further reading

Phillips, R. (1998). *Mushrooms and other fungi of Great Britain and Europe*. Pan Books, London

Courtecuisse, R. and Duham, B. (1995). *Mushrooms and Toadstools of Britain and Europe*. Harper Collins, London.

Courtecuisse, R. (1999). *Collins Wildlife Trust Guide: Mushrooms of Britain and Europe*. Harper Collins, London.

Most of the fungi records from Lancashire are slowly being added to the North West Fungus Group database. This can be accessed from the group recorder web page at: http://ourworld.compuserve.com/homepages/jltaylor2/or via the North West Fungus Group web page at: http://fungus.org.uk/nwfg.htm

Chapter 7

Mammals

Steve Cross (editor)

Introduction

In the wide range of habitats of Lancashire, North Merseyside and Greater Manchester, from coast to hilltop, 58 species of mammals have been found. Mammals are amongst the most familiar of animals, our closest relatives, though many are nocturnal and secretive. Apart from a few pest species, they are universally liked and some such as Otter (*Lutra lutra*) and Red Squirrel are 'conservation flagship' species.

Habitat loss and change has caused decline in many species, but Lancashire is still important for Red Squirrel, Brown Hare and Water Vole.

Bats, by Steve Bradley

Lancashire is fortunate in still having good populations of several species of bats, and our knowledge of them is largely due to several active Bat Groups (Box 7.1). Many of our urban areas are linked to good habitat by river and canal corridors so that bats which roost in buildings during the day are able to forage in nearby insect-rich places at night. The many pockets of semi-natural woodland, parkland and mature trees provide natural roost sites for tree-dwelling species, while the few old mines and natural caves are used by hibernating bats.

Most people will have noticed bats flittering around gardens at dusk, often following a regular route as they catch small insects in flight. These will usually be pipistrelle bats: mostly Common Pipistrelles (*Pipistrellus pipistrellus*) which gather at maternity colonies of perhaps a hundred female bats in the eaves of modern houses from May to September. A second species, the Soprano Pipistrelle (*Pipistrellus pygmaeus*), is more likely to be seen close to rivers – one colony in the Lune valley had over 1200 adult females in June 2001.

Small bats are difficult to identify even in the hand (which requires a licence). This is probably a Whiskered Bat. (Malcolm Edmunds)

Lancashire's rivers provide such an abundance of insect food that hundreds of bats of five or six species can be observed feeding at dusk at favourite sites such as Halton on the Lune and Ribchester on the Ribble. Standing quietly on the river bank on a warm summer evening, one can use a bat detector to listen to their ultrasonic calls as the first Noctules (*Nyctalus noctula*) pass over, soon joined by pipistrelles then Whiskered (*Myotis mystacinus*) and Brandt's (*Myotis brandtii*) bats, and finally the late-emerging Daubenton's (*Myotis daubentonii*) start to skim over the water surface.

One feature of the north of England is the abundance of old stone bridges over rivers, streams and canals. These bridges very often have crevices between the stones which provide a perfect roost site for Daubenton's Bats, and this species can be seen hunting on most waterways in Lancashire: good views of its hovercraft-like flight can be had by briefly flashing a torch across a canal such as the Leeds and Liverpool at Haskayne, especially where trees overhang the water. Daubenton's also use the ponds of the Fylde, the mill lodges of East and South Lancashire, and the flashes of the Wigan area. The latter also attract good numbers of feeding Noctules with spectacular gatherings of fifty or more over Scotsman's Flash in the summer months. The Noctules probably roost in tree holes and may have travelled several miles to feed here.

Whiskered and Brandt's Bats are two very similar species, which perhaps occur more commonly in Lancashire than in many other parts

Box 7.1 Bat Groups

Much remains to be discovered about bats in our area, and there are several bat groups which participate in research and further the conservation of bats. Bat group members may visit bat roosts at houses to give advice and allay the concerns of householders; catch and handle bats under licence; undertake survey work using bat detectors to find out which bats feed where; and look after sick and injured bats until they can be released back into the wild. Much of the survey work is co-ordinated nationally by the Bat Conservation Trust, whilst much of the conservation work is undertaken for English Nature.

117

Mammals:
Bats

of the country. Several breeding colonies of each are known, especially in the north of the county, where they favour older houses close to areas of woodland. They can also be seen at sites such as Birkacre Country Park, Chorley, and in urban areas such as Liverpool's Sefton Park.

Small mammals, by Steve Cross

Despite being very abundant, most of our small mammals are seldom seen because they are nocturnal and adept at hiding when danger threatens. Live-trapping, cat (and dog) kills and animals found dead are just some of the ways of finding out about their distribution in the county.

Pygmy and Common Shrews (*Sorex pygmaeus* and *Sorex araneus*) are widely distributed through most of Lancashire in a range of habitats. Seldom seen, though you can hear their high pitched sounds, these tiny animals with their short, frantic lives constantly search for their own weight in food each day. Cats and other predators may kill but seldom eat them due to their noxious taste. Their black and white relative the Water Shrew (*Neomys fodiens*) is, as its name suggests, usually, though not exclusively, found in waterside habitats scattered across Lancashire. Unusual locations where they have been found include a coal shed in Bolton and woodland near Silverdale.

Hedgehogs (*Erinaceus europaeus*) are widespread in gardens and are often fed to encourage them. Bread and milk should not be given; instead try tinned cat or dog food, minced meat, biscuits, peanuts,

above The Noctule is one our our largest bats, most often seen flying at dusk on warm summer evenings. *(Peter Smith)*

below Common Shrew eating earthworm. *(Michael Leach/Woodfall Wild Images)*

grated cheese and of course plenty of water. Bunn (1970) suggests that the Hedgehog has changed its behaviour in response to cars, so that some animals now 'run for it' instead of curling up; even so the sight of squashed Hedgehogs on the road is still common. Many Hedgehogs are also poisoned by eating pellets put out to kill slugs. Overwintering Hedgehogs in gardens can be helped by putting out piles of brushwood or boxes with dry leaves.

Hedgehogs should be welcome in gardens as they eat slugs as well as earthworms.
(Peter Smith)

Water Shrew.
(Steve Austin/ Woodfall Wild Images)

The Common Mole (*Talpa talpa*) is still seen as a pest in some quarters due to the production of molehills and is still regularly trapped and killed. However it remains widespread and locally common, though declining, and it does avoid urban areas. It is even climbing higher in the Pennines following agricultural changes. There are a few records of partial and full albinos of this 'gentleman in black velvet'.

Bank and Field Vole (*Clethrionomys glareolus* and *Microtus agrestis*) are amongst the most numerous of Lancashire mammals, and are major food items for many predators. Habitat preference is indicated by their names, and its slightly larger ears and eyes, longer tail and reddish fur distinguish the Bank Vole. As with many other small mammals, useful survey techniques include searching for skulls in owl pellets and looking in discarded bottles from which they cannot climb out. The rarer Water Vole is described in Box 7.2.

The House Mouse (*Mus musculus*) is a visitor we would rather not have living with us, it can even bite through electric cables! It is, however, equally widespread outdoors (at least in the summer). This Asian immigrant has a strong mousy smell, small ears and very dark coloured fur which helps distinguish it from its native cousins that will sometimes come indoors in winter. The Wood or Long-tailed Field Mouse (*Apodemus sylvaticus*) occurs abundantly in a range of habitats, though the similar, but larger and more brightly coloured Yellow-necked Mouse (*Apodemus flavicollis*), a species of woodlands of Wales and southern England, has been found at just one site in our area, Chorley.

above Molehills are familiar to everyone, but the Common Mole is only occasionally seen above ground, when its wonderful adaptations for burrowing and capturing earthworms can be admired.
(Peter Smith)

below Its large eyes seem to make the Long-tailed Field Mouse more attractive to many people than either voles or House Mice.
(Peter Smith)

Box 7.2 *The Water Vole* (Arvicola terrestris)

'Ratty' of *Wind in the Willows* is in trouble. It is the fastest declining mammal, down by some 90% across the country due to waterside habitat loss and degradation, pollution and the effects of predation by the American Mink.

Despite its name Britain's largest vole is not particularly adapted to water, lacking webbed feet and its fur soon becomes waterlogged. However it swims and dives well, an essential adaptation to a waterside life. Water Voles live in colonies extending along watercourses, each using a series of burrows. They are herbivorous, feeding largely on the stems and leaves of waterside plants. Habitat preference in their favoured lowlands is for narrow slow-moving watercourses, with lush bank-side vegetation and no extreme water level fluctuations. Canals, water meadows and ponds are also used. In urban situations they are less fussy: a lack of predators can compensate for reduced bank-side cover.

As they are most active during the day you may see them, though sure signs of their presence are their closely cropped 'lawns', and latrines hosting distinctive shiny droppings found along bank sides or floating vegetation. It is such evidence that makes this mammal relatively easy to survey.

Water Voles seem to have been disappearing across our area, even at sites where they were formerly common. Concern over their falling numbers locally, such as at Martin Mere, led to a five-year county-wide survey which started in 1999. The survey, which was aided by volunteers, found that water voles are widespread, though mostly uncommon, throughout the river catchments of Lancashire and North Merseyside. Across the whole region, more than half of the sites surveyed were found to have at least some evidence of water voles. The key catchments were the Lune, Ribble, Alt/Crossens and Sankey/Glaze, with particularly important areas on the Wenning, Greta and Keer systems (Lune), the Hodder and Calder (Ribble) and the Ditton (Sankey/Glaze).

Dominic Rigby

A few minutes spent quietly watching a Water Vole busily feeding or swimming is a delightful experience.
(Peter Smith)

The tiny Harvest Mouse (*Micromys minutus*) occurs at a scattering of sites across Lancashire with the woven nest being one of the best ways of locating it. Changes in farming have meant a decline in this species, though it can thrive in hedgerows, marshes and other tall vegetation habitats as well as in grain fields.

The two species of rats found in Lancashire show contrasting fortunes. The Black Rat (*Rattus rattus*) was introduced from Asia, arriving in Britain by the fifth century AD, and soon became a common

opposite left Our smallest rodent is the Harvest Mouse, so small that the damage it does to a field of wheat is negligible, and it only eats grain for a few weeks of the year.
(Peter Smith)

Mammals:
Small mammals

Rabbits are once again common in the countryside after the massive losses due to myxomatosis.
(Peter Smith)

animal. It was, of course, the carrier of the fleas responsible for outbreaks of plague in medieval times. It is now probably extinct in mainland Britain, apart from transitory imports from ships including at Liverpool, though it does still occur on a few offshore islands. In contrast the Brown Rat (*Rattus norvegicus*) was a late arrival from Asia, not turning up until the eighteenth century, but has since become a major pest, with one probably within fifty metres of you now! Constant war is waged against this adaptable species, yet it is still thriving and has even become resistant to some rodenticides, and its potential to spread Weil's disease can curtail our own waterborne activities in some areas because of the health risks.

Lancashire does not have a lot of suitable woodland to support the Common Dormouse (*Muscardinus avellanarius*). There are records of it from parts of the Ribble Valley and the Silverdale area, but these populations are now extinct. This species may be helped by artificial nest sites, though increases in Cornwall by the use of Pied Flycatcher nestboxes (with occasional eating of the avian nestlings) caused problems for conservationists there!

The Rabbit (*Oryctolagus cuniculus*) is another introduction to this country, probably by the Normans (though some say it goes further back as far as the Romans). It was formerly an important resource, carefully protected and looked after in the 'warrens' of the lord of the manor, especially along the sand dune coasts. It has since spread and became abundant across most of the county. With its grazing and burrowing altering habitats and whole landscapes, to many farmers and others it is a pest. The decline after myxomatosis came to Lancashire in September 1954. This has had a profound effect on the grasslands, dunes and other habitats with extensive scrubbing over of large areas, most critically on limestone pavements, dunes and heathland. There was also a knock on effect on the predators that fed on it. Today it is thriving over most of our area, but with periodic outbreaks of myxomatosis still affecting its numbers.

The Mountain Hare (*Lepus timidus*) is native to the highlands of Scotland, but sportsmen in Victorian times tried to introduce it to northern

England and Wales. All of these attempts failed except for three introductions to the Peak District between 1870 and 1880, and this population still survives in the area around Saddleworth in Greater Manchester.

Brown Hare, by Simon Hayhow

There is no sight more typical of the British spring than the 'mad' March hares boxing and lolloping across our open countryside. Yet this familiar mammal, distinguished from the rabbit by its size, tall and leggy appearance and distinctive black tips to the long ears, is in serious decline. An 80% reduction in the population has taken place during the twentieth century but, thankfully, Brown Hares are still widespread in Lancashire and reasonably numerous in the Fylde and West Lancashire in contrast to other parts of western Britain (Box 7.3).

This is how one usually sees Brown Hares.
Malcolm Edmunds)

Brown Hares (*Lepus europaeus*) are not native to Britain, but have been with us for over 2000 years (Harris and McLaren 1998) and have long featured in folklore and mythology. The hare has always been special to us. In pre-Roman times it appears the hare was considered sacred and Boudicca is reported to have released one in honour of the goddess Andraste before leading her tribe into battle in AD 60/61 (Pinnock 2000). In Celtic mythology there are stories of hares turning into beautiful women, and women, in turn, transforming themselves into hares – a theme which was to re-emerge in the seventeenth century with links to witchcraft (Evans and Thomson 1972).

123

Box 7.3 Brown Hares in Lancashire

Hares are still seen frequently in Lancashire in suitable habitats, but a decline certainly took place during the 1970s and 1980s resulting in their complete absence from some areas (Hayhow 2000). Good information exists on their distribution but the lack of systematically collected data makes assessment of the scale of any decline difficult. Local strongholds are the former mosslands of the Lancashire coastal plain, including the mosses of Thurnham, Cockerham, Pilling, Rawcliffe, Halsall and Downholland, along with Catchdale and Holiday Mosses near St Helens. Other key areas are Freckleton, Newton and Clifton Marshes and the Altcar Estate. To a lesser extent the upland pasture fringe of the Forest of Bowland also appears to be important, especially around Quernmore, Abbeystead and Bleasdale.

Reasons for their decline in Lancashire can only be surmised without detailed survey work. Undoubtedly loss of habitat diversity within the agricultural landscape has contributed to this (Harris and McLaren 1998). Intensification of farming has resulted in decreased crop diversity, larger fields and the loss of conservation headlands and hedgerows. Crop diversity is important because the nutritional requirements of Brown Hares vary according to the season and so they move between different crops. Hedgerows are important diurnal lying-up sites, particularly for the leverets. Other agricultural factors may be the shift from hay to silage cutting and the use of faster silage cutters, as well as the change from winter to spring sown cereals resulting in a shortage of food during the breeding season (Temple et al. 2000). Increased stocking densities and the use of synthetic herbicides may also have contributed to the decline. Other factors could be increased fox predation on leverets, particularly around the urban fringes, a higher level of road casualties, adverse spring weather and disease.

The Brown Hare has long been a game species but there is no close season. It is not clear how much impact coursing and shooting, either by organised game shoots or for pest control, have had on the population. The activities of the Holcombe Harriers, Bleasdale Beagles and the Waterloo Cup have long been part of the countryside calendar. Even if hunting has not caused the decline of the Brown Hare, its impact on a much-reduced population may now be more significant, especially as this tends to take place predominantly during February and March when most females are pregnant. There is also the problem of poaching, and instances of farmers heavily culling their hares to deter poachers, especially those with lurchers (Harris 1996).

Conservation organisations are now addressing the lack of systematically collected data in Lancashire. This survey work is being tackled in conjunction with landowners, farmers and gamekeepers who know a great deal about their local hare population. Positive steps are also being implemented by the agricultural industry to encourage wildlife conservation on farmland. Through schemes like Arable Stewardship there are incentives that encourage farmers to increase habitat diversity, and these should help our hares. More also remains to be discovered about their behaviour. We do know that the spring 'boxing'

is not between rival males but is almost always a female fending off the advances of too amorous males (Tapper 1987).

Let us hope we have now arrested the drastic decline of the Brown Hare, as it is an important 'flagship' conservation species within our agricultural countryside. However, it is also an enigmatic and mysterious animal, which has interested and inspired us for thousands of years. We must ensure that it continues to do so for centuries to come.

Squirrels, by Fiona Robertson

The tale of the British Red Squirrel (*Sciurus vulgaris*) is not one with a fairy tale ending. It has become a 'flagship species' – our equivalent of China's giant panda or Asian tigers. All very dramatic, but it is the true, sad story of a species on its way to likely extinction in Britain.

The Red Squirrel was one of the last mammals to make it to Britain before the disappearance of the land bridge with Europe 10,000 years ago. The species evolved in dense conifer forests, which it still occupies over much of mainland Europe and Russia. This left it poorly adapted to Britain's predominantly oak woodlands, but in the absence of a competitor species it successfully occupied all types of

And this is the sort of place where Brown Hares rest up during the day.
(Malcolm Edmunds)

125

above Red Squirrels are a favourite with almost everyone, but they will only survive in their stronghold on the Sefton coast if the Grey Squirrel is controlled. (Peter Smith)

below Some people think Grey Squirrels are delightful animals to have in parks and gardens, while others see them as exotic pests which should be controlled or killed. (Peter Smith)

woodland. Then in the nineteenth century the Grey Squirrel (*Sciurus carolinensis*), an animal which had evolved in the broadleaved forests of North America, was deliberately introduced. The first known introduction was at Henbury Park in Cheshire in 1876 but it was from later introductions at Woburn Abbey in Bedfordshire in 1889 and Regents Park in London in 1904 that it began its inexorable spread.

It became clear very early on that as Grey Squirrels occupied an area the Red Squirrels disappeared, usually within 15 to 30 years. The exact mechanisms for this displacement of Reds by Greys is still not known; identifying it remains a major conservation priority. The simple truth is that the 'alien' Grey is better adapted to Britain's woodlands than the 'native' Red. To make matters worse, Grey Squirrels are known to carry North American strains of diseases, and the Red Squirrel may have no defence against these. For example, the parapox virus is lethal to Reds; Greys can carry this but are rarely affected themselves.

The first published record of Grey Squirrels in Lancashire was in 1954 at Winkley Hall, Pendle Hill. In 1971 North Merseyside was reported by MAFF to be still free of Grey Squirrels, but by this time they had undoubtedly spread throughout central Lancashire. By the late 1980s Greys had penetrated as far north as Silverdale, being first seen at Warton Crag in 1989, and within two or three years Reds were extinct there. Red Squirrels continue to disappear to our north and are now absent from the southern Lake District.

The extinction took longer in West Lancashire, probably due to the relative isolation of its scattered woodlands, but breeding colonies at the Trust's Mere Sands Wood Reserve and at Ruff Wood (Ormskirk) were hit by parapox virus in 1995. The last breeding record at Mere Sands Wood came in 1998, but wandering individuals from unknown colonies continue to be seen there occasionally. Small populations still persist in Ormskirk and Aughton.

The situation remains more optimistic in Merseyside, although Grey Squirrel numbers are on the increase. The main population of Reds is in the pine plantations of the Sefton Coast, centred around Formby. Its origins are unknown but it is thought likely to have been established, or at least supplemented, by the introduction of central European animals. However, smaller populations continue to thrive in other areas of Merseyside, particularly in south Sefton, Knowsley Park and Fazakerley in Liverpool, from where no introductions have been recorded.

Conservation effort is organised through Red Alert North West, which was established in 1993, and now centres upon establishing

Red Squirrel 'refuges' – large, isolated areas of conifer woodland from which Grey Squirrels can be excluded. Red Squirrels have undoubtedly persisted in Merseyside because of the lack of continuous woodland on the surrounding mosslands, and the Sefton Coast woodlands have been designated as a refuge site in the hope that the Grey Squirrels can continue to be excluded.

below Badgers are still widespread throughout our countryside though rarely seen unless you are prepared to sit quietly and brave the midges on a summer evening.
(Peter Smith)

bottom Badger sett in Lancashire wood showing how they profoundly alter the vegetation.
(Malcolm Edmunds)

Carnivores, by Steve Cross

Badgers (*Meles meles*) are to be found across much of Lancashire, but moorland setts in the uplands, such as around Rossendale, are much less conspicuous than those in lowland woodland, farmland and gardens. Though worms make up most of their food, Badgers are omnivores and in some areas garden feeding of cat and dog food can bring them very close to us. Lancashire cattle (and thus Badgers) seem to be clear of bovine tuberculosis. Badger baiting and snaring however, are still major issues, and Badgers often become casualties on the roads. Worryingly Lancashire Badgers seem to be declining, against the national trend, which is up.

Box 7.4 Urban Foxes

The Red Fox (*Vulpes vulpes*) is a widespread species across the county, with hands turned against them in the rural areas, yet welcomed by many people in the urban areas. They are now a familiar sight and sound of many towns and cities. They will of course feed at bins and other rubbish, take food left out for the cat or birds, as well as taking 'more natural' food (such as small birds and pigeons) to be found in the urban environment. Urban life is not all fish and chips or curry leftovers – up to 50% of urban foxes face death on the roads and the introduction of wheelie-bins will curtail some of their feeding. Diseases such as fox mange are also a possible threat.

Foxes are elusive animals to see unless you roam our urban streets in the early hours before dawn or are able to sit quietly downwind of an earth where a vixen has her cubs.
(Peter Smith)

Stoat (*Mustela erminea*) and Weasel (*Mustela nivalis*) can be found throughout the county in a range of habitats from coastal dunes to suburban cemeteries and up to the Bowland fells. Rabbits are the main prey for the stoat while the smaller Weasel is a fierce predator of small rodents, though both will also feed on other small animals. Stoat rarely acquire their white winter coat of ermine in lowland Lancashire, though they may do so in the uplands, but Weasels never change to white.

Introduced American Mink (*Mustela vison*) are now the bane of the watercourses. These fierce predators take a range of animal prey including fish, birds and small mammals. They are now well established through much of the county, though the location of the first record for Bolton was unusual – the gents toilets in Derby Street in 1956 !

Does its relative the Pine Marten (*Martes martes*) remain in Lancashire? Tantalising recent records of one found dead near Chorley in 1994, one in the Pennine Moors in 1996 and signs of one in North Lancashire suggest that this enigmatic mustelid is still present.

Stoat.
(Mike Lane/Woodfall Wild Images)

Otters used to be widespread across most of Lancashire, and were once hunted in the north of the area by the Kendal and District Otter Hounds. There was a decline, which by the 1960s and 1970s had seen it nearly disappear from the county, just Leighton Moss keeping hold of them. Following protection in 1981 and projects to reverse that decline, the Otter is starting to appear again on some of the river catchments. The Lune, Hodder and Ribble have all been visited by Otters with around a dozen animals now in the county.

Both British seals occur in Lancashire coastal waters, though the Common or Harbour Seal (*Phoca vitulina*) is actually very rare with just a handful of confirmed records from Morecambe Bay to Lytham St Annes and Formby over the years. The Grey Seal (*Halichoerus grypus*) is

Thanks to the efforts of the Lancashire Wildlife Trust and other conservation organizations, Otters are returning to quiet stretches of many of our rivers.
(Peter Smith)

The Grey Seal can quite often be seen along our coast but it does not breed here.
(Peter Smith)

regular in ones and twos from watch points at Jenny Brown's Point, Heysham, Blackpool and Formby. However, this 'roman-nosed' seal does not breed any nearer than the Isle of Man, Scotland or Wales, though immatures and non-breeders are to be found with their heads poking out of the sea seemingly watching the watchers. The sandy beaches of Lancashire do not seem to be suitable for hauling out, unlike the West Hoyle Bank near Hilbre Island on the River Dee. Grey Seals take a wide range of fish and thus they can come into conflict with fishermen. On the occasions when they ascend miles up the rivers they can often hit the headlines in the local press. The arctic Harp Seal (*Phoca groenlandicus*) has been recorded just once, in Morecambe Bay, during the nineteenth century.

Cetaceans, by Simon Hayhow

Whales, dolphins and porpoises, known as cetaceans, are mammals that are specially adapted to life in the sea (see Box 7.5). Like all mammals cetaceans breathe air, are warm blooded and give birth to live young which are suckled with the mother's milk. Twenty-five species have been recorded around British coasts (Evans 1990) and so they make up one quarter of all British mammal species. Almost half of these have been found along the coast of Lancashire and

Wildlife of
Lancashire

top left
Harbour Porpoise.
(Mick Baines/
Woodfall Wild
Images)

Cetaceans are divided into two Orders: Odontoceti (toothed whales) and Mysticeti (baleen whales) (Watson 1985). Accurate identification at sea is not easy and, sadly, most contact is through strandings. In the fourteenth century whales were declared 'fishes royal' (they are not fish) and this gave the sovereign rights to all cetaceans stranded or caught around British coasts. Strandings were initially required to be reported to the Crown, but from 1913 this duty was taken over by the British Museum, now the Natural History Museum (Corbet and Southern 1977). Since that date a wealth of information has been amassed from reports by H.M. Coastguard and H.M. Receiver of Wrecks. Today, data is also collected by voluntary societies and groups as well as national and regional museums.

Merseyside but only eight species have been recorded with any regularity in the Irish Sea in recent years (Northridge 1990). Although many people will never see live whales in their natural environment, most species are familiar to us through programmes on television, videos and magazines.

Among the toothed whales the smallest and most frequently seen along the Lancashire and Merseyside coast is the Harbour Porpoise (*Phocoena phocoena*). There are regular records every year in all months. They rarely exceed 2 metres in length and breed from May to August, newly born young occasionally being found dead along the Lancashire coast. There are no estimates of population size in the Irish Sea and no distinct peak in sightings. Northridge (1990) reports a peak in March but other records suggest a later peak in the period June to October, more typical of other British coasts.

The most frequently seen dolphin is the Bottle-nosed (*Tursiops truncatus*) with records in most years and a peak in August or

Bottle-nosed Dolphin.
(Paul Thompson/ Woodfall Wild Images)

Fin Whale stranded
at Heysham in
2000.
(Mark Woombs)

September. Common Dolphins (*Delphinus delphis*) are rarely recorded but may be increasing in the southern Irish Sea (Northridge, 1990), and when seen, they may be in larger numbers than other cetaceans as they congregate in schools. There are also occasional records of White-beaked and Risso's Dolphins (*Lagenorhynchus albirostris* and *Grampus griseus*) (Ellison 1959, M. Jones pers.comm.). The Northern Bottle-nosed Whale (*Hyperoodon ampullatus*) appears to have been more frequent in the nineteenth century (Coward 1910, Ellison 1959) but has reappeared recently, probably because of more observers. The Long-finned Pilot Whale (*Globicephala melaena*) is occasionally seen in schools off the Welsh coast, but there are no recent Lancashire or Merseyside records. There is a historical reference to Killer Whales (*Orcinus orca*) being 'seen fairly regularly at the mouth of the Lune' (Ellison 1959) but the only recent record was of one in the Mersey in 2001.

None of the baleen whales is at all numerous in the Irish Sea, although the Minke Whale (*Balaenoptera acutorostrata*) is the most frequently recorded and could be seen annually with more observer effort. Fin Whales (*Balaenoptera physalus*) have been found dead at Seaforth in 1985 and Heysham in 2000, while Sei Whales (*Balaenoptera borealis*) have been found at Sunderland Point in 1980 and a stranding at Pilling Sands in 2001. There is also a record of three Humpbacked Whales (*Megaptera novaeangliae*) breaching at Heysham in 1938 (Ellison 1959).

Among the cetaceans it is more than likely that the numbers of some of the whale species which inhabit the Irish Sea have decreased

Box 7.6 *Conservation of Cetaceans*

The conservation of cetaceans presents some extremely intractable problems. Our current level of knowledge of the status and abundance of different species around our coast, and indeed the threats they face, makes it very difficult to develop conservation strategies (Papastavrou 1991). A danger is that paucity of management information might be used as an excuse to do nothing. A further complication is that cetaceans migrate making their conservation an international issue.

Concern for the plight of cetaceans has been voiced by an ever-larger number of people over the last thirty years. In the 4,000 years humans have known about whales we have hunted most species to the brink of extinction. For centuries their lives have remained an almost complete mystery to us whilst we have exploited them. Only now are we beginning to give them the respect they deserve as we unravel some of their fascinating secrets.

132

due to past whaling activities. The scarcity or absence of some of the piscivorous baleen whales, such as Minke, Fin and Humpbacked could also be related to declines in fish stocks (Northridge 1990). Of the smaller cetaceans, population trends are less clear but it is generally agreed that Harbour Porpoises have declined since the 'large shoals' reported by Ellison (1959). The exact reasons are unclear at present but may include pollution and environmental degradation as well as over-fishing (see Box 7.6).

What is needed is more systematic collecting of data by a network of observers along the coast and at sea using modem electronic communication to help monitor movements. Such a network is being established in the region (N. Hammond pers.comm.) but any casual sightings of live animals or strandings are very valuable to help build up the big picture.

Deer, by Nigel Pickering

No large predators now occur in Lancashire: Brown Bears (*Ursus arctos*) have been extinct since Roman times while the last Wolf (*Canis lupus*) in Lancashire was probably round about 1305 (Yalden 1999), but neither of these predators would be welcomed back by some people. So for the larger mammals such as deer there is no check on numbers apart from food shortages, disease and people. The total deer population has been increasing over the past 50 years, and to prevent serious agricultural and forestry damage deer are managed by stalkers with high velocity rifles. Feral and escaped deer have even managed to find their way in to towns and cities and have occasionally caused traffic chaos.

The diminutive Muntjac (*Muntiacus reevesi*) was introduced from China to Woburn in Bedfordshire in the nineteenth century, and they have since spread through much of England as far north as Cheshire. It is the size of a small dog, only 45 cm at the shoulder. Muntjac have not been reliably reported from Lancashire, but could be present, so keep an eye out for them!

The Red Deer (*Cervus elaphus*) is our largest native land mammal, with big stags 1.4 m at the shoulder and weighing up to 200 kg. The main population centre is in the Arnside-Silverdale area especially around the Leighton Hall Estate and Leighton Moss, where up to about forty animals can be present. A few also occur in the Forest of Bowland area, but occurrences elsewhere are usually escapes from deer farms of which there are several in the county.

In Lancashire the Sika Deer (*Cervus nippon*), up to 95 cm high, was

A Red Deer stag is an impressive sight, especially during the autumn rut.
(Peter Smith)

introduced to be the quarry for the Ribblesdale Buckhounds by the Ormerod brothers of Wyresdale and Lord Ribblesdale of Gisburne Park. It proved unsuitable for the chase, but inevitably some escaped and formed the feral population that in 1979 numbered some 300 animals around the Ribble and Hodder Valleys.

The Normans created Parkland and introduced the Fallow Deer

(*Dama dama*) to inhabit them. Fallow Deer are intermediate in size between Red and Roe Deer, up to 95 cm high at the shoulder, with broadly palmated antlers in the males. This species is now the most widespread deer in lowland England, but your best chance of seeing one in Lancashire is in the Silverdale area. These grazers live in single sex herds except during the autumn rut, and the single fawn is born in June or July. The smallest indigenous deer is the Roe (*Capreolus capreolus*), at just 70 cm high. It is also our most widespread deer, present throughout most of the county, including some remarkably urban sites, despite it being the species least tolerant of disturbance.

Further reading

Arnold, H. R. (1993). *Atlas of Mammals in Britain*. HMSO, London.

Corbet, G. B. and Harris, S. (Eds.) (1991). *The Handbook of British Mammals*. (3rd edn) Blackwell, Oxford.

Macdonald, D. and Barrett, P. (1993). *Mammals of Britain and Europe*. Collins Field Guide. Harper Collins, London.

Morris, P. A. (1993). A *Red Data Book for British Mammals*. Mammal Society, London.

Pinnock, J. (2000). Ancient Tales of the Mystic Hare. *The Field*, 295 (No. 7146), IPC Magazines, London.

Serjeant, T. (Ed.) (2000). *Lancashire's Biodiversity Action Plan*. Lancashire Biodiversity Partnership, Preston.

Shorten, M (1957). *Squirrels in England, Wales and Scotland*. Collins, London.

Skelcher, G. (1981). Ecological survey of red and grey squirrels at the interface of their present range in NW England. Report for Lancashire Trust for Nature Conservation.

Strachan, R. and Jefferies, D. (1993). *The water vole in Britain 1989–1990: its distribution and changing status*. The Vincent Wildlife Trust, London.

Tapper, S. (1987). *The Brown Hare*. Shire Publications, Aylesbury.

Temple, R., Clark, S. and Harris, S. (2000). *The National Hare Survey*. University of Bristol, Bristol.

Watson, L. (1985). *Whales of the World*. Hutchinson, London.

Mammal contacts

Mammal Society The Mammal Society, 15 Cloisters House, 8 Battersea Park Road, London SW8 4BG Tel. 020 7498 4358 Fax. 020 7622 8722 Website www.mammal.org.uk

Lancashire Badger Group P. O. Box 58, Lancaster LA1 5AF

Badgerline 07980 630250 (24 hrs) Website www.geocities/lancashirebadgergroup/

The Bat Conservation Trust, 15 Cloisters House, 8 Battersea Park Road, London SW8. Website www.bats.org.uk

English Nature Bat Helpline 01704 385735

Merseyside and West Lancs. Bat Group, Phil Witter, Section of Birds and Mammals, Liverpool Museum, William Brown Street, Liverpool L3 8EN. Tel. 0151 478 4248

South Lancs. Bat Group, Angela Graham, 15 Lakeland Crescent, Bury, BL9 9SF. Tel 0161 7974745 Website www.slbg.org.uk

Birds

Dominic Rigby and Steve White

Introduction

Lancashire's rich variety of estuaries, coastal dunes, wetlands, agricultural land, woodlands and moorland make it one of the most diverse ornithological regions in Britain. 356 different species have been reliably recorded out of a British total of 557. Many of these are rare vagrants, seen only a handful of times in the last 150 years, while about 210 species are seen every year. Annual totals in the order of 230–240 species are the norm, but a birdwatcher would be very lucky (or profligate with petrol) to accumulate a 'year list' approaching this. There is a slight upward trend in the number of species seen each year, mostly as a result of more and better-informed observers, but partly due to range extensions of a small number of species (see recent Lancashire and Greater Manchester Bird Reports).

Since the nineteenth century 152 species of wild birds have bred in Lancashire – plus a handful of escaped species. A number of these are rare breeders in the UK including Black-necked Grebe (*Podiceps nigricollis*), Bittern (*Botaurus stellaris*), Spoonbill (*Platalea leucorodia*), Pochard (*Aythya ferina*), Hen Harrier (*Circus cyaneus*), Goshawk (*Accipiter gentilis*), Spotted Crake (*Porzana porzana*), Ruff (*Philomachus pugnax*), Black-tailed Godwit (*Limosa limosa*), Black Redstart (*Phoenicurus ochruros*) and Bearded Tit (*Panurus biarmicus*).

As elsewhere in Britain, some breeding species are increasing while others are declining, mostly as a result of loss of habitat. In general, birds of woodlands and wetlands together with birds of prey are on the up, while most farmland birds are registering dramatic losses.

Conservation efforts have largely been focused upon rare species and have met with considerable success, so it is perhaps not surprising that recent extinctions have been outnumbered by new colonists (see Box 8.1).

Birds whose breeding habitats can be protected by nature reserves or special conservation measures seem unlikely to suffer further extinctions. However, some species of the wider countryside are suffering alarming declines for which remedies may be hugely costly and difficult to achieve. Our most endangered species are probably Twite, Hen Harrier and Ring Ouzel (*Turdus torquatus*) in the uplands;

Box 8.1 *Gains and losses*

Just three breeding species have been lost since World War II:

* Corncrake (*Crex crex*), which used to nest in abundance in lowland crops but is now, at best, sporadic.

* Black Grouse (*Tetrao tetrix*), which was probably introduced into the Forest of Bowland and was last reliably recorded in the early 1990s.

* Nightjar (*Caprimulgus europaeus*), which disappeared when the last of its heathland habitat was destroyed by peat extraction at Simonswood Moss in 1980 and Astley Moss in 1983.

Set against these, nine new breeding species have appeared during the same period:

* Black-necked Grebe (up to five pairs have nested at two sites in Greater Manchester since 1992).

* Eider (*Somateria mollissima*), which first bred on Banks Marsh in 1984 and is now established on the Ribble, Wyre and Lune estuaries.

* Spoonbill (one pair on the south Ribble marshes in 1999).

* Marsh Harrier (*Circus aeruginosus*), which first bred at Leighton Moss in 1987 and probably in the Merseyside mosslands around the same time.

* Hobby (*Falco subbuteo*), no nest of which has been located in the region but which probably bred in the Lune Valley from the 1990s and in central Lancashire in 2001.

* Avocet (*Recurvirostra avosetta*), which first nested on Carnforth Marsh in 2001 and has become firmly established there, and has now also nested at Marshside, Martin Mere and the south Ribble marshes.

* Mediterranean Gull (*Larus melanocephalus*), which first bred successfully at Leighton Moss in 1990 and has since established itself at several other sites.

* Kittiwake (*Rissa tridactyla*), which has nested on a gas platform in Morecambe Bay since 1998.

* the now ubiquitous Collared Dove (*Columba decaocto*) which first bred at Ormskirk in 1961.

* Bearded Tit, which colonised the Leighton Moss reed beds in 1973.

Turtle Dove, now a rare species in the Trust area.
(Stan Craig)

The Peregrine Falcon can be found wherever there are cliffs or quarry faces where it can nest, or even tall buildings in Liverpool.
(Peter Smith)

Turtle Dove (*Streptopelia turtur*), and Yellow Wagtail (*Motacilla flava*) in the lowlands; and Lesser Spotted Woodpecker (*Dendrocopos minor*), Wood Warbler (*Phylloscopus sibilatrix*), Spotted Flycatcher (*Muscicapa striata*) and Hawfinch (*Coccothraustes coccothraustes*) in woodlands.

Climate change and conservation measures may encourage potential new colonists to extend their range northwards from southern England or westwards from continental Europe. The most likely candidates are Little Egret (*Egretta garzetta*), Honey Buzzard (*Pernis apivorus*), Osprey (*Pandion haliaetus*), Yellow-legged Gull (*Larus cachinnans*), Woodlark (*Lullula arborea*), Cetti's Warbler (*Cettia cetti*), Dartford Warbler (*Sylvia undata*) and Common Rosefinch (*Carpodacus erythrinus*).

A handful of established breeding species have spread spectacularly in the past 10 to 20 years. Sparrowhawks (*Accipiter nisus*) and Peregrines (*Falco peregrinus*) have made come-backs after organochlorine pesticides were withdrawn from widespread use. Buzzards (*Buteo buteo*) and Ravens (*Corvus corax*) have benefited from reduced persecution, spreading southwards from the northern Pennines and northwards from north Wales. Two woodland species, Nuthatch (*Sitta europaea*) and Long-tailed Tit (*Aegithalos caudatus*), have also become far more widespread.

Estimating the total number of breeding birds in the region is tricky, but a million pairs is probably about right. Adding in the season's young would give a post-breeding population of perhaps five million individuals – roughly the same as the region's human population.

The number of birds spending the winter in Lancashire is probably not far different, with birds that migrate southward (mostly warblers) being replaced by others coming in from more northerly breeding grounds (mostly wildfowl, waders, thrushes and finches). Sometimes these huge displacements pass unnoticed as British-breeding birds are replaced by populations of the same species from further north – the Blackbird in your winter garden is as likely to have nested in Sweden as in Lancashire.

It is, however, difficult to miss the winter invasion of our estuaries, coasts and wetlands by tens of thousands of swans, geese, ducks and wading birds from the Arctic and central and northern Europe. North West England is by far the most important part of Britain for these birds, and the five main sites (two shared with neighbouring counties), the Mersey, Alt and Ribble estuaries, Morecambe Bay and Martin Mere, hold an average of 600,000 birds each winter (about 450,000 of which are in Lancashire) (see Box 8.2).

Buzzards are birds of the upland Pennines, but have been seen more frequently in recent years in lowland farmland.
(Peter Smith)

Box 8.2 Internationally important wetland birds

Twenty-four species of wetland birds winter in Lancashire in internationally important numbers (>1% of the East Atlantic or Western European populations).

These are:

Bewick's Swan (*Cygnus columbianus*)
Whooper Swan (*Cygnus cygnus*)
Pink-footed Goose (*Anser brachyrhynchus*)
Shelduck (*Tadorna tadorna*)
Wigeon (*Anas penelope*)
Teal (*Anas crecca*)
Pintail (*Anas acuta*)
Pochard (*Aythya ferina*)
Oystercatcher (*Haematopus ostralegus*)
Ringed Plover (*Charadrius hiaticula*)
Grey Plover (*Pluvialis squatarola*)
Lapwing (*Vanellus vanellus*)
Knot (*Calidris canutus*)
Sanderling (*Calidris alba*)
Dunlin (*Calidris arctica*)
Black-tailed Godwit (*Limosa limosa*)
Bar-tailed Godwit (*Limosa lapponica*)
Curlew (*Numenius arquata*)
Redshank (*Tringa totanus*)
Turnstone (*Arenaria interpres*)
Black-headed Gull (*Larus ridibundus*)
Common Gull (*Larus canus*)
Lesser Black-backed Gull (*Larus fuscus*)
Herring Gull (*Larus argentatus*)

above Dunlin are one of the commonest wading birds on our estuaries in winter, busily probing for food on the mudflats.
(*Stan Craig*)

below As their name implies, Turnstones differ from most other wading birds in searching underneath stones for food.
(*Stan Craig*)

Seabirds

Lancashire's lack of coastal cliffs means that few seabird species breed although some ground-nesting gulls and terns do so in considerable numbers. In 1989 the south Ribble salt marshes supported the country's largest coastal colony of Black-headed Gulls – more than 20,000 pairs. This colony has shrunk since then, but, together with others – mostly at Leighton Moss and Stocks Reservoir – the county still holds about the same number of pairs.

Even more significant in national terms is the Lesser Black-backed Gull. About a quarter of the UK population breeds in the county, the overwhelming majority of them at Tarnbrook Fell in Bowland (c. 17,000 pairs) and the Ribble marshes (c. 4,000 pairs). Much smaller numbers of Herring Gulls and Great Black-backed Gulls (*Larus marinus*) breed in these gulleries. Common Terns (*Sterna hirundo*) are the only other seabirds to nest in significant numbers; they are largely confined to the Ribble marshes (c. 100 pairs) and to Seaforth Nature Reserve (c. 160 pairs) with smaller colonies on Pennington Flash and the Wigan Flashes.

Gulls are far more conspicuous in winter when hundreds of thousands, mostly Black-headed and Herring, are attracted to inland rubbish tips and the coast. Whenever winter gales wash up large 'wrecks' of starfish and shellfish, beaches become white with gulls; estimates of 250,000 along the Sefton and Fylde coasts are perhaps conservative.

top left The Lesser Black-backed Gull breeds in the Ribble marshes.
(Peter Smith)

above The Black-headed Gull breeds regularly in Lancashire and is widespread in winter when it lacks the chocolate head.
(Peter Smith)

141

Information on species that remain at sea during winter is much harder to obtain, but recent aerial surveys have begun to reveal unsuspected numbers of seabirds offshore – especially diving birds which feed on fish in the open water column or shellfish from the sea-bed. The most numerous are Common Scoter (*Melanitta nigra*), a sea-duck for which the shallow seas off the Fylde coast are amongst the most important sites in the country, supporting in excess of 40,000 birds. Three other species winter in smaller but nationally important numbers: Red-throated Diver (*Gavia stellata*) (in both Liverpool and Morecambe Bays), and Great Crested Grebe (*Podiceps cristatus*) and Red-breasted Merganser (*Mergus serrator*) (at the southern end of Morecambe Bay).

Most of these wintering birds are too far out to be seen from the shore and the same is almost certainly true of migratory seabirds – storm-petrels, shearwaters, skuas and terns. Birdwatchers scan weather forecasts waiting for autumn gales which blow these birds into view. In particular they wait for the right conditions to bring one

below Little Gull.
(*Steve Young*)

Box 8.3 *The Little Gull* (Larus minutus)

This is the world's smallest gull and one of just a few that truly deserve the epithet 'seagull', since it spends most of its life on the open sea where it feeds on fish and crustaceans close to the surface. However, it usually nests far inland on freshwater marshes where it feeds on small flying insects.

Most of Europe's population breed in Finland, the Baltic States and around St. Petersburg. Their wintering grounds are poorly known but most are probably in the Mediterranean. One sub-population winters in the Irish Sea, mostly off County Wicklow to the south of Dublin Bay.

Each spring 800 or more appear to follow a regular route towards Finland, arriving at Seaforth Nature Reserve and Crosby Marine Park in early April, then crossing the Pennines and the North Sea and entering the Baltic. They linger in Liverpool for about a fortnight as they complete their moult into their smart black, grey and pink breeding plumage. They are probably drawn to the site by the proximity of its marine and freshwater habitats which may facilitate their switch between winter and summer diets. Certainly the key attraction appears to be the swarms of chironomid midges

that hatch from the freshwater lagoons at this time of year, which the Little Gulls deftly pick from the surface film in low-level flight.

This spring gathering is unique in England, although far smaller numbers congregate at a similar site in Tayside.

of Lancashire's speciality birds, Leach's Storm-petrel (*Oceanodroma leucorhoa*) onshore in September. This starling-sized bird breeds on the remote islands around St Kilda and spends the winter in the middle of the South Atlantic, feeding in foot-pattering flight from the ocean surface. Prolonged westerly gales exhaust them and produce an almost annual spectacle at the main seawatching stations of Heysham, Blackpool, Formby Point and, especially, the mouth of the Mersey, which is rarely seen elsewhere in Britain.

The spring migration often requires quite different weather conditions – calm and misty – to bring birds onshore. Arctic Terns (*Sterna paradisaea*) are the stars, moving past the Morecambe Bay headlands of Heysham and Jenny Brown's Point in early May *en route* from their Antarctic wintering grounds to breed in northernmost Europe by the thousand. Another, very local, spring migrant is the Little Gull (Box 8.3).

Estuary birds

There are few more thrilling sights for the birdwatcher than watching a prime estuary around high tide. Clouds of tightly knit waders wheel through the air with choreographed precision, settling on one of the

Unlike most other owls, Short-eared Owls commonly hunt for voles during the day. They nest on moors, as here, but can be seen during winter on salt marshes.
(Peter Smith)

Whooper Swans flying in to roost on a freshwater lake.
(Peter Smith)

Wigeon are often the most abundant duck in the Ribble estuary, and the drake has gorgeous colours in winter sunshine.
(Peter Smith)

few remaining exposed sand flats, in incredible closeness, only to be joined by more! They take to the air again as the tide moves in, rolling through the sky over large flocks of ducks, the latter displaced from the sea-cropped salt marsh by the persistent in-coming tide. A Twite calls among a large flock of Linnets (*Carduelis cannabina*) which are looking for salt marsh seeds, then a Peregrine stoops towards them. Kestrels (*Falco tinnunculus*) hover over patches of greenery, evenly spaced above the tideline, waiting for voles to flee the enveloping saltwater. Several Short-eared Owls (*Asio flammeus*) quarter the marsh, and a Barn Owl (*Tyto alba*) joins them, interrupting its nocturnal routine to take advantage of the feeding bonanza provided by the spring tide. As dusk approaches skeins of noisy Pink-footed Geese whiffle down to safe waterside roosting sites, and the piping and whooping of migratory swans leaving the coastal marshes for inland roosts rounds off a birdwatching experience for which Lancashire excels.

Estuaries are constantly moving systems receiving fresh nutrients from the sea, rivers and the land with every tide. The Ribble is the most important estuary for birds in Britain with internationally important numbers of wildfowl and waders visiting it each year to feed on the vast sandflats, pools and grazing marshes.

However the Ribble estuary system extends beyond its tidal reaches. In the south the freshwater havens at Martin Mere and Mere Sands Wood provide feeding areas for many of the estuary's birds. These sites are separated from the coast by a rich farmed landscape of peat mosslands. An intricate network of reedy ditches crosses this farmland linking the inland wetlands to a series of important protected sites and nature reserves on the coast stretching from Ainsdale to Blackpool. Birds move between the different sites in the system; each site is a piece of the jigsaw, important in its own right but when linked to the whole picture its true value is seen.

Teal, for example, return from their northerly nesting grounds in autumn and concentrate at Martin Mere, where up to ten thousand feed on a rich, floating seed bonanza of recently cut weedy, marshland. By the winter many will have moved to Mere Sands Wood to shelter from the worst of the weather. At dusk, as winter progresses, increasingly more birds move out to the estuarine salt marshes, returning in ever smaller numbers to the flooded inland sites at dawn. By New Year the majority will be spending their whole time on the coast. Early spring sees the Teal beginning to disperse to distant breeding grounds, but those that remain favour the flooded marshes at Marshside, where over 500 may still be present in April. A cold snap at any time can send the birds from their frozen freshwater habitats to the unfrozen waters of the estuary.

Lancashire hosts some of the country's most important estuaries for birds. The southern section of Morecambe Bay, the Ribble and Alt estuaries and the northern part of the Mersey lie within our region and all are significant for their waterfowl. Over 110,000 Wigeon were recorded on the Ribble estuary in the mid-1990s, the second highest count ever in Europe. The sanctuary conditions provided by the National Nature Reserve allow the ducks to nibble the short-cropped turf of the coastal grazing and salt marshes. Numbers are swelled most winters by Wigeon using the Ribble as a stopping off point on their way to Irish estuaries. Among the Wigeon can be several thousand Pintail. The drake Pintail is perhaps our most elaborately plumaged dabbling duck, but when outnumbered twenty to one they can be hard to detect among the Wigeon! Pintail numbers vary enormously as they move round the coast with inland incursions in some years. Teal also occur in high numbers in winter. Individuals of their American cousin, the Green-winged Teal (*Anas carolinensis*), have appeared among the wintering flocks in both the Ribble and Morecambe Bay systems in recent, consecutive winters. Studying the movements of these individuals has led to the belief that Teal move little between the estuaries in winter, but there is considerable movement *within* each estuary system (see Box 8.4).

Birds:
Estuary birds

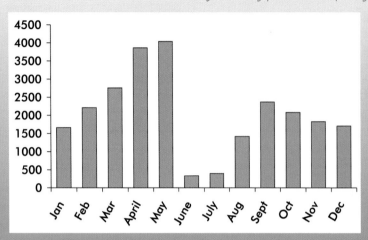

Grey Plovers breed on the Arctic tundra and winter in western Europe and south into Africa. Two Lancashire estuaries, the Ribble and Alt, support internationally important numbers while Morecambe Bay is of national importance. The chart shows a clear pattern of annual occurrence. A few non-breeding birds are present during June and July and birds begin to return from their breeding grounds in August. Autumn numbers peak in September, leaving a relatively stable wintering population. February and March see a steady increase, culminating in a surge of migrants from southern Europe and Africa in April and May.

(*Source: Wetland Bird Survey*)

Morecambe Bay also attracts impressive numbers of fish-eating birds in winter. It is one of the top sites in Britain for Great Crested Grebe (see p. 278), with counts regularly approaching 200, and a similar number of Red-breasted Mergansers in the Lancashire section is the highest count in England.

The sand flats of Lancashire's estuaries attract massive numbers of wintering wading birds, which leave their arctic breeding grounds in late summer. Unlike many of the ducks, the waders tend to be more mobile, frequently moving between different estuaries. The most abundant wader is the Knot; the majority of the Icelandic-race of Knot winter on British estuaries and over a third of these can occur at Morecambe Bay, the Ribble and Alt. The peak at Morecambe Bay can exceed 75,000, and our knowledge of its winter diet has been acquired from studies here in the early 1970s (Cramp and Simmons

Knot are often the most numerous wader in our estuaries during winter.

(*Stan Craig*)

1983). The next commonest wader on our estuaries is the Dunlin which may outnumber the Knot in some winters. Less abundant but equally significant nationally is the population of the energetic Sanderling. The Ribble and Alt are the only sites in Britain where winter numbers

Sanderling are almost always on the move probing for food at the edge of the tide.
(Stan Craig)

Chart 2   Annual fluctuations in peak Bar-tailed Godwit numbers on the Ribble and Alt Estuaries, 1978–2002

Like many arctic birds the breeding success of Bar-tailed Godwits varies from year to year. This is partly connected to huge annual changes in populations of Lemmings and other small mammals and their predators. At the start of the 'lemming cycle' there are huge numbers of Lemmings, so Arctic Foxes and other predators feed on Lemmings and ignore breeding birds. At the end of the year both birds and predators have produced many young. The following year Lemming numbers crash and the large predator population concentrates on young birds with the result that few young are successfully reared.

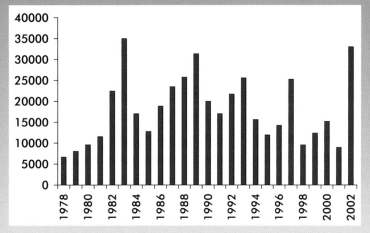

However, because of a shortage of prey, many predators also die. The next year Lemming numbers increase a little and with fewer predators around the birds have a moderate breeding season.

The 'lemming cycle' usually takes three or four years to complete and this is reflected in the number of Bar-tailed Godwits wintering on Lancashire coasts over the past 25 years, which have shown little overall change but large annual fluctuations.

(Source: *Wetland Bird Survey*)

regularly reach internationally important numbers (1,000), while on autumn and spring passage nearly 10,000 can occur on the Ribble, easily eclipsing all other sites.

Perhaps the most obvious wader is the Oystercatcher. This large black and white bird with bright orange bill has been mistaken for a penguin before now! Over 50,000 regularly winter in Morecambe Bay, the top site in Britain, a title this estuary holds for two of the other larger and particularly vocal waders, Curlew and Redshank. Lapwings retreat to the coast in winter, where combined January totals on the Ribble and Morecambe Bay regularly reach 50,000. They often form flocks with several thousand Golden Plover (Pluvialis apricaria), while the Grey Plover also visits the Ribble and Alt in significant numbers.

As the tide recedes the birds spread across the expanding flats. Shelducks feed purposefully in the muddy pools left by the tide, and wonderfully camouflaged Turnstones live up to their name, looking for tiny invertebrates; Morecambe Bay attracts more of this charming wader than any other site in Britain. Ringed Plovers, virtually unnoticed during the frenzy of high tide, are now dotted across the sandy expanse. There may only be a few hundred in winter, but the Ribble

The Ribble estuary and Morecambe Bay provide excellent breeding conditions for Shelduck.
(Stan Craig)

attracts several thousand in spring as they stop off to re-fuel on their way north. Adding character to the busy sandflats are the Bar-tailed and Black-tailed Godwits, elegant, long-legged waders whose long bills probe deep into the sand for food. The Ribble, Alt and Morecambe Bay can hold up to half the 40,000 Bar-taileds that winter in Britain, while 3,000 or more Black-taileds, 10% of the British population, winter on the Ribble. This species has regularly attempted to breed in the Ribble Estuary since 1988 (Pyefinch and Golborn 2001), and with a national breeding population of fewer than thirty pairs in some years, it is one of Lancashire's most important birds in summer and winter.

During the breeding season our estuaries are much quieter. Many Shelducks occur, often nesting in rabbit burrows, but they can be hard to spot on the wet sands in the shimmering sunlight. Calling Redshank and Oystercatchers penetrate the delicate, descant background provided by singing Skylarks (Alauda arvensis) and Meadow Pipits (Anthus pratensis) over the salt marshes, while drumming Snipe (*Gallinago gallinago*) may be joined by the primitive percussive sounds of drake Gadwall (*Anas strepera*) (on the Ribble) and Shelduck.

Freshwater birds

Lowland Lancashire provides some of the most important havens for birds in Britain. The lakes, pits and wet marshes hold internationally important concentrations of wildfowl in winter and some of our most enigmatic breeding birds in summer.

Nationally famous sites at Leighton Moss, Martin Mere and the Greater Manchester Flashes host many of the key species, but there are also many smaller excellent freshwater sites, many restored or created following industrial use.

Many birds, particularly wildfowl, move daily between freshwater and salt and brackish-water areas. Bewick's Swans, for example, regularly feed on the cereal fields on the south side of the Ribble estuary, but during the coldest parts of winter the majority move inland at dusk to roost at Martin Mere, only to leave again at first light. Their western relations the Whooper Swans are less adventurous: in mild weather they will venture to the coast with the Bewick's, but for much of the winter the thousand-plus herds stay close to food and sanctuary at Martin Mere.

Many Pink-footed Geese roost at Martin Mere in winter, with large numbers also on the Ribble and Pilling sands and smaller roosts on the Alt. Up to 40,000 could be counted in Lancashire in a day in the early 1990s, but a shift in distribution to take advantage of sugar beet stubbles in Norfolk has reduced the Lancashire population by a third.

Dabbling ducks characteristic of estuaries in winter can also reach important numbers inland. Counts of 15,000 Wigeon, 10,000 Teal, 5,000 Mallard (*Anas platyrhynchus*) and 7,500 Pintail at Martin Mere with 3,000 Teal at Mere Sands Wood all underline the importance of these havens. Gadwall are less inclined to flock to the coast in winter; but 50 or more are regularly seen in autumn at the Wigan Flashes, Pennington Flash and Hope Carr Nature Reserve. The freshwater

The Pintail is well worth looking out for among the wintering ducks on our estuaries.
(Stan Craig)

149

Tufted ducks are usually our commonest fish-eating diving duck on freshwater reservoirs and lakes.
(Peter Smith)

lakes also attract high numbers of our most familiar diving ducks. The largest counts of Pochard in North West England are regularly at Martin Mere with peaks of over a thousand, and 400 occur each winter at Chorlton Water Park. This site had twice as many in the late 1980s, but Pochard seem to have changed their habits, possibly because global warming allows them to remain closer to their breeding grounds. Tufted Ducks (*Aythya fuligula*) also visit these sites and other reservoirs with flocks of several hundred in winter.

Coot (*Fulica atra*) counts rose dramatically in the 1990s with winter peaks of 500 or more at the Wigan Flashes, Martin Mere and Pine Lake (Carnforth), and smaller numbers at many other sites. Moorhens (*Gallinula chloropus*) are an ubiquitous feature of freshwater wetlands, seemingly able to survive on some of the least fruitful looking ditches and ponds, as well as the most productive waters. Some of Britain's highest counts have been at Martin Mere with 750 or so each winter, the birds taking advantage of supplemented food and predator-free conditions provided for the captive exotics in the Waterfowl Gardens.

The open water habitats in the east of the county tend to be less nutrient-rich and consequently less popular with the majority of wetland birds. However over 100 Goosander (*Mergus merganser*) are occasionally seen in winter from central sites such as Anglezarke and Alston Reservoirs.

Wading birds also concentrate at some wetland sites with up to

Coot are easily recognised and then overlooked as dull and uninteresting birds, but their energetic behaviour is well worth watching.
(Peter Smith)

150

Chart 3 Annual sightings of Ospreys In Lancashire, 1953–2001

The Osprey was a very rare bird in Lancashire throughout the twentieth century until a marked increase in sightings began in the mid-1970s. This was partly due to the increased number of birdwatchers, but it also reflects real changes in the fortunes of Ospreys in Britain. Sustained conservation efforts have brought the Scottish breeding population (to which most Lancashire migrants probably belong) back from the brink of extinction. Ospreys have recently begun to colonise the Lake District and it is probably just a matter of time before this magnificent fish-eating bird nests once again in Lancashire.

(Source: Lancashire Bird Reports)

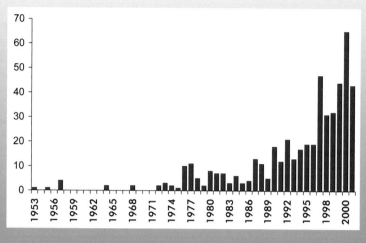

two hundred Ruff at Martin Mere each winter, putting it among the top sites in Britain, while up to 500 have been seen there on autumn passage. Another passage wader is the Curlew's northern-breeding relative, the Whimbrel (*Numenius phaeopus*) with peak counts usually during the first week of May. Over a thousand were recorded at Barnacre Reservoir, on the western edge of Bowland, in the early 1990s, but by the end of the decade numbers had fallen by about a third, perhaps because they were spread over other sites including Longton Marsh, Windy Harbour (on the Wyre), Brockholes Quarry and Formby Moss.

The handsome drake Goosander is our largest fish-eating 'sawbill', and it breeds on the Ribble.

(Stan Craig)

151

Bittern, superbly
camouflaged
among reeds.
(Steve Young)

Box 8.5 *Bittern*

The Bittern is fully adapted to life in the reed bed. A little smaller than a Grey Heron (*Ardea cinerea*), it is perfectly camouflaged by its streaked brown plumage. If disturbed it stretches its neck and points its bill skywards with posture and streaks aligned to the reeds, thus perfecting the camouflage. The presence of Bitterns is often only realised when an individual flies over the reed bed, or when a territorial male gives its haunting boom, like blowing across the top of a milk bottle.

The Bittern eats a range of fish, especially Eels and Roach at Leighton Moss, together with amphibians, rodents and invertebrates. Availability of food within a reed bed is one of the most important factors for successful breeding.

The Bittern was lost as a regular breeder in Lancashire in 1820 when the last areas of the once enormous Martin Mere were drained for agriculture. It remained a relatively common wintering species in Lancashire according to Mitchell who wrote *The Birds of Lancashire* in 1882. He also commented on how useful the feathers were for making trout flies. Re-colonisation took place at the RSPB reserve at Leighton Moss sometime in the mid twentieth century, and now two to four booming males breed here, each with one or more females. More recently Bittern have been recorded from other reed beds in winter including Marton Mere (Blackpool), the Wigan Flashes, Martin Mere and Mere Sands Wood. This has prompted the Wildlife Trust to join with other partners to encourage breeding by developing larger and better quality reed beds, especially at the Wigan Flashes.

Every naturalist should experience a dusk or dawn visit to one of the county's key wetland sites in summer, and Leighton Moss is arguably the best. Three of Britain's most specialised breeding birds nest here: Bittern, Bearded Tit and Marsh Harrier (see Boxes 8.5 and 8.6).

Water Rails (*Rallus aquaticus*) also like reed beds with 132 territorial males at Leighton Moss in 2000 (based on responses to tape-recorded calls), and much smaller numbers elsewhere including the Wigan Flashes and Abram Flashes. Another species that prefers reeds in Britain is the aptly named Reed Warbler (*Acrocephalus scirpaceus*).

Box 8.6

Bearded Tits and Marsh Harriers

These are two more reed bed specialists which have recently spread to Leighton Moss as breeding species.

Bearded Tits first colonised Leighton Moss in 1973 and by 2000 the population of this dry reed bed specialist had reached 65 pairs; recent increases are thought to coincide with the provision of wigwam-style nest boxes, allowing breeding incursions into the wetter parts of the reed bed. However, this peak breeding season was followed by a dramatic crash triggered by the very wet autumn in 2001, but with good quality habitat numbers should increase again.

The breeding population of the stunning Marsh Harrier in Lancashire is centred at Leighton Moss, a long way from its British headquarters in East Anglia. Over a hundred years ago it inhabited the mossland at Pilling and Martin Mere, but eventually became extinct. It returned to breed at Leighton Moss in 1987, and between 1987 and 2000 76 young harriers have been reared (Pyefinch and Golborn 2001). Looking to the future, the arable-cropped mosslands in the south-west of the county should prove suitable for Marsh Harriers to expand: 10% of the East Anglian population now nests in similar habitats.

One normally sees Bearded Tits at Leighton Moss flying up in small groups and then diving back into the reeds. This is a male. *(Peter Smith)*

Unlike the Bittern and Bearded Tit, this warbler will colonise small patches of reed and many canal sides and ditches in the county now host one or two pairs. However, where the habitat is especially good they thrive, with a staggering 410 pairs at the Wigan Flashes in 2001 and around 300 pairs at Leighton Moss.

Other interesting wetland birds breed in areas lacking reed beds, for example in 1994 42 broods of Shelduck were counted at Martin Mere, at the time the densest breeding population in Britain. Five per cent of Britain's Pochard regularly nest at just five sites in our region; and five percent of Britain's breeding Goosanders come from the Rivers Lune and Ribble.

The post-industrial landscape of extraction pits and mining sub-sidence has also contributed to the county's breeding wetland birds. Little Ringed Plovers (*Charadrius dubius*) almost exclusively choose such sites as do almost half of the county's Great Crested Grebes. Since 1992 there has been a small but possibly expanding breeding population of Black-necked Grebes in the Manchester region. With only around 20 breeding localities in Britain (Ogilvie *et al.* 2001), this tiny water bird must rank as another of our county's ornithological highlights.

153

Birds:
Freshwater birds

Kingfishers (*Alcedo atthis*) are usually seen as a disappearing flash of electric blue, but anglers who sit quietly see them more often.
(*Peter Smith*)

Little Ringed Plovers nest on the shingle close to gravel pits.
((*Peter Smith*)

Farmland birds

Lowland farmland has changed dramatically over the past fifty years, leading to major declines in some once familiar lowland birds (see Box 8.7).

Box 8.7 Declining farmland birds

Lancashire breeding birds suffering from long-term declines due to changes in farming practices include Kestrel, Grey Partridge (*Perdix perdix*), Lapwing, Turtle Dove, Skylark, Yellow Wagtail, Tree Sparrow (*Passer montanus*), Linnet, Yellowhammer (*Emberiza citrinella*), Reed Bunting (*Emberiza schoeniclus*) and Corn Bunting (*Miliaria calandra*).

Factors which have caused these declines include simplification of the farmed landscape by reduction of ponds, trees, hedges and un-cropped field margins, abandonment of crop rotations, increased use of pesticides, intensification of grassland management and a switch from spring to autumn grown cereals. The finches, buntings and Tree Sparrow, for example, depend on cereal grains and seeds from grasses and arable weeds, but during the summer most switch to an invertebrate diet. Simplifying the farming landscape and rotations has reduced available breeding habitats. Perhaps the most startling loss is the Skylark with a 55% decline in Britain in the twenty years since 1975. In the Lancaster area there was a range contraction of 15% in the 1990s. Popularised in much of our pastoral culture, the rich song of the lark is now rarely heard on intensively farmed arable land and improved pastures. This ground nesting bird has been dealt a double blow by the trend towards autumn sown crops: the crucial second-brood nesting becomes difficult in the tall vegetation and then those that do succeed are deprived of winter stubbles for feeding, these being ploughed then cropped in the autumn.

Yellow Wagtails favour mixed farming plots with late summer hay cropping where they feed on insects attracted to marshy pools, cattle dung and nectar. This type of agriculture is not a profitable management of land in the twenty-first century, so the species has been in rapid decline in our region, following a slow longer-term contraction of range first noted in the 1930s. Breeding Yellow Wagtails now remain on the upper Lune, a band of mossland stretching from the Ribble estuary into northern Merseyside and on Chat Moss. On the West Lancashire mosslands it has long been associated with cabbage fields, and more recently with carrot fields, and this adaptation may help it retain its tenuous county-foothold.

155

Chart 4 Declining fortunes of the Yellow Wagtail

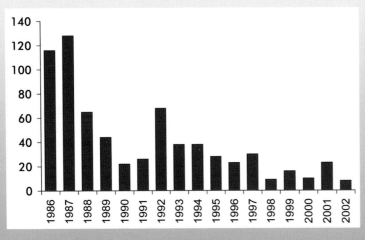

This graph shows the total number of sightings of migrant Yellow Wagtails each spring from 1986 to 2002 at Seaforth Nature Reserve, based on daily counts. British breeding Yellow Wagtails belong to the race *flavissima* and their numbers are declining sharply. From mid-April they return from Africa to breed, mostly on farmland. In Lancashire, at the northern edge of its breeding range, its breeding distribution has shrunk by 60% in the past 30 years: in the 1970s several hundred pairs bred in 45 10 km squares, while by the late 1990s only about 70 pairs bred in just 19 squares. At Arkholme, on the River Lune, 28 breeding pairs in the 1970s have reduced to only six. Sadly, it appears just a matter of time before Yellow Wagtails disappear completely from the county.

Changing agricultural practices are probably to blame, particularly the loss of small farms with a mixture of low-intensity crop fields and pastures and the consequent reduction in insect numbers upon which Yellow Wagtails depend.

(*Sources: British Trust for Ornithology Atlases, Lancashire Atlas, K. Briggs, Seaforth Bird Reports*)

Yellow Wagtail.
(*Stan Craig*)

Some species, however, are proving more adaptable to agricultural changes than others: Linnets, Reed Buntings and Sedge Warblers (*Acrocephalus schoenobaenus*) are increasingly using oil seed rape fields. This crop is harvested in late summer and provides dense cover; its eye-aching acres, characteristic of modern lowland agriculture, may yet compensate for some of the losses caused by modern production methods. Tree Sparrows have suffered major losses, again linked to herbicide use and losses of winter-feeding on stubbles. The breeding range has contracted rapidly since the 1980s and there was a 20% loss in the 1990s. The species is commonest on the mosslands south of the Ribble estuary. A series of nestbox schemes and appropriate all-year round supplemental feeding has helped populations in West Lancashire, the Lune Valley and

Preesall/Pilling. The continued expansion of nestbox schemes and support for garden feeding may provide some hope for this enigmatic hole-nester.

For other species it is difficult to be optimistic. Turtle Doves will soon be lost while Yellowhammer and Corn Bunting will continue to decline unless there is a major change in agricultural practice. Lapwings too are struggling; could any Lancashire naturalist imagine a March morning without the sound of 'Tuwit'? They are in steep decline nationally and local losses in Lancashire reflect this. Recent trends for mid-spring silage cropping, increased rolling of grasslands in April and high stocking rates of farm animals all take their toll on Lapwing chicks. The Grey Partridge has suffered serious chick mortality in recent years linked to declines in their insect food caused partly by insecticides and partly by herbicides reducing plant diversity with knock-on effects on nectar and insects. Simplification of farmland habitats also leaves birds more vulnerable to ground predators.

Game birds are still part of the farmland scene, however, with Red-legged Partridges (*Alectoris rufa*) being released in large numbers, and

left The Yellowhammer has been hit by modern farming practices and its song 'a little bit of bread and no cheese' is now rarely heard.
(Peter Smith)

right The Corn Bunting is a bird of arable farmland, most easily recognised by its call that has been likened to the closing of a rusty gate.
(Peter Smith)

Birds:
Farmland birds

Pheasants (*Phasianus colchicus*) continuing to be re-stocked annually. Surprisingly Lancashire is also a popular county for the diminutive Quail (*Coturnix coturnix*), Britain's only migratory game bird. It is rarely seen but has a far-carrying whiplash call. In most summers there may be just four or five pairs, but every five or so years a massive influx leads to perhaps as many as fifty breeding birds. During invasions the distinctive call might be heard on a calm evening from any lowland site, but otherwise Quail are restricted to West Lancashire and north Fylde mosslands.

Some birds have adapted well to modern agriculture with Woodpigeons (*Columba palumbus*) and Carrion Crows (*Corvus corone*) particularly successful. Other species have over-spilled from their specialist niches and adapted well. Oystercatchers started nesting on arable fields in the mid 1960s; this habit is now commonplace on our southern mosslands and those of north Fylde, and seems to be spreading into Greater Manchester. Shelducks, too, have discovered arable mossland breeding sites, but the majority of females still prefer to raise their crèched young on the coast, so they have not spread as prolifically as Oystercatchers.

above The once common Grey Partridge has suffered from modern farming practices but is still present on some farms.
(Peter Smith)

below Pink-footed Geese feeding on an arable field.
(Peter Smith)

Where stubbles remain many of our farmland breeders are still present in winter. Influxes of birds from the Continent, where agricultural change has been less dramatic, swell populations. Finches, buntings, sparrows, starlings, pipits, larks and wagtails can form impressive flocks. If there are a few trees nearby Mistle Thrushes (*Turdus viscivorus*), Fieldfares (*Turdus pilaris*) and Redwings (*Turdus iliacus*) may form large gatherings, fleeing to the trees whenever disturbed. Stubbles and un-harvested potato and carrot fields attract large flocks of Pink-footed Geese on the western mosses, and in the south Whooper Swans and smaller herds of Bewick's Swans accompany them.

A cold snap during the winter may be the best time to see Barn Owls which continue hunting for voles during the day in hard weather.

Upland birds

Most birds flee the uplands in winter but, although the number of species is lower than in other major Lancashire habitats, our moorlands support an interesting assemblage of breeding birds.

Pride of place goes to the Red Grouse (*Lagopus lagopus*), a bird which is almost synonymous with moorland dominated by heather, its main food. More than 200 km² of managed grouse moors in the Bowland Fells, West Pennine Moors and South Pennines support almost all of these birds. This population varies cyclically, mostly in response to disease, probably reaching 10,000 pairs in the best years. The Black Grouse, a bird of the moorland fringe, was never common in Lancashire and is probably now extinct although occasional sightings are reported from far-flung areas of Bowland.

It is passerines (songbirds), however, that predominate. Just two, Meadow Pipit and Skylark, outnumber all other upland birds several times over and can be found on both heather and grass moorland and agricultural in-bye land. These species are so numerous that they tend to be taken for granted and little studied, but there is increasing evidence that numbers of both may be in steep decline, possibly as a result of agricultural intensification.

Joining these on the moorland fringe are Wheatears (*Oenanthe oenanthe*), one of the earliest birds to return in spring from Africa to seek out nesting sites in dry-stone walls.

Uncultivated areas with tall heather, bracken and scrub, found throughout the uplands, continue to support about 150 pairs of Whinchats (*Saxicola rubetra*), but their numbers are declining rapidly. In contrast, the closely-related Stonechat (*Saxicola torquata*), which

Much of the Pennine and Bowland moorland is managed for the Red Grouse.
(Peter Smith)

159

Birds:
Upland birds

inhabits broadly similar habitats, is thriving. The late 1990s saw a dramatic – perhaps as much as threefold – upsurge to around 50 breeding pairs which shows no sign of abating. The reasons for this are not known but recent mild winters may have benefited the partially-migratory Stonechat over the African-wintering Whinchat, or it may be due to subtle habitat changes. It is interesting to note that Stonechats completely 'replaced' Whinchats on the Sefton coast in the 1980s – will the same happen in the uplands?

Two passerine species are particularly endangered, Twite (see Box 8.8) and Ring Ouzel. The Ring Ouzel is amongst the most elusive of British birds. Closely related to the Blackbird (*Turdus merula*), it spends the winter in southern Europe and North Africa but returns in early spring to breed in rocky gullies and cloughs where its far-reaching song is often the only sign of its presence. A handful of birds hang on in the South Pennines but the bulk of Lancashire's population is found in Bowland. Their breeding range has shrunk by at least a quarter in the past 25 years, and a mere 35 or fewer pairs remain in the county. Conservation efforts are focused on discovering the reasons for their decline – candidates include increased competition from other thrush species due to climate change, increased recreational disturbance in the breeding season and losses of their favoured winter food resource, juniper berries.

Although songbirds dominate the uplands numerically it is often waders that are more noticeable, none more so than the Curlew, whose song dominates the open moors. Curlews are the most wide-spread and numerous upland waders with about 4,500 pairs in Lancashire, where numbers appear to be stable. Most nest on grass moorland but often feed on enclosed in-bye land.

The other open-country specialist is the Golden Plover, which breeds unobtrusively in short vegetation in Bowland, the West Pennine Moors, Pendle and the Boulsworth Hill area. The Lancashire population of around 130 pairs is insignificant nationally, but it is a charismatic bird. Fortunately, it appears to be holding its own in the county but it is particularly sensitive to disturbance and increased recreational pressure may pose a future threat.

The other upland plover is the Lapwing. In many areas of Britain Lapwing populations are under threat but Lancashire remains one of the species' strongholds, although numbers are undoubtedly declining. Lapwings breed throughout the county with an estimated population in Lancashire and North Merseyside of more than 13,000 pairs (figures for Greater Manchester are not known), about half of which breed in the uplands.

Box 8.8 *The Twite* (Carduelis flavirostris)

The Twite is the archetypal 'little brown job' – a small, dark finch whose only distinguishing feature is the bright pink (but rarely visible) rump of the male. Perhaps that's why birdwatchers are so infatuated with it! Sometimes known as the 'Mountain Linnet', in England it breeds mostly on the edge of grass moorlands.

It remains relatively common in northern Scotland, where it is associated with crofting, but is disappearing fast from its English stronghold in the South Pennines (see Map 10, overleaf).

Although one or two pairs may breed in Bowland, most Lancashire birds are found in the Burnley and Rossendale areas and on the West Pennine Moors. The decline has been sudden and dramatic. Ten years ago the annual birdwatching pilgrimage up Pendle Hill to see migrant Dotterels (*Charadrius morinellus*) in early May would be sure to turn up numerous Twite – now the area has just a couple of pairs. In the 1970s one Rossendale site held up to 17 breeding pairs; all were gone by the late 1980s. During the 1990s their breeding range contracted by a third and their population shrank by a half to about 40 pairs. Without rapid action, extinction looms.

Why have they declined? Twite nest on the moorland edge but require access to a succession of seed sources on nearby agricultural land in the breeding season. They switch from dandelions to sorrels to thistles as the season progresses. Sorrel seeds are probably critical, being fed as a crushed 'porridge' to their young, and the loss of hay meadows to silage-production and intensive sheep-pasture is probably the cause of the Twite's decline. Conservation efforts are concentrated on restoring hay meadows in areas where Twite remain.

Most Pennine birds are thought to spend the winter on the English east coast, although some remain in the uplands, e.g. the 40 or so that have wintered at a feeding station at Light Hazzles in recent years. The origins of the 200 or more birds which winter on the south Ribble, Lune and Fylde coast marshes were unknown until recently but sightings of ringed birds in 2003 suggest that they breed in the Hebrides and perhaps other parts of Scotland.

Wintering Twite, now threatened with extinction as a breeding bird in our uplands.
(Peter Smith)

161

Birds:
Upland birds

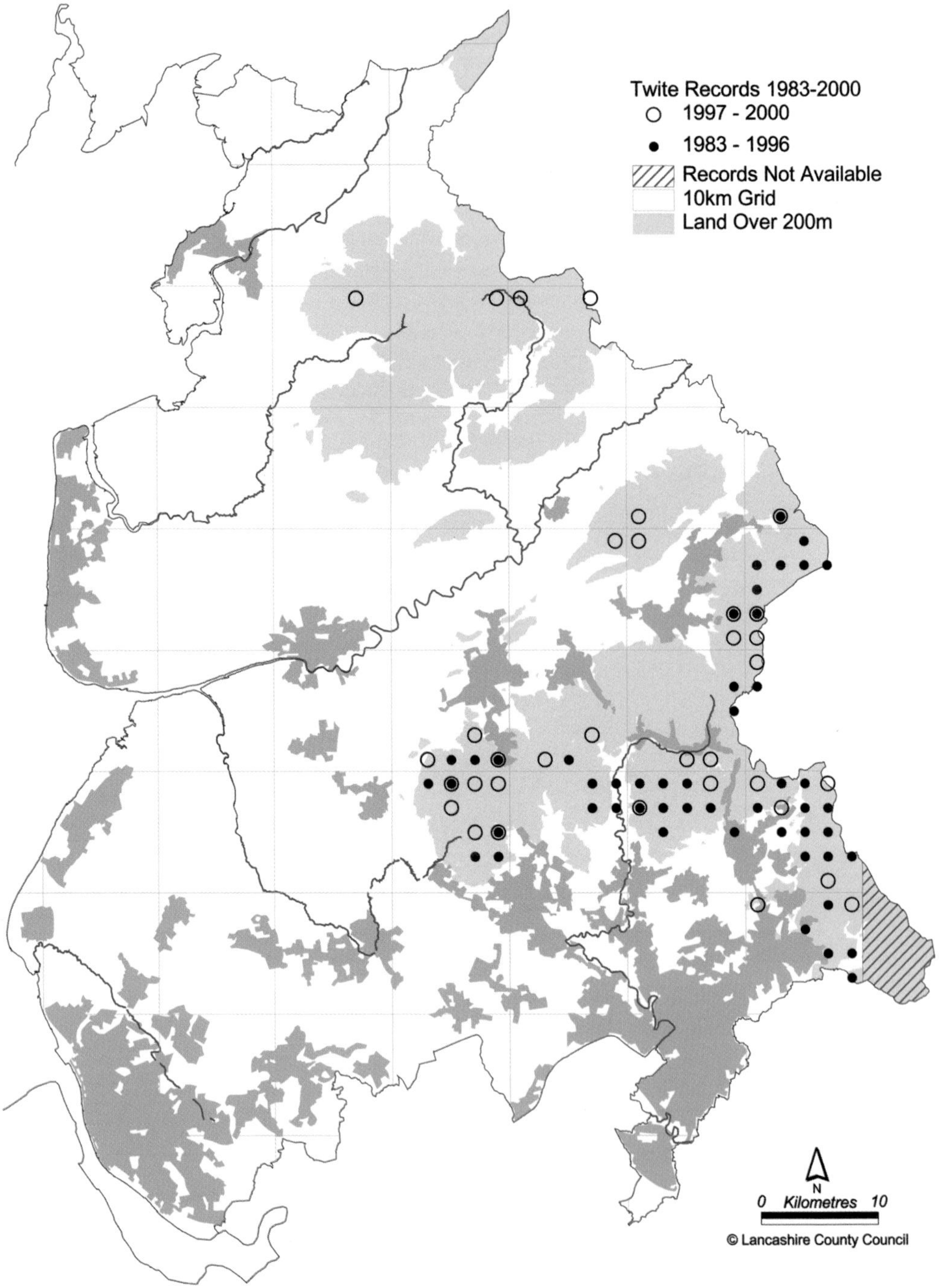

Map 10.
Records of Twite in the Wildlife Trust area.
(Nik Bruce)

Twite Records 1983-2000
○ 1997 - 2000
● 1983 - 1996
▨ Records Not Available
10km Grid
Land Over 200m

0 Kilometres 10

© Lancashire County Council

Source: Lancashire and Cheshire Fauna Society,
Greater Manchester Bird Recording Group

top left The song of the Curlew resonates throughout our uplands in summer, and on many lowland farms too.
(Peter Smith)

top right Lapwing, emblem of the Wildlife Trust, still breed in much of our countryside, though in reduced numbers.
(Peter Smith)

left Golden Plovers breed in our uplands but are shy and easily frightened away.
(Stan Craig)

Birds:
Upland birds

Sharing similar habitats, particularly tussocky pastures, is the Redshank. Most of Lancashire's 850 or so pairs breed on coastal marshes or wet grassland, but Bowland alone supports 250 pairs, and smaller numbers can be found in the Pennines. Numbers have probably declined slightly in the county in recent years in line with the national trend but Lancashire remains a stronghold of the species.

Snipe favour permanently wet areas on the open moors and in pastures. They require soft ground to probe for food, and have suffered from agricultural improvement and increased drainage. Around 450 pairs remain in Lancashire with major populations in the West Pennine Moors and areas of Bowland, but they are rarely seen except when accidentally flushed or when displaying at dawn and dusk.

At the top of the avian food chain are the birds of prey. Hen Harriers are arguably Lancashire's most important breeding bird – they are certainly its most controversial. Ten or so pairs nest in their only regular breeding area in England. All proven recent breeding records have been in Bowland but one pair may have nested in the Pennines in 2001. The problem with Hen Harriers is that they favour grouse moors and they undoubtedly take some young grouse. Recent research has

top Snipe thrive in marshy areas of moorland and pastures.
(Stan Craig)

bottom The Hen Harrier has one of its British strongholds in the Forest of Bowland where it is occasionally (and illegally) persecuted. Here the male is on the nest hidden in heather; the female is brown.
(Peter Smith)

shown that they rely heavily on small songbirds, especially Meadow Pipits, and that they are not a major factor in regulating grouse numbers. However, there is a long history of persecution of Hen Harriers by shooting interests nationally that has contributed heavily to their present precarious situation.

The Merlin (*Falco columbarius*) is the other specialist moorland raptor (Britain's smallest), feeding predominantly on Meadow Pipits and Skylarks which it catches in flight. It is notoriously shy on its breeding grounds where it usually nests amongst heather. There appear to be at least 25 pairs in Lancashire, where its main threats today are probably afforestation and egg-thieves.

Wildlife of Lancashire

Several other birds of prey hunt the moorland edges, but the only other species that is mainly confined to the uplands in Lancashire is the Short-eared Owl. Britain's only day-flying owl, it specialises in hunting voles in rough grassland, a habitat which has now largely disappeared from the county's lowlands. Numbers fluctuate in line with the changing abundance of its prey, but about 30 pairs are now thought to breed in Lancashire. Upland afforestation has undoubtedly reduced the population but it is quick to reoccupy clear-felled areas.

Woordland birds

Just over 50 species breed regularly in Lancashire's woodlands, roughly a third of the total. Only a handful of additional species visit the habitat in winter; most notable are Redwing, Fieldfare and Brambling (*Fringilla montifringilla*) – Scandinavian immigrants whose numbers depend on the size of berry and beech-mast crops.

Woodlands contain most of the birds that people know well: many are widespread, abundant and regular garden visitors, indeed, nine of our commonest ten species are largely woodland birds. Of all avian habitats, broad-leaved woodlands have suffered the least in recent times and most resident species are thriving. Extensive conifer plantations have helped the spread of species such as Goldcrest (*Regulus regulus*), Siskin (*Carduelis spinus*) and Crossbill (*Loxia curvirostra*). There

above Dippers breed on most of the fast-flowing streams coming off the fells. (Peter Smith)

left Britain's smallest bird, the Goldcrest, breeds in conifer plantations and joins parties of tits in winter. (Stan Craig)

165

Birds:
Woodland birds

are four exceptions to this rosy picture – all associated with mature broad-leaved woods: Willow Tit and Marsh Tit (see Box 8.9); Lesser Spotted Woodpecker and Hawfinch.

Seeing a Lesser Spotted Woodpecker has become something of an obsession for many birdwatchers, partly because of its secretive behaviour but mainly because they are so scarce. A cluster of pairs breeds in the Chorley area but elsewhere they are extremely thin on the ground.

The Hawfinch, with a population of about ten pairs, is one of our rarest birds. It was once seen fairly regularly in the Chorley and Blackburn areas, but is now down to perhaps one or two pairs. One pair has recently bred near the Cheshire border in Greater Manchester. The only reliable site is Silverdale, an area which supports all the remaining birds, with Woodwell being the favoured watch-point.

Resident birds are joined by migrant breeders from April onwards. The most widespread and numerous are Willow Warbler (*Phylloscopus trochilus*), Chiffchaff (*P. collybita*), Blackcap (*Sylvia atricapilla*) and Garden Warbler (*S. borin*). Species with more specialised habitat requirements, such as those associated with mature, predominantly oak woodlands, are far less common, but their numbers are relatively stable: Wood Warbler, Redstart (*Phoenicurus phoenicurus*) and Pied Flycatcher (*Ficedula hypoleuca*), whose numbers have been stimulated by the provision of nestboxes in several woodlands. The Spotted

*Wildlife of
Lancashire*

left The Willow Warbler is one of our commonest woodland warblers. *(Peter Smith)*

below The Wood Warbler is easiest to find in woodland in eastern Lancashire. *(Stan Craig)*

Box 8.9 *Marsh and Willow Tits*

upper Marsh Tit.
(Steve Young)

lower Willow Tit showing the pale patch on the wing which distinguishes it from the otherwise similar Marsh Tit.
(Dorothy Holt)

Marsh Tit (*Parus palustris*) and Willow Tit (*Parus montanus*) are so similar they were thought to be a single species until just over 100 years ago, but their calls are distinctive. Both are sedentary and take more seeds than do other tits.

Marsh Tits nest in ready-made holes in drier deciduous woods and trees in parks and gardens, whereas Willow Tits excavate their own holes and favour damp woods and riverine environments.

If you see a brown tit north of the Ribble it is almost certainly a Marsh Tit, while south of the Ribble it will be a Willow Tit. The focal area for Marsh Tits is the limestone woodland at

Silverdale, especially the yew woodland whose berries they eat in autumn. Willow Tits are virtually confined to the lowlands south of the Ribble from the coast to Wigan and Bolton. There are also small declining populations of Marsh Tits in the Lune and Ribble valleys, where Willow Tits have also been found.

Marsh Tits have declined nationally over the past 20 years (Gibbons *et al.* 1996). They are on the Red List of Birds of Conservation Concern, but the Silverdale population appears to be stable with

around 300 pairs which is now of national significance (Pyefinch and Golborn 2001). Willow Tits are also declining: of 17 sites on the south western mosses that hosted pairs in 1978, only one pair remained in 1997.

The reasons for their declines are not fully understood. Loss of habitat has certainly affected Willow Tits whose nests are also vulnerable to weasels, but this does not explain all the losses, and there may be different reasons for each species. However, it is of particular concern when sedentary birds are in decline, as there is less chance of migratory influxes from areas of stable or increasing populations swelling the local stock. It would be sad if we were to lose either of these charming woodland birds from our county.

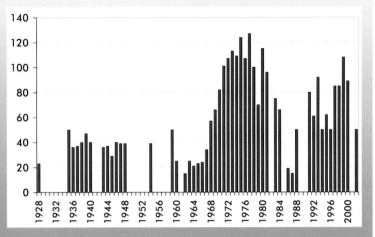

Chart 5 *Changing fortunes of Herons at the Brock Valley Heronry between 1928 and 2002*

Red bars are numbers of pairs attempting to breed each year. Blanks indicate no count was made, blue bars mean only part of the heronry was counted. The earlier figures are probably less accurate than the later ones.

(By kind permission of the Fitzherbert-Brockholes family)

Flycatcher is the odd one out. Despite being fairly catholic in habitat requirements, its numbers are in steep decline nationally and it has disappeared from many parts of Lancashire in the last decade, presumably because of problems in its wintering grounds.

Urban birds

Most birds in our towns and cities are really woodland and hedgerow species that have adapted to breeding in gardens and parks. These include many of our favourite familiar birds: Robin (*Erithacus rubecula*), Great and Blue Tits (*Parus major* and *P. caeruleus*), Wren (*Troglodytes troglodytes*), Dunnock (*Prunella modularis*), Chaffinch (*Fringilla coelebs*), Blackbird and Song Thrush (*Turdus philomelos*). Here they find plentiful food but a combination of scant nest cover and high densities of predators (cats and to some extent Magpies (*Pica pica*)) means that breeding success is often low.

However, as intensified farmland diminishes in value for birds, urban areas may take on increasing importance. Two species in particular have become true suburbanites with some of their highest breeding densities in generously-gardened urban areas: Greenfinch (*Carduelis chloris*), which has enthusiastically taken to a diet of peanuts and sunflower seeds, and Song Thrush, whose earthworm food is readily available on well-tended lawns.

Box 8.10 *Black Redstart*

One of Britain's rarest breeding birds with around 100 pairs, the Black Redstart first colonised in numbers from continental Europe after the Second World War when it took to nesting in crevices in bomb-damaged cityscapes as a substitute for its usual semi-montane rocky habitat.

While nesting the birds become extremely inconspicuous and often the only evidence of their presence is the song of the male from high buildings in competition with the noise of traffic below.

According to published records, Black Redstarts first bred in both Manchester and Liverpool in 1977 but were almost certainly present before that. Derelict Liverpool docklands continued to be used by up to three pairs until at least 1998 while a single pair breeds in central Manchester in most years.

Sporadic breeding has occurred elsewhere, most recently in Bolton and Blackpool in 1997 and Blackburn in 2000, and regular sightings near Pendle Hill and on the West Pennine Moors are suggestive of breeding. However, it seems unlikely that the total population has ever exceeded five pairs. It is even more unlikely that such numbers will be regained as urban regeneration destroys the habitat of our most elusive urbanite.

Black Redstart.
(*Steve Young*)

Wildlife of
Lancashire

The real urban-dwellers are those that have adapted to using buildings. Two are quite recent colonists: Peregrines and Ravens, both traditionally associated with sea-cliffs, have adopted tall buildings and gasometers as surrogate nest-sites and appear to be thriving on diets of feral pigeons and discarded take-away food respectively. Herring and Lesser Black-backed Gulls have acquired the habit of nesting on flat roofs in Liverpool, Fleetwood and other coastal towns. Strangest of all are the large winter rooftop roosts of Lapwings with some Golden Plovers in urban areas of Greater Manchester and east Lancashire. The much smaller Black Redstart also has a tenuous foothold in some of our cities (Box 8.10).

Other species have a longer history of cohabiting with people: Feral Pigeons (*Columba livia*) (the domestic version of the cliff-dwelling Rock Dove) inhabit empty buildings, House Sparrows (*Passer domesticus*), Starlings (*Sturnus vulgaris*) and Swifts (*Apus apus*) share our roof-spaces, while House Martins (*Delichon urbica*), once cliff-nesters, now breed exclusively under our eaves. The recent decline of the urban House Sparrow has received much publicity but Starlings too are much reduced in numbers – due to similarly unknown causes.

Further reading

Pyefinch, R. and Golborn, P. (2001). *The Atlas of Breeding Birds in Lancashire and North Merseyside*. Hobby Publications, Liverpool.

Chapter 9

Reptiles and

Lancashire is of national importance for amphibians with breeding sites throughout the area for Smooth, Palmate and Great Crested Newt (*Triturus vulgaris*, *T. helveticus* and *T. cristatus*) as well as Common Frog (*Rana temporaria*) and Common Toad (*Bufo bufo*). Over much of its European range the Great Crested Newt is severely threatened and is protected by European legislation, so the large Lancashire population is of international importance. The coastal population of the much rarer and local Natterjack Toad (*Bufo calamita*) is also of national importance. In contrast reptiles are much scarcer, but we do have small populations of Common Lizard (*Lacerta vivipara*), Sand Lizard (*L. agilis*), Slow-worm (*Anguis fragilis*), Adder (*Vipera berus*) and possibly Grass Snake (*Natrix natrix*). Our threatened populations of amphibians and reptiles can be helped by attracting them to our gardens (see Box 9.1)

Common Frog.
(Mike Atkinson)

Male newts in the spring are brightly coloured and the Great Crested is brilliant orange-red with black spots on the belly. Frogs and

Amphibians

Rick Parker

Common Frogs spawning.
(Peter Smith)

toads are camouflaged, mottled with green, olive, brown and grey, but the Natterjack has a characteristic yellow line down its back.

In the 1980s it was realised that some species of amphibians were declining. This led to statutory protection for the Great Crested Newt and Natterjack Toad under the Wildlife and Countryside Act of 1981, and the Nature Conservancy Council launched a national amphibian survey. Handling these two protected species requires a licence from English Nature. In 1988 the Lancashire Trust for Nature Conservation established the Great Crested Newt Group of volunteers to co-

Common Toads paired up on the way to a breeding pond.
(Mike Atkinson)

ordinate systematic amphibian surveys. Two survey methods were adopted, netting and torching, but both failed to show the presence of the Great Crested Newt, the most threatened species. Careful research revealed the reasons for this failure. Most of the ponds surveyed in our area were old marl pits, but these had developed large areas of marginal vegetation and the water was usually cloudy with suspended clay. With disturbed newts retreating to deeper waters neither torching nor netting proved effective, especially for Great Crested Newts.

Great Crested Newt.
(Peter Smith)

Assisting with amphibian surveys is easy to do and your results can help to locate and protect the remaining amphibian strongholds. Newts lay eggs singly on aquatic vegetation and fold the leaves of aquatic plants around them. Eggs of Great Crested Newts are twice the size of those of Smooth and Palmate Newts, with a yellowish white instead of grey embryo in the centre. It is also possible to distinguish the more similar eggs of Smooth and Palmate Newts. Start the search at the south facing side of the pond and look for water plants, especially sweet-grasses (*Glyceria* spp.), water forget-me-not (*Myosotis* spp.) and Water Mint, which are the most favoured plants for egg laying. Look for folded leaves and gently open the fold to find the eggs. Opening folds makes eggs more vulnerable to predation so only unfold the minimum necessary to confirm presence.

Egg search is a quick, efficient, easy technique for determining the presence or absence of newts, particularly the Great Crested, and a large number of ponds can be surveyed in a day. Prolonged periods of warm weather stimulates egg laying and increases the chances of successful egg search which is best carried out from April to June.

The Lancashire newt group therefore devised a new survey method of searching for eggs on vegetation (see Box 9.2) which has now revealed hundreds of breeding ponds for Great Crested Newt, many of which contain all five of our amphibian species, and this method has since been taken up nationally. More survey work is still required in Lancashire since there are an enormous number of ponds, and the amphibian fauna of each pond is not necessarily the same today as it was when surveyed 10 or 20 years ago. Ponds also undergo natural succession and can become choked by vegetation or too shaded by overhanging trees for tadpoles to mature. Many amphibian ponds are threatened by development, but if the presence of the protected Great Crested Newt can be confirmed, then mitigation can be demanded and replacement ponds dug out.

The few colonies of Natterjack Toads in Merseyside and Cumbria are at the northern edge of the species range, but one of the largest populations is on the Sefton coast. Nevertheless this population too appeared to be declining, so conservation work was initiated in the 1970s. New pools were dug for tadpoles and scrub was cleared to ensure there were sufficient mobile dunes which are favoured by the adults. The pools must be shallow otherwise Common Toads and Frogs invade them, and their tadpoles outcompete the Natterjack. With careful monitoring and habitat management the population is now thriving. The Natterjack has also been introduced at Cockerham (Box 9.3).

Reptiles and
Amphibians

Box 9.3 *Natterjack Toads return to Lancashire*

Although fairly common on the Sefton dunes the Natterjack Toad is one of our rarest amphibians. Eighty years ago it could be found as far inland as Wigan, but since then its populations have declined, mainly due to loss and degradation of habitats, particularly its dune slack and salt marsh strongholds. A well established colony was discovered on a salt marsh near Cockerham in 1969, midway between the Sefton and Cumbria colonies, and the site was designated a Site of Special Scientific Interest ten years later. However, local flood defence works in 1981 together with consequent changes to vegetation severely affected the site's hydrology, so that the population dwindled with the last Natterjack being seen in 1990.

Natterjack Toad.
(Phil Smith)

Plans to reintroduce Natterjacks at Cockerham were prepared by the Environment Agency, English Nature, The Herpetological Conservation Trust and a local landowner. Extensive restoration work was carried out at the site to make it suitable for Natterjacks, including the creation of two new ponds.

Natterjack spawn was then taken from Sandscale in Cumbria and introduced to the Cockerham Marsh site in Spring 2002. Toadlets were seen leaving the ponds in the summer, so the signs are encouraging that in a few years time there will once again be a thriving population at this Lancashire site.

All five reptile species are rarely seen in Lancashire: maybe our northern climate is simply not warm enough in spring and summer, though all but the Sand Lizard occur into Scotland. This coastal Sand Lizard population is some 300 km from the nearest southern colony (Box 9.4). Common Lizards also occur on the coast, on the moors, on some of the remnant mosslands and especially on the limestone and other areas in northern Lancashire.

What of the Grass Snake, Adder and Slow-worm? They are very rarely seen, which is probably just as well since many people still think that snakes are dangerous and should be killed. Slow-worms are the commonest of the three, though probably not as widespread as the Common Lizard: they are most often seen on the Morecambe Bay limestones but occur elsewhere in gardens and rough ground, and there is even a small population in Fulwood (north Preston). There are

Common Lizard.
(Mike Atkinson)

Box 9.4 *Sand Lizards*

The beautiful emerald green male Sand Lizard is one of our most attractive animals, while the female is mottled brown; both sexes have a median dark grey stripe down the back bordered by paler grey lines. In the early part of the nineteenth century it was commonly seen on the Sefton dunes, and even at the start of the second world war there were still 8–10,000 in the area. However by 1991 the population had plummeted to less than 500, and today these shy reptiles are very rarely seen. The decline is probably mainly due to loss of suitable habitat to housing, forestry and growth of scrub, but there is hope for the

Male Sand Lizard.
(Phil Smith)

future. Sand Lizards require south facing dune slopes with low or sparse vegetation. They rely on the warmth of the sun to hatch their eggs, unlike the Common Lizard which gives birth to live young. So long as the dunes are safeguarded and managed carefully for the benefit of the Sand Lizard the small population should survive and possibly increase, with the main threat being from domestic cats on the nearby housing estates.

Malcolm Edmunds

*Reptiles and
amphibians*

Slow-worm.
(Peter Smith)

reliable recent records of Adders in the Forest of Bowland and on the northern limestones, but they appear to be rare. The Grass Snake is the rarest of all our reptiles and may no longer exist in our area.

Global warming is now affecting the distribution of our flora and fauna with a northern shift in species of butterflies, dragonflies and birds. This just might help our threatened reptiles. But we need to know in much more detail what our reptile populations are now so that conservation measures for threatened species can be put into place. Volunteer surveyors for both amphibians and reptiles are always welcome and the techniques are easy to learn with help from the British Herpetological Society and the Wildlife Trust.

Further reading

Beebee, T. (1985). *Frogs and toads*. Whittet Books, London.
Wisniewski, P. J. (1989). *Newts of the British Isles*. Shire Natural History, Aylesbury.

Adder.
(Peter Smith)

Chapter 10

Freshwater life

David Turnbull and Darren Bedworth

Invertebrates, by David Turnbull

Life probably originated in the sea and plants and animals later moved into freshwater and colonised the land. The organisms that we find in freshwater today are the result of millions of years of adaptation to their environment. Some invertebrate groups still contain both saline and freshwater species, for example snails, mussels, crabs and shrimps, and a few of these which live in estuaries can tolerate a wide range of salinities.

Fresh waters cover a large variety of environments including streams, rivers, ponds, lakes, canals, reservoirs, marshes and bogs, all of which occur in Lancashire. Within natural river systems there are huge variations in habitat. For example gravel beds are common in upland streams throughout the Pennines, and are not only important spawning grounds for salmonid fish, but usually support diverse populations of mayflies and stoneflies. Gravel bars, which are depositional features on the sides of river channels, may support a range of invertebrates such as shrimps and beetles that can cope with winter flooding and low flows in the summer by burrowing into the substrate. Eroding banks may provide nesting locations for birds including ducks and Kingfishers and offer suitable habitats for the pupae of many aquatic flies and beetles. There are numerous other habitats (or micro-habitats) in rivers including riffles, pools, backwaters, the floodplain and a range associated with aquatic and marginal vegetation. Of these it is probably riffles

Greater Pond Snail.
(Andy Harmer)

179

that host the greatest diversity of freshwater life: nearly all orders of macro-invertebrate can be found within them, including the aptly named riffle beetles (belonging to the family Elmidae).

Molluscs

Freshwater molluscs include gastropods (snails and limpets) and bivalves (mussels and cockles). The 40 or so species of snails commonly found in Lancashire are of two types: operculate snails, with the opening plugged by a trap-door (or operculum), and with gills that are reminiscent of marine molluscs e.g. Jenkins' Spire Shell (*Potamopyrgus jenkinsi*); and pulmonate snails with a simple lung that return to the water surface whenever they need fresh air e.g. the Greater Pond Snail (*Lymnaea stagnalis*). The former occurs in many small streams and brooks throughout our region whilst the latter is readily found in densely vegetated ponds. The mud snail *Lymnaea glabra* is one of Britain and Lancashire's rarest snails but occurs in a pond in Lytham. It favours ponds that periodically dry up and is never found where there is a diverse snail population. Tiny River Limpets (*Ancylus fluviatilis*) are common on rocks in streams. All of the air-breathing snails are hermaphrodite and their eggs are often seen as strands of jelly attached to submerged vegetation. The jelly coating acts as a food source for the developing young, a barrier to prevent desiccation (as water levels vary) and a useful protection to clog up the jaws of possible predators. Bivalves are an interesting group that includes species that can live for over one hundred years (Box 10.1).

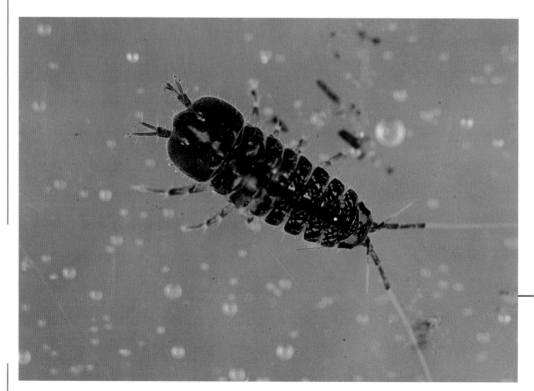

A relative of woodlice, the Hoglouse is abundant in organic-rich sediment in ponds and streams. (*Andy Harmer*)

Box 10.1 Clams

British bivalves range in size from the tiny pea mussels (*Pisidium* spp.) to the long-lived Swan Mussel (*Adononta cygnea*) which can grow to 25 cm in length. The former are found in a wide range of habitats from ponds to rivers whilst Swan Mussels prefer still water and are common in Lancashire's canals. Mother-of-pearl provides a beautiful lining to the shells of both the Swan Mussel and the Pearl Mussel (*Margaritifera margaritifera*). In the nineteenth century the pearls found in the latter formed the basis of a lucrative fishery in some Scottish rivers. Nationally this species is now quite rare, however it has recently been reported from a new site on the River Lune. The distinctive stripes of the Zebra Mussel (*Dreissena polymorpha*) clearly distinguish it from other species. It is believed to have been introduced over one hundred years ago with imported timber from the Baltic. They are sometimes considered a pest because they form large clumps that can block pipe entrances within reservoirs. Locally the Zebra Mussel occurs at Longton Brickcroft where it is probably not a problem.

Swan Mussels partly buried in mud.
(G. I. Bernard/NHPA)

Crustaceans

The crustaceans most commonly found in ponds and rivers throughout the region are the Hoglouse (*Asellus aquaticus*) and freshwater shrimps (of which *Gammarus pulex* is the commonest). *Gammarus* has a most interesting courtship; the male carries his mate beneath him for weeks or even months until the female moults and is thus able to be fertilised. This pairing can be observed through most of the year. *Asellus* closely resembles a woodlouse and has the same habit of carrying its eggs in a sack on its belly. Both *Gammarus* and *Asellus* feed on detritus and are often found amongst decaying leaf matter. Recent research has pointed to them occupying similar ecological niches but with *Asellus* having the competitive edge in organically enriched environments. Consequently the ratio of *Gammarus* to *Asellus* has been proposed as a possible indicator of pollution (see also Box 10.2). A much rarer and larger crustacean is the Common Crayfish (Box 10.3).

Freshwater life:
Crustaceans

Box 10.2 *Pollution and water quality*

Freshwater macro-invertebrates have long been used as indicators of water quality and this pattern is nowhere more evident than downstream of an organic source such as a sewage outfall. In the immediate vicinity of the outfall the fauna is typically limited to worms and midge

larvae. Further downstream, detritivores including *Asellus* and *Gammarus* become more numerous. Once the natural processes of biodegradation of the waste and re-oxygenation of the water are complete a diverse fauna can re-establish. Typically this community will include stoneflies, mayflies, caddisflies and beetles. These characteristic changes in the community reflect the different tolerances of species to oxygen levels.

These differences have been partly quantified and have led to the development of biological indices that help us assess the pollution status of our rivers. The system currently used in Britain (and recently adopted in other countries such as Spain) is the Biological Monitoring Working Party (BMWP) Score. Animals such as the freshwater worms (Oligochaeta) and the larvae of non-biting midges (e.g. *Chironomus*) are given a low score; *Asellus* and *Gammarus* have intermediate scores, whilst most species of mayfly and stonefly score the most highly. However one family of mayfly, the Baetidae, includes species such as *Baetis rhodani* with an intermediate score, indicating its tolerance to moderate levels of organic pollution. As a consequence it is very common in mildly polluted urban and suburban rivers throughout Lancashire. By consulting the Environment Agency's web site you can view maps showing river water quality in our region.

top left Freshwater shrimp (*Gammarus* sp., probably the widespread *G. pulex*).
(Stuart Crofts)

left The pollution tolerant mayfly *Baetis rhodani*.
(Stuart Crofts)

Box 10.3 Crayfish

Lancashire's (and Britain's) largest freshwater invertebrate is the lobster-like crustacean, the Common or White-clawed Crayfish (*Austropotamobius pallipes*) which grows to about 10 cm in length. Apart from an introduced population near Edinburgh, it is at the most northerly part of its range in North West England. Once seen as a culinary delicacy (and still consumed in vast quantities in France), its numbers have dramatically declined in recent years due to the fungal disease 'crayfish plague' carried by non-native North American crayfish (e.g. *Orconectes limosus*). A small number of non-native crayfish have been found in Lancashire and may represent a threat to the native population because of direct competition and possible disease transmission. They are currently mainly confined to a small number of ponds but with one record from the River Hodder. The River Lune is one of the White-clawed Crayfish's most important refuges in the country and other local populations occur in stretches of the rivers Ribble, Mersey and Weaver.

Common Crayfish.
(Roy Waller/NHPA)

Worms

Of the worm-like animals leeches are probably the best known group. Leeches are hermaphrodite, lay eggs in oval-shaped cocoons and often carry their young until they are capable of living independently. Sixteen leech species occur in Britain most of which are predators of other invertebrates, but three are parasitic on fish or water birds. The author has to-date found seven species in Lancashire and several more are probably present. *Glossiphonia complanata*, *Helobdella stagnalis* and *Erpobdella octoculata* are by far the most commonly found species. True aquatic worms (order Oligochaeta) are ubiquitous with more than 200 species, and in polluted waters they are often the most abundant animals present (Box 10.2).

One of the most striking groups of animals are the aquatic

No photographs of *Prostoma jenningsi* have ever been taken, but it is very similar in colour to *Lineus ruber* (shown here), though smaller and more slender. *Lineus ruber* is a marine ribbon worm that occurs in Morecambe Bay. If you find a freshwater ribbon worm resembling this animal in a pond, it might be a new locality for *Prostoma jenningsi*, or it could be a new and as yet undescribed species.

above *Lineus ruber*, similar to *Prostoma jenningsi*.
(Ray Gibson)

flatworms which swim with a grace reminiscent of marine jellyfish with gently undulating bodies that slowly propel them through the water. Ten of Britain's twelve species are found in the Lake District and may occur in Lancashire. Two species are restricted to running waters (*Crenobia alpina* and *Polycelis felina*) and occur in Lancashire's fast-flowing upland streams. However, a different type of worm is quite possibly Lancashire's rarest animal (Box 10.4).

The flatworm *Dugesia tigrina* is commonly found in streams.
(Andy Harmer)

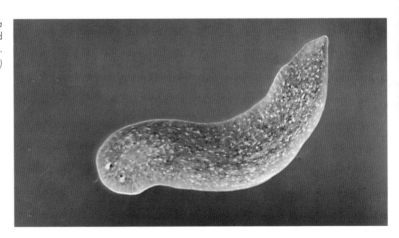

Wildlife of Lancashire

Insects

The aquatic insects make up the largest group of freshwater macro-invertebrates. Water beetles and bugs spend all of their lives in water, apart from adults occasionally flying from one pond to another. Britain has more than 200 species of water beetle of which the commonest large one throughout our region is the Great Diving Beetle (*Dytiscus marginalis*) which reaches 32 mm in length. It is very aggressive and will attack tadpoles, small fish and even fingers. Perhaps the rarest water beetle in North West England is another member of the Dytiscidae family, the tiny (3 mm long) *Laccophilus ponticus*, which occurs in fresh or slightly brackish coastal ponds and ditches. It has recently been recorded on the Sefton coast, and is classified as being vulnerable in the Red Data Book of Great Britain.

The Hemiptera (bugs) contain some of the strangest looking invertebrates. Water boatmen (forty-two British species), water crickets (fifteen species) and pond skaters (there are ten British *Gerris* spp.) are familiar inhabitants of most ponds. There are two water scorpions in Britain but it is only the ferocious looking *Nepa cinerea* that occurs in Lancashire. It can be found at the margins of ponds and ditches amongst dense vegetation. It waits there motionlessly observing its

above The voracious larva of the Great Diving Beetle. *(Mike Atkinson)*

prey before it rapidly attacks using its two huge scorpion-like pincers before impaling its victim and sucking it dry through its beak. In common with other bugs it possesses wings and in moonlight its stunning flight can be observed.

left *Hesperocorixa sahlbergi* is one of several common species of water boatman in ponds and canals throughout the Trust area. *(Andy Harmer)*

right The water scorpion *Nepa cinerea*. *(Tim Mitcham)*

185

Freshwater life:
Insects

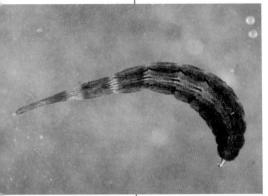

above Larva of the soldierfly *Stratiomys furcata*, which lives in organic rich pools.
(Andy Harmer)

right Flattened nymph of the mayfly *Ecdyonurus torrentis*, of the family Heptageniidae, which thrives in clean fast-flowing streams.
(Stuart Crofts)

The remaining insects all spend their larval lives in water and then emerge to spend their adult lives on land. The true flies (Diptera) are a huge order that includes the unpopular midges and mosquitoes. Fortunately in the UK these do not transmit the terrible diseases prevalent in tropical regions. *Anopheles* mosquitoes occur commonly in Lancashire, and although in the tropics they often carry malarial parasites, they do not do so here. One of the most ingeniously adapted of the Diptera is the rat-tailed maggot larva of droneflies (*Eristalis* spp.). It has a telescopic tube which can be extended out of the water to obtain oxygen and it can thus be found in highly polluted waters that are unfit for most other animals. The most commonly observed Diptera are the falsely named bloodworms (*Chironomus* spp.) which are distinctive because of their vivid red colour and are widely used by anglers as bait. Like red sludgeworms (*Tubifex* spp.) they carry haemo-

The mayfly nymph *Paraleptophlebia submarginata* has long filamentous gills and lives in clean streams.
(Stuart Crofts)

186

globin in their blood that enables them to extract oxygen from the very low concentrations found in organic rich water (see Box 10.2).

The mayflies (Ephemeroptera) are aquatic for nearly all of their lives, only living for a few days at most as flying adults, during which time they mate and deposit their eggs. Forty-eight species occur in British rivers, eighteen of which can also be found in still waters. All are herbivorous and possess three tails, which distinguishes them from the two tailed stoneflies. The large 'alien-like' flattened mayflies (there are eight species belonging to this Heptageniidae family in our region) have very strong limbs, streamlined bodies and are widely found in upland rivers and the stony shores of some lakes. In some ponds and slow flowing rivers lives the burrowing mayfly, the Green-drake (*Ephemera vulgata*). Its gills are characteristically held over its back to protect them whilst digging.

The most abundant and widely distributed mayflies are the 'swim-mers', most of which belong to the Baetidae family, and can be found in ponds, lakes and rivers throughout the region. The sensitivity of mayflies to water quality is well documented and the group are widely used as pollution indicators (Box 10.2). Even waters without obvious pollution can be impoverished in their mayfly fauna, for example in the Ribble catchment the River Hodder has a much smaller diversity of mayflies than one would expect, possibly due to acidification from coniferous plantations.

The Neuroptera (alderflies and spongeflies) are a group of insects which as adults possess large delicate heavily veined wings. Only

Freshwater life:
Insects

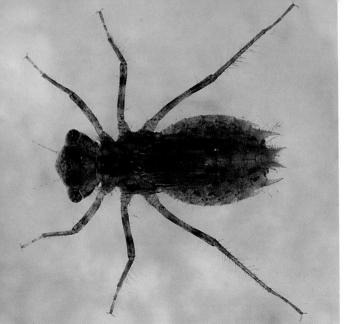

above The Common Darter nymph has a much shorter body than a hawker dragonfly. *(Andy Harmer)*

right Stonefly nymphs have two tails, and all require clean oxygen-rich water. This is *Dinocras cephalotes*. *(Stuart Crofts)*

seven UK species have aquatic larvae of which the Alderfly (*Sialis lutaria*) is by far the most commonly observed in both its aquatic and terrestrial stages, and it can be found in ponds and streams throughout the region.

Caterpillars of the china mark moths are uniquely aquatic amongst the Lepidoptera. There are five British species with the Brown China Mark (*Nymphula nymphaeta*) the commonest. They are usually found in still waters with plenty of floating vegetation.

The Odonata (dragonflies and damselflies) spend most of their lives as aquatic larvae and are amongst the largest and fiercest freshwater predators. An account of all of the species found in our region is given in Chapter 11.

The Plecoptera (stoneflies) are the invertebrates most characteristic of Britain's upland rivers, though they can also be found at the margins of some stony lakes and reservoirs. Twenty-five species have been recorded in North West England including Britain's largest species up to 33 mm long, the carnivorous creeper (*Perla bipunctata*). This has a distinctive 'tiger-like' pattern of yellow stripes on its black body, and can be found throughout the Pennines and the Lake District. It may spend three years as a nymph before emerging for just a few days as an adult. Other species are given common names (such as Yellow Sally, Willow Fly and Needle Fly) by anglers who use imitations as lures when fishing for Salmon and Trout. As with most of the macro-invertebrates discussed here the Lake District has a

Wildlife of Lancashire

particularly well-studied, rich and varied fauna many of which also occur in the Lancashire Pennines.

The Trichoptera (caddisflies) include some of the most ingeniously adapted macro-invertebrates. The case-building caddis are largely vegetarian and each species makes its own distinctive case using a variety of materials (e.g. silk, sand grains, silt or plant fragments) in a fascinating variety of structural forms. The largest British family is the Limnephilidae with fifty-eight species. Some, such as *Anabolia nervosa* and *Halesus radiatus*, often attach long sticks to their cases; the reason for this is unclear, possibly they act as vanes giving the animal greater stability in the current. The cases of the three British Goeridae species are made of sand grains with larger rock particles attached that appear to act as ballast.

There are also forty-six British species of caddis that do not build cases. These are largely carnivorous and many of them spin silk nets to filter the water for prey. One of the most commonly found caseless caddis in fast flowing upland rivers in Lancashire is the free-moving predator *Rhyacophila dorsalis*. It has elaborate and very distinctive fleshy gills down each side of its body.

Ecology

Aquatic invertebrate ecology is a vast subject and includes a huge number and diversity of species. There are over 3,500 different

Rhyacophila dorsalis is one of the commoner caddis larvae in streams which do not build elaborate cases.
(Andy Harmer)

189

Box 10.5 *Animals in the plankton*

Many of our smallest freshwater animals, the zooplankton, live in the water column and so are abundant in ponds and large rivers but quickly get washed away in fast flowing streams. The larger ones include copepods (such as the Cyclopoida), and water fleas (Cladocera), two groups of small crustaceans with jerky swimming movements, and water mites (Hydracarina), relatives of spiders which use 8 long legs to run through the water. Some of these larger planktonic animals also thrive close to food rich detritus at the bottom of ponds and canals or in pockets of streams where dead leaves accumulate out of the current. These animals are so small that they often prove too difficult for the amateur naturalist to identify without using specialist equipment. But there is a wonderful world of even smaller microscopic animals in freshwater that will repay study including the fascinating rotifers, or 'wheel animalcules' of the early microscopists, so called because of their rotating semicircles of vibrating ciliary bristles, and the elegant single celled relatives of the protozoan *Amoeba*, the Heliozoa or 'sun animalcules'.

Malcolm Edmunds

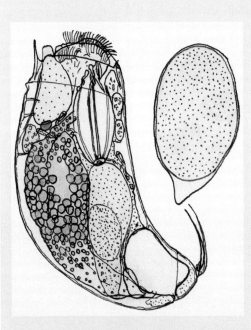 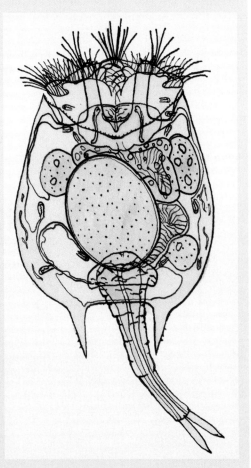

These two drawings of living rotifers from a pond were made with a magnification of 350x using a microscope.

left *Diurella* sp. swims in the plankton using cilia on the head (*top*) which also draw minute algae into the mouth. There is a red light-sensitive spot, and to its right the large jaws. A recently laid egg is on the right.

right *Platyias quadricornis* lives in the debris at the bottom of the pond but can also swim. The mouth is top centre, and below it the jaws, gut and a huge egg.

species of British freshwater macro-invertebrates, so in this account only a handful of the commonest or most interesting have been mentioned. There are many more smaller animals and plants which swim or drift in the water column; these are the planktonic animals and plants (Boxes 10.5 and 10.6). However, nearly all bodies of freshwater will reveal interesting life to those willing to explore them and new regional discoveries are waiting to be found amongst this vast and under-recorded group of species.

below Spirogyra is a common filamentous alga often forming a thick scum in ponds during the summer.
(Jackie Parry)

bottom Diatoms are the commonest algal component of biofilms, the slimy covering on stones and other surfaces in water.
(Jackie Parry)

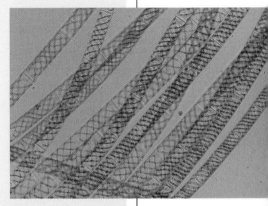

Box 10.6 *Algae and other microbes*

The major food for aquatic animals are microbes. The microbial world is one that is truly alien to the amateur, unless s/he possesses a microscope. Here the diversity of organisms is unrivalled, with single-celled plants (algae), 'germs' (bacteria) and animals (Protozoa) making up a substantial and complex community that exists beyond the naked eye. Microbes come in a variety of shapes and sizes, usually ranging from between 0.0005 and 0.3 mm in length, and even though they exist in the water itself, they are more commonly found in the 'slime' on rocks and man-made surfaces.

Algae are particularly sensitive to water quality and while some thrive on man-made pollutants, others do not. Algae in the 'slime' (or 'biofilm') are now being used to monitor the quality of our rivers and lakes, as it involves a simple scrape of a surface followed by microscopic examination rather than sampling and killing the macro-invertebrate community to give a BMWP Score (see Box 10.2).

It is not widely appreciated that these microbes fuel the whole of the aquatic food web. The algae take up carbon dioxide from the water and photosynthesise, just like higher plants. They produce organic carbon in the form of simple sugars that are secreted into the water and used as a food source by the bacteria. These bacteria (together with the algae) are eaten by protozoan animals, which are then eaten by the larger aquatic animals. If anything disrupts the functioning of the microscopic algae, e.g. pollution, the microbial food web is affected and this will ultimately affect the functioning of the rest of the aquatic food web.

Jackie Parry

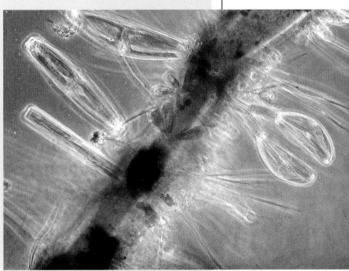

Freshwater life:
Ecology

Fish and Fisheries, by Darren Bedworth

Freshwaters in Lancashire range from tumbling moorland streams, sluggish rivers and canals to ponds, lakes, reservoirs and gravel pits, and the fish that live in them are equally diverse (see Box 10.7). The North West contains some of the highest quality Salmon rivers in England, but it is also rich in coarse fish (see Box 10.8).

Rudd.
(Derek Lippett)

Box 10.7 *Fish from still and running waters*

Still-waters, such as the extensive large lakes of the Wigan Flashes formed after mining subsidence, contain species such as Carp (*Cyprinus carpio*), Tench (*Tinca tinca*), Roach (*Rutilus rutilus*) and Rudd (*Scardinius erythropthalmus*), though farm ponds often contain equally diverse fisheries. Typical fish of rivers include Barbel (*Barbus barbus*), Dace (*Leuciscus leuciscus*), Chub (*Leuciscus cephalus*), Pike (*Esox lucius*), Salmon (*Salmo salar*), Sea Lamprey, Lampern (or River Lamprey), Brook Lamprey (see Box 10.9), Brown Trout and Sea Trout (both *Salmo trutta*), Eels (*Anguilla anguilla*), and Minnows (*Phoxinus phoxinus*).

Box 10.8 *Coarse fish and salmonid fish*

'Coarse' fish is a general description used to describe 'non-salmonid' fish. One theory is that the gentry fished for Salmon and Trout (game fish) and the 'coarse man' fished for 'coarse fish'. Historically anglers have valued salmonid fish more than coarse fish, perhaps because of the flavour of salmonid flesh compared to the often 'earthy' taste of coarse fish as well as the spirited fight given by salmonid fish. This value has largely changed now with some coarse fisheries having higher values than salmonid fisheries, and individual coarse fish such as Carp, having phenomenal value (an individual Carp weighing over 35lbs can be worth over £3,000, in terms of a fishery's day-ticket sales income from anglers). Specialist Carp fisheries can charge similar permit fees to Trout and Salmon.

Carp.
(Derek Lippett)

Wildlife of Lancashire

Salmonid fish prefer fast flowing, well oxygenated, cool water, clean gravel in which to lay eggs, and plenty of cover for young fish, conditions which are found in many of the streams running off the Pennines. As we move down river we see a gradual shift towards species such as Chub, Dace, Grayling and Barbel. These coarse fish also require well oxygenated water with clean gravel on which to spawn but cannot tolerate quite as fast flowing water as Trout and Salmon. Moving further down river we reach the slower flowing zones where there is more silt than gravel, the water tends to be a little warmer and flows more slowly. Bream (*Abramis brama*) and Roach, which are not such strong swimmers, live here and lay their eggs in the denser aquatic vegetation.

Salmon and Trout populations have declined due to overfishing and deterioration of habitat and water quality, but now in many areas they are increasing. Understanding the problems facing salmonids requires knowledge of their life cycles. Salmon spend most of their adult life maturing in the sea but return to the upper limits of rivers to spawn. If water quality is poor, a Salmon may not return to the river or perhaps not recognise the 'smell' of the particular river where it was born. Once Salmon eggs have hatched the young fish spend about 2 years in the river, often hiding behind boulders, tree roots and undercut banks. At 2 years old these young 'parr' go through a physiological change (smoltification) to become 'smolts' as they travel downstream to the sea. They remain at sea for between 1 and 5 years, before returning to the same river (often the same stretch) to spawn. The returning Salmon are often between 5 and 20lbs in weight, although the current British record is 64lb.

Salmonid fish are good indicators of the quality of the freshwater ecosystem. In many areas of the North West, salmonid habitat has been degraded through past flood defence works, poor farming practices and industrial pollution. Structures such as weirs, that many people would consider a normal part of a river, can have disastrous effects on fish populations and river ecology by acting as a barrier to fish moving upstream and because of silting above the weir. Fortunately the efforts of the Environment Agency, North West Water Authority (now United Utilities), Mersey Basin Campaign and smaller angling-lead initiatives, have dramatically improved the rivers of Lancashire in recent years.

Lancashire is dominated by three large rivers, the Mersey, the Ribble and the Lune. The Mersey was a good Salmon river in the mid 1800s, but by the 1870s it was in decline due to increasing pollution from industry and growing human populations. In the early 1960s,

Fish pass on Losterdale Brook, Trough of Bowland.
(Darren Bedworth)

Roach.
(Miran Aprehamian)

193

Box 10.9 *Lampreys*

Lampreys belong to an ancient group of fish whose fossils date back 450 million years. They are quite distinct from other British freshwater fish as they lack a lower jaw, have cartilage instead of bone, only one nostril and no scales. Adult lampreys are parasitic on a variety of fishes and

marine mammals and seek the largest individuals of a species. They attach using a suctorial mouth, which has pointed teeth arranged in concentric circles. Once attached, the lamprey opens wounds on the prey's skin using a rasping tongue and sharp teeth and feeds on blood and other tissues.

Lampreys have a life cycle which is not unlike that of Salmon. The adults migrate upstream to reach stony or gravely spawning areas (Maitland and Campbell 1992). They dig holes in the gravel by picking up stones with their suckers. Eggs are then laid in the holes and covered over with gravel. Adults die soon after spawning. The young blind lampreys, called ammocoete larvae, migrate downstream and spend the next few years living in tunnels in silt feeding on bacteria and single celled plants. At around two years old they change over a period of two weeks, developing the characteristic sucker filled with teeth while the skin over the eyes thins so they can see. These adult lampreys then move down river to areas away from the nursery places or in the case of Sea Lampreys, out to sea.

The smallest lamprey in the North West is the Brook Lamprey.
(Paul Frear)

when water quality checks were first carried out, the condition of the water in the Mersey estuary was atrocious, but at last it has begun to improve, and Roach, Chub and Pike now thrive above the tidal limit of Howley weir in Warrington. In November 2001 three Salmon were found in a trap upstream of Woolston weir, Warrington, providing the first conclusive proof that Salmon could gain access to the River Bollin where they will attempt to spawn. The lower part of the Mersey, particularly the estuary, has improved dramatically over the last decade, in no small part due to the efforts of the Mersey Basin Campaign, which has won a European award for its efforts.

The Ribble carves through central Lancashire and is one of the longest rivers in North West England. Two major tributaries join the Ribble south of Clitheroe, but while the Hodder draining the Forest of Bowland is clean like the Ribble itself, the Calder crosses east Lancashire, and is only now recovering from minewater and industrial

waste as well as run-off from contaminated land and sewage discharges.

In the nineteenth century the Ribble was an important Salmon river, but the numbers caught declined between 1900 and 1930 as a result of industrial pollution, and again during the 1960s when many fish were killed by the disease ulcerative dermal necrosis. Reduced water flow during the drought years of 1976, 1995, and 1996 are also thought to have had a major impact on the fish populations. However, since 1995 both the Salmon and Sea Trout populations have gradually increased.

The Ribble also supports net fisheries for Eels and elvers and a recreational fishery for Brown Trout and coarse fish such as Grayling. Other coarse fish in the Ribble include Roach, Chub, Pike, Barbel and Dace.

In the north of Lancashire we find the most untouched of the three main rivers, the Lune. Most of the catchment is used for grazing sheep and cattle and for producing hay and silage. The Lune was also a very important salmonid river, but populations decreased during the 1960s due to ulcerative dermal necrosis. They have since recovered and the River Lune is now considered to be the second best Salmon river in England. Like the Ribble, the Lune also supports net fisheries for Eels and elvers, a recreational fishery for Brown Trout, and in the lower reaches coarse fish comprising mainly Bream, Dace, Roach, Gudgeon (*Gobio gobio*), Perch (*Perca fluviatilis*) and Eels. Anecdotal evidence from catch reports suggests that in certain areas which often have poor habitat, coarse fish recruitment is poor. The Environment Agency works with local interested parties wherever possible to rehabilitate spawning areas and recruitment/nursery areas for coarse fish in the lower parts of the river. One such project upstream of the Lancaster Canal aqueduct created an 'off river support unit' (effectively a ditch)

Freshwater life:
Fish and fisheries

top Pike.
(Derek Lippett)

above Barbel.
(Chris Gardner)

Gudgeon
(Peter Smith)

which now provides refuge for species such as Dace during times of high water. Dace numbers are now reported to be 10 times higher in the local area.

Throughout the North West there are many lakes and ponds ranging from very small farm ponds through to the larger 'flashes' and sand and gravel quarries. Where these ponds or lakes are connected to rivers and streams they have often developed the same fish populations as fish move from one to the other. Where lakes are isolated from rivers they are usually stocked by anglers. Anecdotally, fish found in isolated ponds are often attributed to birds, such as herons, carrying fish eggs stuck to their feet, but it is more likely that anglers have moved the fish.

Historically these fisheries have contained Perch, Roach, Tench and Rudd, as well as Bream, Eels and Three-spined Sticklebacks (*Gasterosteus aculeatus*). Barbel populations in the UK are thought to have all come from the Rivers Thames and Lee (the Thames was originally a tributary of the Rhine) and now reside not only in rivers such as the Ribble but also in some ponds. In the last 30 years, as angling has developed, new species have been introduced. Carp, originally introduced by monks for food, are now considered to be one of the hardiest and hardest fighting fish. They have been introduced into most water bodies and are now considered a 'naturalised' species (the largest UK fish caught weighed over 60lbs). In the last 10 years or so more species have been introduced by anglers to ponds including Sterlet (*Acipenser ruthenus*) (related to Sturgeon), Grass Carp (*Ctenopharyngodon idella*), Silver Carp (*Hypopthalmichthys molitrix*), Wels

Catfish (*Silurus glanis*) (weighing up to 100lbs in Britain but up to 660lbs in France), Channel Catfish (*Ictalurus punctatus*), Golden Orfe (*Leuciscus idus*) and Topmouth Gudgeon (*Pseudorasbora parva*).

Canals usually contain a mix of river and still-water fish species, as they are often fed by rivers but have relatively still water. However the overall density of fish in canals is often lower than in still waters as a result of boat traffic which stirs up sediment and destroys submerged vegetation.

The usual reason for stocking coarse and game fish is to improve angling in new ponds or to supplement existing fish stocks. Game anglers also often stock Trout and juvenile Salmon into rivers in order to improve catches. Sometimes fish will be introduced into sites where there is no angling in order to improve biodiversity and provide food for piscivorous birds. The Environment Agency will sometimes stock fish into rivers to replenish fish populations following a pollution incident where fish have been killed. Sometimes, where a river has been improved by enhancement works, fish may also be stocked to give the fish populations a quick boost as the river habitat improves.

As people have moved fish over the years, it has become increasingly difficult to differentiate between naturally occurring fish and those artificially stocked. However, people with experience of particular rivers can still tell the difference between a true 'wild' Trout and one raised in a fish farm. The same may be true of 'wild' and raised coarse fish, though the differences are much more subtle and disappear as the fish age and mix with 'wild' populations.

Perch.
(*Derek Lippett*)

Further reading

Allan, J. D. (1995). *Stream Ecology. Structure and Function of Running Waters*. Chapman & Hall, London.

British Ecological Society (1990). *Ecological Issues – No. 1 River Water Quality*. Field Studies Council, Shrewsbury.

Clegg, J. (1956). *The Observer's Book of Pond Life*. Frederick Warne, London.

Fitter, R. and Manuel, R. (1986). *A Field Guide to the Freshwater Life of Britain and North-West Europe*. Collins, London.

Fryer, G. (1991). *A Natural History of the Lakes, Tarns and Streams of the English Lake District*. Freshwater Biological Association, Cumbria.

Haslam, S. M. (1992). *River Pollution, an Ecological Perspective*. John Wiley, Chichester.

Jeffries, M. and Mills, D. (1994). *Freshwater Ecology: Principles and Applications*. John Wiley, Chichester.

Maitland, P. S. (1977). *A Coded Checklist of Animals Occurring in Fresh Water in the British Isles*. Institute of Terrestrial Ecology, Edinburgh.

Maitland, P. S. Campbell, R. N. (1992). *Freshwater Fishes*. HarperCollins, London.

Mason, C. F. (2001). *Biology of Freshwater Pollution*, 4th edn, Prentice Hall, London.

197

Chapter 11

Land Invertebrates

Front end of Dog Tapeworm. Hooks and suckers at the front end attach the worm to the wall of the dog's intestine. Just behind the suckers the worm proliferates thin segments which grow into rectangular units, each with a full set of reproductive organs, and at the back end of the worm these drop off as bags full of eggs which are voided with the dog's faeces.
(© OSF/ Photolibrary.com)

Introduction, and lesser known animals, by Malcolm Edmunds

Invertebrate animals living on land are sometimes divided into the wiggly-wagglies and the creepy-crawlies, the former comprising worms and snails, the latter various insects, spiders, centipedes and millipedes. However, the diversity of different types of animals on land and in the soil is much greater than this. The best known groups are given separate sections in this chapter, but there are several others which deserve mention.

There are many single celled protozoans, scarcely visible without a microscope, and particularly common in damp soil. Some are parasitic in the guts of invertebrates, but more serious is *Toxoplasma gondii*, a common parasite of cats. The larval cysts lodge in rat brains and alter the rat's behaviour to make it less cautious and so more likely to be caught and eaten by a cat. Unfortunately we can pick up parasites either from cat faeces or by eating rare infected beef, and the cysts can lodge in our brains where they make us less cautious and so more likely to be involved in traffic accidents.

Parasitic flatworms include the flukes and tapeworms of vertebrates. Liver Flukes (*Fasciola hepatica*) are still common in boggy Pennine pastures where they infect sheep. The Dog Tapeworm (*Dipylidium caninum*) is very common in dogs and cats; its larva lives in fleas, especially the Human Flea (*Pulex irritans*) and the Cat Flea (*Ctenocephalides felis*), which frequent the dirt in kennels and dog-baskets, and this tapeworm sometimes gets into children. Less common is the minute tapeworm *Echinococcus granulosus* which is relatively harmless in dogs. Its larval stage, however, occasionally forms tennis-ball sized 'hydatid' cysts in Lancashire sheep and (fortunately more rarely) in people who pick it up from dogs licking infected faeces and then licking their hands or faces. The Beef Tapeworm (*Taenia saginata*) lives in humans and can be acquired from eating undercooked infected steak, and the cysts are found quite often in meat inspected in

Lancashire abattoirs. Rather less common here is the Dwarf Tapeworm (*Hymenolepis nana*): it lives in rats and other mammals but can infect humans if they inadvertently eat flour beetles or other insects that carry the larvae.

Many roundworms (Nematoda) are also parasites, including the common eelworms which kill garden plants and numerous larger ones in the intestines of domestic animals. The earthworm-sized *Ascaris lumbricoides* is exceedingly common in tropical countries but fortunately only occasionally crops up in Lancashire folk, particularly children, who have picked it up overseas through not washing hands before eating. The smaller *Toxocara canis* is a parasite of dogs but occasionally infects children and may damage their eyesight. They pick up larvae from residual dirt from where there was infected dog faeces. There are enormous numbers of parasitic roundworms living in other animals from insects to fish and birds, and perhaps even more free living roundworms only a millimetre or so long living in the soil.

More noticeable to the gardener are the larger invertebrates such as harvestmen (Opiliones). These 8-legged relatives of spiders have

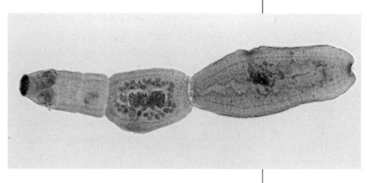

Echinococcus granulosus is a minute tapeworm with only three or four segments behind the head with its hooks and suckers. It is these whitish segments in your dog's faeces that tell you that he (or she) has worms. (© OSF/ Photolibrary.com)

Mitopus morio is a common harvest-man on low vegetation and shrubs. (Peter Wilson/ Woodfall Wild Images)

199

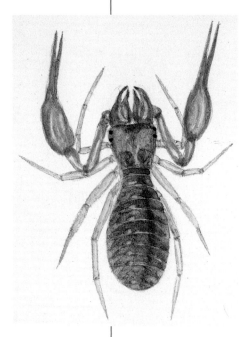

eyes set on little turrets. They become abundant in gardens in late summer and several species are widespread in our area, e.g. *Mitopus morio*, with a dark pattern and long legs. There are probably a dozen species of harvestman in our area and a similar number of the much smaller false scorpions (Pseudoscorpionida). These diminutive but fearsome looking arachnids have pincers just like a real scorpion, and species of *Chthonius* can be found in any soil rich in leaf litter. They are fascinating creatures to watch as are the far more numerous and diverse soil mites (Acari). Unlike the larger ticks which are parasitic on dogs and wild animals, the majority of mites are only really visible with a strong hand lens or a low power microscope. They are very abundant in rich soil where some are herbivores, others carnivores feeding on springtails, but the diversity of body shapes and designs adapted to evading predation is fascinating.

Much larger is the 10 cm long leech *Trocheta subviridis* which occurs in waterlogged garden soil in Preston and elsewhere where it eats earthworms. More unusual is a recent immigrant from Australia, the amphipod crustacean (or sandhopper) *Arcitalitrus dorrieni*, which is abundant in a garden at Clayton-le-Woods, near Preston.

The false scorpion *Chthonius ischnochelus* at just 2 mm long is one of our commonest false scorpions.
(Malcolm Edmunds)

Earthworms, by Kevin Butt

Most of the 28 native species of earthworm in Britain occur within Lancashire. For example, preliminary survey work at Mere Sands Wood Nature Reserve (Rufford) revealed 11 species of which 9 were found in a single grass/heathland habitat. Gardens would easily be

Mating Lob Worms with their front ends stuck together in a slimy sheath.
(Kevin Butt)

capable of producing a similar diversity of species and any keen gardener will be aware of the different colours of earthworms – purple, red, grey and even green – that can be seen when turning over the soil.

Our largest species, the Lob Worm (*Lumbricus terrestris*), reaching 20 cm, is relatively common and often found in rich grassland and woodland habitats. It feeds above ground by pulling leaves into its vertical burrow. In autumn the burrow entrance is often conspicuous due to leaf stalks poking out, giving a wigwam-like appearance. This earthworm also mates at the soil surface and copulation, lasting up to 4 hours, may extend beyond dawn revealing the animals together but with tails still in their burrows ready for a quick retreat.

Green Worms tend to live in wet soils and have been found in lakes, streams and caves.
(Kevin Butt)

The commonest soil dwelling species have non-permanent horizontal burrows a few centimetres below the soil surface. A*porrectodea caliginosa* (the Grey Worm) and *A. rosea* (the Rosy-tip Worm), both up to 10 cm long, are typical of this group. A species with a similar habitat requirement, but preferring wetter soils and often found associated with the roots of plants, is *Allolobophora chlorotica*. The common name of this species, the Green Worm, gives its most obvious characteristic. It is also quite short (5 cm) and moves very little when disturbed. Another small but colourful species is the Tiger Worm (Box 11.1).

Tiger Worms, excellent for breaking down kitchen waste.
(Kevin Butt)

Box 11.1 Tigers in the garden

One species of earthworm, *Eisenia fetida*, is probably better known to gardeners and organic waste managers as the Brandling or Tiger Worm. It is easy to keep, breeds rapidly and thrives in most types of organic waste, including kitchen peelings, garden green waste and manure. Kept in a suitable container with adequate moisture and warmth, Tiger Worms will produce castings that can be used as fertiliser or even as a plant growth medium. Such worm-worked material is reputed to contain plant hormone-like substances.

Land Invertebrates:
Earthworms

Earthworms produce casts on the soil surface which are most often seen in spring and autumn. During very dry spells or very cold periods species such as L. *terrestris* retreat to the bottom of their 2 m deep burrows, but others such as *Aporrectodea longa* (the Black-headed or Long Worm) coil up into a ball and rest up in a spherical chamber until soil conditions improve. Unlike L. *terrestris*, A. *longa* is a 'bottom-up' earthworm: under normal conditions it tends to rest with its head pointing down its burrow, and this is the major species responsible for casting.

Earthworms help to aerate soil and recycle nutrients in gardens and agricultural land, but they can also be used on industrial waste sites (Box 11.2). They can be encouraged by provision of organic matter

Box 11.2 *Restoration engineers*

Soil dwelling species of earthworm such as those found in Lancashire may be put to good use on sites reclaimed after industrial usage. Where new 'soil' is created from subsoil and organic materials the introduction of appropriate earthworms can be the catalyst required for pedogenesis (soil formation). The earthworms intimately mix the soil constituents by feeding and casting whilst aerating and draining the soil through burrowing. These behaviours have led to earthworms being described as ecosystem engineers. Trials of this type are already underway around the county e.g. at Bidston Moss on Merseyside. Research suggests that adding a mixture of species gives rise to more rapid soil improvement.

Box 11.3 A *threat to earthworms*

One predator of earthworms now present in Lancashire is the New Zealand Flatworm (*Arthurdendyus triangulatus*). This introduced species devours earthworms, particularly *L. terrestris*, by lying alongside them in their burrows, exuding enzymes, and sucking up the resulting 'earthworm soup'. These dark invaders are a serious threat and could decimate earthworm populations. One garden in Clayton-le-Woods now has practically no earthworms but New Zealand Flatworms can often be found resting under bricks on the soil. Unlike earthworms, these flatworms have no positive effects on soil quality.

New Zealand Flatworm.
(Kevin Butt)

(e.g. not sweeping away fallen leaves) and their presence may encourage other wildlife. Numerous mammals, including Badgers and Hedgehogs, as well as birds feed on earthworms as, excluding water, they are 70 % protein. Garden birds like the Blackbird listen for them, head cocked on one side, before pecking them from the soil, whereas others, like the Herring Gull, employ 'foot-trembling'. This stamping on the spot brings worms to the surface, possibly because it mimics rainfall. However, they are now under threat from a much more serious predator from New Zealand (Box 11.3).

Snails and Slugs, by Jennifer Newton

Introduction

Terrestrial molluscs are an important element of Lancashire's bio-diversity, albeit one that is more often derided than appreciated. The slugs and snails which attack our tender young seedlings have learnt where to come for a good meal, but they are a minority of Lancashire's molluscs, most of which do a vital job of recycling dead plant material, and returning organic matter to the soil. They are important in the diet of various birds, Hedgehogs, frogs and toads as well as some beetles.

Woodland Snails

Most molluscs readily dry out and so thrive best in damp, mild climates. Lancashire supports a high proportion of Britain's molluscs,

203

Land Invertebrates:
Snails and Slugs

including some which are confined to the north and west of the British Isles and are rare in England. Many of the rare snails are minute woodland animals, less than 5 mm in diameter, and special techniques of sieving and sorting leaf litter are needed to find them. Only under a microscope can the attractive detail of shell structure and ornamentation be fully appreciated. The Prickly Snail (*Acanthinula aculeata*) has an amazing array of spines over the surface of the shell, while the Silky Snail (*Ashfordia granulata*) and the Hairy Snail (*Trichia hirsuta*) are densely covered in hair-like filaments, unexpected in snails. The Plated Snail (*Spermodea lamellata*), a tiny snail of ancient woodlands, has miniature plates over the surface of the shell, which glint in the light. It is rare in England but commoner in Wales and Scotland, and has been found in a few woodlands in north Lancashire. Tiniest of all is the Dwarf Snail (*Punctum pygmaeum*), a mere 1½ mm in diameter. It looks like a speck of sand until under a microscope you can see the typical spiral of a snail shell in miniature. Surprisingly it has been recorded from many woodlands in Lancashire, so it is perhaps less readily overlooked than many larger but more active invertebrates. The glass snails (*Oxychilus* spp.) have very thin, almost translucent shells. One of the smallest, the Garlic Snail (*Oxychilus alliarius*), is distinctive for the very strong smell of garlic which it emits on disturbance.

Turret Snails

The snails mentioned so far all have a spiral shell which is broader than tall. Snails with this type of shell range from the almost flat (and very common) Rounded Snail (*Discus rotundatus*) to the almost globular Silky Snail. In another group of snails the spiral grows upwards to form an elongate turret. These turret snails are particularly adept at

*Wildlife of
Lancashire*

climbing walls and trees, for example the Common Door Snail (*Clausilia bidentata*) which feeds on algae on walls. It is rare in the industrial centre of England, perhaps because of the lack of algae and lichens on trees and walls as a result of air pollution. It is common on walls in north Lancashire and it will be interesting to see if it spreads south with the reduction in sulphur pollution and gradual return of lichens and algae. Other elongate snails include the Slippery Moss Snail (*Cochlicopa lubrica*), common in damp places throughout the County, and the Common Chrysalis Snail (*Lauria cylindracea*), a very common inhabitant of stone walls. The Large Chrysalis Snail (*Abida secale*) is now very rare on open limestone cliffs, but fossilised shells show that it was much more widespread in the past, from the end of the Ice Age until woodland spread over the country. Molluscs are useful indicators of climate and habitat in the past because, unusually among invertebrates, they provide good fossils.

Snails of sand dunes

Coastal sands on the Sefton, Fylde, and Heysham coasts, support a different set of snails, which can survive hot, dry conditions. They often do this by climbing up vegetation in the heat of summer to aestivate. In this way they can escape from the even hotter sand surface, and by covering the mouth of the shell with a thin film they can slow down the loss of water and spend summer in a dormant state. Snails often found dormant on coastal vegetation in summer include the Striped Snail (*Cernuella virgata*) and the Wrinkled Snail (*Candidula intersecta*). On the other hand the widespread Brown-lipped Banded Snail (*Cepaea nemoralis*) is also common on the coast but prefers damper conditions and climbs vegetation only in damp weather.

The Brown-lipped Banded Snail with Early Forget-me-not on the Ainsdale dunes. The shell of this snail can be yellow, pink or brown with from zero to five black bands (this one is pink with bands). On sand dunes most shells are banded pink or yellow, while in woods most are unbanded pink or brown, and on grassland the commonest colour is yellow with bands. These colours give good camouflage on the different coloured backgrounds.
(Malcolm Edmunds)

left The large Great Grey Slug (*Limax maximus*), with black and grey stripes, is widespread in gardens and elsewhere.
(*Ken Blamire*)

right Two Large Black Slugs mating; these are the common garden form which is brownish with an orange edge to the foot.
(*Ken Blamire*)

below Narrow-mouthed Whorl Snail.
(*Bob Marsh*)

Slugs

Slugs, which are snails without external shells, are perhaps even more damned as pests than snails. One of the commonest and most widespread is the Large Black Slug (*Arion ater*). In gardens it frequently appears in an orange form, but it is generally considered the same species as the large all-black slug, which may be found in many wild

Box 11.4 *Whorl snails* (Vertigo species)

Whorl snails are tiny but distinctive snails, about 2 mm in diameter, identified by the number and position of 'teeth' projecting into the 'mouth', or opening of the shell. They are very demanding in their habitat requirements and most British species appear to be declining. There are 5 species in Lancashire, including the nationally rare Narrow-mouthed Whorl Snail (*Vertigo angustior*) known only from the limestone pavements of Gait Barrows and a handful of other sites in South Wales and Suffolk. The nationally scarce Wall Whorl Snail (*V. pusilla*) and the Mountain Whorl Snail (*V. alpestris*) are typically found in dry stone walls in limestone areas in the north of England. Both are included in the Lancashire Biodiversity Action Plan.

places including high on moorlands. Similarly large and black but with a pointed tail is the Ash-black Slug (*Limax cinereoniger*), a nationally scarce species found in several of Lancashire's woods. *Limax* species frequently climb, and one of the best climbers is the Tree Slug (*Lehmannia marginata*, formerly *Limax marginatus*). It requires damp conditions, and flourishes on cave walls and tree trunks in woods. The beautiful yellow Slender Slug (*Malacolimax tenellus*, formerly *Limax tenellus*) is a very rare woodland species which has not been recently recorded in Lancashire.

Dragonflies, by Dominic Rigby

Introduction

Dragonflies and damselflies (belonging to the insect order Odonata) are among the most spectacular and popular of insects. The order includes the larger and more robust true dragonflies (sub-order Anisoptera) and the smaller slender-bodied damselflies (sub-order Zygoptera). They are primitive insects, originating over three hundred million years ago, and fossil records suggest they have changed little since then. There are around 5,000 species globally, but only 2.5% of these occur in Europe. Britain is further impoverished with just forty regularly breeding species, twenty-three have been recorded in Lancashire, nineteen of which have bred.

Southern Hawkers mating: the male grips the neck of the female with appendages at the tip of his abdomen. Then the female curls beneath him and with the tip of her abdomen removes sperm from a pouch just behind his legs.
(Malcolm Edmunds)

Box 11.5 Odonata of Lancashire

Breeders

Banded Demoiselle	Calopteryx splendens	Local breeder
Common Emerald Damselfly	Lestes sponsa	Local breeder
Large Red Damselfly	Pyrrhosoma nymphula	Common breeder
Blue-tailed Damselfly	Ischnura elegans	Abundant breeder
Common Blue Damselfly	Enallagma cyathigerum	Abundant breeder
Azure Damselfly	Coenagrion puella	Abundant breeder
Red-eyed Damselfly	Erythromma najas	Rare, one breeding site
Common Hawker	Aeshna juncea	Local breeder
Brown Hawker	Aeshna grandis	Common breeder
Southern Hawker	Aeshna cyanea	Common in south
Migrant Hawker	Aeshna mixta	Uncommon but increasing breeder
Emperor Dragonfly	Anax imperator	Uncommon but increasing breeder
Golden-ringed Dragonfly	Cordulegaster boltonii	Uncommon and local breeder
Broad-bodied Chaser	Libellula depressa	Uncommon but increasing breeder
Four-spotted Chaser	Libellula quadrimaculata	Common breeder
Black-tailed Skimmer	Orthetrum cancellatum	Uncommon but increasing breeder
Common Darter	Sympetrum striolatum	Abundant breeder
Ruddy Darter	Sympetrum sanguineum	Uncommon breeder
Black Darter	Sympetrum danae	Local breeder
Red-veined Darter	Sympetrum fonscolombi	Has bred at Middleton since 2001. Vagrant elsewhere

Non breeders

Lesser Emperor	Anax parthenope	One record, Middleton 2001
Yellow-winged Darter	Sympetrum flaveolum	Several records in 1995 and 1999, including on Sefton coast and at Heysham/Middleton in both years
Beautiful Demoiselle	Calopteryx virgo	Single males at Leigh and St Annes in 2003

Several species have expanded their ranges northwards in recent years, probably due to the warming of our climate and the occurrence of weather patterns conducive to dispersal. The number of observers has increased recently too, aided by the publication of several new field guides and advances in close-focusing optics. All these factors probably account for the discovery of seven new species of Odonata in Lancashire since 1995, a staggering 31 per cent increase in six years. Nineteen dragonflies and damselflies breed in Lancashire, leaving just three rare vagrants (see Box 11.5).

Damselflies

The commonest and most widespread species in our county is the Blue-tailed Damselfly. It can tolerate mildly polluted and slightly brackish waters so will venture into ditches, canals, rivers and open waters, including those otherwise bereft of odonates. Two other abundant 'blue' damsels are the very similar looking Common Blue and Azure Damselflies. The Common Blue is a stronger flyer and is most abundant on large water bodies, while the Azure prefers smaller, unshaded, unpolluted ponds. The next commonest zygopteran is the Large Red Damselfly which is widespread in the north

Red-veined Darter, a rare species possibly spreading north into our area.
(Ken Blamire)

and east of the county. In recent years it has expanded across the western mosslands and can now be seen on small ponds and clean ditches across the region. This is usually the earliest species to emerge in spring, appearing from mid to late April in mild weather.

The other damsels are more local in their distribution. The Common Emerald is perhaps overlooked because its dark-green, metallic abdomen can be hard to detect as individuals characteristically perch

Large Red Damselfly feeding on mayfly.
(Phil Smith)

Land Invertebrates:
Dragonflies

Box 11.6 *The spread of the Banded Demoiselle*

The Banded Demoiselle is unusual among the county's Odonata in its fluttering flight, more like a butterfly than a damselfly, and in rarely occurring away from rivers. It has long been established on the River Lostock, where it is abundant between Clayton-le-Woods and Wade Hall (Smith 1999). There are smaller but increasing populations along Savick Brook, west of Preston, and on the Ribble close to the M6 which is believed to be the original population from which the impressive Lostock colonies spread. Since 1995 it has been seen further afield, along the Lancaster Canal north of Preston, on the Wyre near Churchtown and on the Leeds and Liverpool Canal at Withnell Fold. There have been sightings in Litherland (North Merseyside) and Parbold (West Lancashire) along the Leeds and Liverpool Canal in recent years, which, together with records from Mere Sands Wood since 2000 and Martin Mere in 2002, suggest there may be an undiscovered colony somewhere nearby. Further north there is much suitable habitat, particularly on the Lune; will the insect eventually appear there too?

above Male Banded Demoiselle.
(Peter Smith)

with wings semi-parted among favoured stands of rushes, spike-rushes and Wood Club-rush. Sefton coast sand dunes are the county hot spot for this species, but there is a large population at Highfield Moss, Golborne (St Helens) and smaller colonies in appropriate habitats in St Helens, Burscough, the Wigan Flashes, Mere Sands Wood and Heysham/Middleton.

The Red-eyed Damselfly was first discovered in Lancashire in 1998. The species had been gradually moving north for several years, but the jump to Eccleston Dams in St Helens from its nearest colony 50 km to the south-east was a great surprise. Perhaps equally surprising is the fact that it did not continue its spread until it appeared at Ochre Flash, Wigan in 2001. This robust damsel prefers clean ponds with lily pads from where it aggressively defends its territory. There are many suitable sites ripe for colonisation in west Lancashire and then further north in Chorley and the Fylde.

Our final damselflies are the large, colourful and spectacular demoiselles. The Beautiful Demoiselle has been seen only twice, both times in gardens. The Banded Demoiselle occurs in clean, running waters, particularly around Cuerden Valley Park, but recent years have seen a large increase in the population and an expansion in range (See Box 11.6).

True dragonflies

Thirteen species of Anisoptera (true dragonflies) breed in Lancashire. The largest are the slender bodied hawkers (Aeshnidae), which favour standing water but also occur some distance from it, patrolling hedgerows or drying their wings in tree canopies. The most widespread is the Brown Hawker, a distinctive insect with golden wings, which is often found by urban ponds. Its highest densities are in lowland wetlands, where several make an impressive sight hawking smaller insects along pond and lake margins. Southern Hawkers are less common across the county, but from the end of July dragonfly enthusiasts would expect to come across it in the south of our region. This inquisitive insect often hawks late into the evening, although like most odonates, they require a temperature of at least 17°C to fly. The Migrant Hawker emerges even later in summer, and is commonest in late August and September when the small Lancashire breeding population is swelled by continental migrants, hence its English name. The first confirmed sighting was as recent as 1997, but the species appears firmly established now, at least in the west of the county.

left Brown Hawker. (Peter Smith)

right Migrant Hawker. (Peter Smith)

The Common Hawker, by contrast, is far commoner in the east of the county, where it finds more of its favoured acid waters and boggy habitat. The largest of our dragonflies is the Emperor which first appeared in Lancashire on the Sefton coast during the long, dry summer of 1976 (Hall and Smith 1991). It was the similarly dry summer of 1995 before there was another incursion. This time the species spread further north and east from strongholds at the Sefton coast and Mere Sands Wood. Now naturalists from more central and northern sites in the county can enjoy this striking insect. The Golden-ringed Dragonfly is an upland specialist in Lancashire, most often reported from Bowland, patrolling fast running streams, but it can wander some distance away from water.

There are seven breeding species of the family Libellulidae in Lancashire: four darters (*Sympetrum* species), two chasers (*Libellula*) and one skimmer (*Orthetrum*). The Four-spotted Chaser is abundant on the mosslands in the south and common on sites close to More-cambe Bay, but apparently absent from many sites in between. The closely related Broad-bodied Chaser, whose male is a beautiful pale

*Wildlife of
Lancashire*

Ruddy Darter.
(Phil Smith)

blue, is on its northern limit in Lancashire, where it favours newly dug ponds in the south of the county. This is another species that has expanded its range northwards in recent years, but not so strikingly as the Black-tailed Skimmer. The skimmer first appeared in Lancashire in 1997, a 100 km leap from its existing range in the north Midlands. The first sightings were at Mere Sands Wood which remained the only site for the species for two years. Since 1999, however, range expansion has continued apace, with sightings from as far north as Heysham. Evidence from Mere Sands Wood suggests that the species has adapted to a one year life cycle, perhaps in response to milder winters, whereas in the past the aquatic nymphal stage has tended to take two years to develop.

Our commonest dragonfly is the Common Darter which occurs throughout our region from summer to late autumn. The territorial, orange-red males often occur in gardens, well away from water, where they can be approached closely. The similar looking Ruddy Darter is uncommon, but since its first occurrence at Ainsdale NNR in 1989, it has gained a foothold in the west but so far no further east than Wigan Flashes (Smith 1997). The Black Darter is a specialist of peatland and more acidic waters, often sharing habitats with the Common Hawker. Its known breeding sites are near Bolton, Wigan, St Helens, Middleton (near Heysham), and Carnforth, however in most years there are sightings elsewhere as this is a migratory insect (Smith 1998). Red-veined Darters colonised Middleton in 2001 and have persisted here until 2004, at its most northerly breeding site in Britain.

Male Broad-bodied Chaser at the Wildlife Trust's reserve at Summerseat.
(Geoff Higginbottom)

213

Black Darter.
(Peter Smith)

Conclusions

There are large gaps in our knowledge of Odonata distribution in Lancashire, particularly in central and eastern areas; moreover there have been significant changes in distributions in recent years. In conservation terms it is important that these gaps are filled and changes monitored. The most important information is proof of breeding which usually requires hunting through rigid, emergent vegetation at watersides to collect and identify exuviae, the larval casts left by emerged insects.

The information gathered so far in our region has enabled a number of key sites to be identified. (See Box 11.7)

Box 11.7 Key sites for Odonata in Lancashire

Site	Total species seen	Regular breeding
Heysham/Middleton	19	12
Mere Sands Wood, Rufford	17	12
Seaforth	17	6
Bold Moss, St Helens	16	12
Wigan Flashes	16	10
Sefton Coast (Ainsdale/Birkdale)	16	11
Cuerden Valley Park	14	10
Amberswood, Hindley*	14	9
Cambourne, St Helens	13	11
Red Moss, Bolton	12	10
Highfield Moss, Golborne*	11	9

* Limited data since 1997.

214

Grasshoppers and crickets, by Jennifer Newton

The sound of the cricket on the hearth, so familiar in the past that it was used by Charles Dickens as the title of a novel (1846), is now very rarely heard, being largely confined to a few coastal refuse tips. But grasshoppers and crickets, belonging to the insect order Orthoptera, are the one group of insects which attract attention mainly by sound, though the decline in grasshopper sound with time may be as much due to the ageing of our hearing as to actual decline of the insects. Grasshoppers need sun and warmth to encourage them to 'sing', or stridulate, by rubbing their hind legs across their wing-cases. They do so primarily in courtship, the male's way of attracting a mate. Our generally cool summers limit the number of species found here, and only four of the thirteen British species occur in Lancashire.

In the upland parts of the county the commonest species is the Common Green Grasshopper (*Omocestus viridulus*) which produces a

Two colour forms of the Common Green Grasshopper, the typical green form and the much rarer variety, green with purple sides, found only in females. Many species of grasshopper have several different colour forms whose frequency varies with the colour of their environment.
(Mike Atkinson, above, and Ken Blamire, below)

215

left Nymph of
Mottled
Grasshopper.
(Jennifer Newton)

right Field Grasshopper.
(Pat Livermore)

continuous buzz lasting for several seconds. By contrast the Field Grasshopper (*Chorthippus brunneus*), common along the coast and on waste land and warm slopes, produces short, well-spaced chirps. Our smallest species, the Mottled Grasshopper (*Myrmeleotettix maculatus*), unusual in having the tips of its antennae slightly thickened, likes very open ground with plenty of bare soil, while the Meadow Grasshopper (*Chorthippus parallelus*) is more often found in unshaded, damp or wet ground, such as damp grassland, lowland mosses and upland sphagnum bogs. It is the only one of the four with very reduced hind wings, rendering it unable to fly, though it can still jump remarkable distances.

In addition to the true grasshoppers, three bush crickets are found in a few scattered localities. Bush crickets are large, bulky insects with very long antennae, which can produce high pitched sounds by rubbing their wing cases together. Many are wingless, and in general they live in coarse dense vegetation or on trees, and are remarkably difficult to see in spite of their large size. The Bog Bush Cricket (*Metrioptera brachyptera*), a nationally scarce species, is found in reasonable numbers in tall grass and heather on Winmarleigh and Cockerham Mosses. Its shrill prolonged call may be heard from some distance with the aid of a bat detector to lower the pitch of the sound. The Oak Bush Cricket (*Meconema thalassinum*), a long winged green insect, known

in Lancashire only from the Ribble Valley woods, produces a very quiet sound, but may be attracted to lights at night and is sometimes blown out of trees in autumn storms. Roesel's Bush Cricket (*Metrioptera roeselii*) was first found quite recently in the Fleetwood area, a long way from its previously known localities. It is one of a group of bush crickets which appear to be spreading north and west, probably as a result of warmer summers.

Finally there are two groundhoppers, *Tetrix undulata* and T. *subulata*, tiny hopping insects which feed on mosses and algae and may be present in large numbers on old bonfire sites with a good covering of mosses. They do not produce any noise, are generally dull browns and greys and are readily overlooked, but are widespread at least in the Silverdale area.

Although the number of species is small, Orthoptera are not very mobile and dislike enriched soils, so their presence forms a useful indicator of habitats rich in bio-diversity.

Land Invertebrates:
Grasshoppers and crickets

Bugs, *by Simon Hayhow and Steve Judd*

Introduction, by Malcolm Edmunds

Bugs belong to the insect order Hemiptera, but this includes two suborders which some experts consider are sufficiently unrelated that they should be separated into different orders. These are the Homoptera (including aphids and froghoppers) and the Heteroptera (including the larger shieldbugs and assassin bugs) (Box 11.8). All have piercing and sucking mouthparts, and it is unfortunate that many people (particularly across the Atlantic) use the word 'bug' loosely and derogatively for almost any insect.

Homopteran bugs, by Simon Hayhow

The most familiar homopteran bugs are aphids including the familiar garden pests Greenfly (or Rose Aphid, *Macrosiphum rosae*) on roses and Blackfly (or Black Bean Aphid, *Aphis fabae*) on broad beans. These aphids overwinter on different plants where they do little obvious damage. There are many other common aphids including the Sycamore Aphid (*Drepanosiphum platanoidis*), important food for tits and warblers, but which descends in showers if you inadvertently brush against Sycamore branches on a warm summer's day.

Aphid populations can build up quickly in hot dry weather as the females often give birth to live young (viviparity) without the need for insemination by males (parthenogenesis), and not all adult aphids have wings. Other common homopterans with similar habits, some of which are pests, include psyllids, whiteflies and scale insects. Leafhoppers and froghoppers, with powerful jumping hind legs, are

Box 11.8 *Homopteran and Heteropteran bugs*

These can be distinguished by their wings and mouthparts: homopterans have membranous wings and a piercing beak arising between the front legs whereas heteropterans have the forewings partly hardened and protective while the beak arises from the front of the head.

Homopterans all feed on the juices of plants whereas some heteropteran bugs feed on plants while others feed on animals. There are about 1,700 species of bug in Britain, most of them homopterans, but species in Lancashire are poorly known even though some are easy to identify.

larger; the best known is the Common Froghopper (*Philaenus spumarius*) whose larva secretes the white bubbly 'cuckoo-spit' in which it hides.

Heteropteran bugs, by Steve Judd

The heteropteran, or 'true' bugs are a fascinating group of insects but unfortunately are very poorly studied in Lancashire. There is plenty of opportunity for an enthusiastic field naturalist to play a major role in extending our knowledge of their distribution within the county and nationally. They are very variable in shape and colour and occupy a wide variety of habitats including freshwater.

Heteropterans are predominantly a southern group of insects in Britain, and Lancashire has about 40% of the British fauna, with just over 200 species recorded. Box 11.9 describes some of the commoner ones. There are also nine nationally scarce species and two Red Data Book species. The records of two nationally scarce plant bugs,

Box 11.9 Some common Lancashire bugs

Anyone searching for true bugs in Lancashire will soon encounter a number of very common species. The small, shiny, brown, black and grey-white Common Flower Bug (*Anthocoris nemorum*) has a distinctive circular, black blotch on its wing, and must be close to the top of any list of frequently encountered insects in the county. It is a general predator of small insects and mites, and can be found on most deciduous trees and rank herbage. If you don't find it, it might find you, because there are many records of it 'biting' people.

Also very common is the yellow-brown, long and slender Common Damsel Bug (*Nabis rugosus*). This aggressive predator uses its front legs and noticeably curved mouthparts to capture a wide variety of small insects and spiders. It can be found on most patches of waste grass and is often found in gardens.

A close search amongst the spines on the flower heads of Spear Thistle (*Cirsium vulgare*) in early or late summer should quickly reveal adults of the grey-coloured Spear Thistle Lacebug (*Tingis cardui*). This species should be examined under a hand lens to reveal the intricately sculptured pronotum and wings that gives rise to the family name.

The elusive, oval, brown-black Common Shorebug (*Saldula saltatoria*) lives amongst the flies and other insects around the edge of any muddy pond. Be careful – this predatory bug is very difficult to approach and quickly runs, jumps or flits away, when disturbed.

Well over half of all the True Bugs found in Lancashire are members of the predominantly plant-feeding Miridae. These insects are sometimes known as capsid bugs and are often difficult to distinguish apart. Two of our commonest capsid bugs are the mainly green-coloured Potato Capsid (*Calocoris norvegicus*), which occurs on mixed herbage, and the smaller, drab-coloured *Plagiognathus arbustorum*, which is especially abundant on Nettles.

Land Invertebrates:
Bugs

Amblytylus brevicollis, a typical species of dry grassland and *Halticus saltator*, a poorly known species, both require confirmation and must be regarded as doubtful. The record for the Red Data Book seedbug *Acompus pallipes* also needs confirmation while the Red Data Book shieldbug *Odontoscelis fuliginosa* was last seen in Lancashire a hundred years ago. Other rare shieldbugs are described in Box 11.10.

Box 11.10 Lancashire Shieldbugs

Shieldbugs are among the most colourful and attractively shaped insects, and with practice, most of the county's 15 known species can be easily identified.

Hawthorn Shieldbug. (Phil Smith)

The Hawthorn Shieldbug (*Acanthosoma haemorrhoidale*) is large, triangular, and green with a blackish red triangle on the back. It is common in gardens throughout the summer on Hawthorn, although it also lives on other trees.

Probably the most frequently encountered shieldbug in Lancashire is the Birch Shieldbug (*Elasmostethus interstinctus*). This is a smaller version of the Hawthorn Shieldbug and is particularly abundant on birches with catkins.

The female Parent Bug (*Elasmucha grisea*) guards her eggs and newly hatched young against predators and parasites. It is small, greyish-brown tinged with orange, and is usually on birch.

The Gorse Shieldbug (*Piezodorus lituratus*) is about 10 mm long and yellowish-green in spring, becoming darker later (a melanic specimen was recorded from Pex Hill, Cronton in 1984). Young adults have a reddish tinge, especially on the wings, from their emergence until hibernation time in autumn. Whilst most frequent on Gorse, it also lives on Broom (*Cytisus scoparius*) and other shrubby legumes.

New county records are:

* The Sloe Bug (*Dolycoris baccarum*), first discovered in Lancashire at Heysham Nature Reserve in 1997. It is similar to the Gorse Shieldbug, but more yellowish-brown, tinged with red and distinctly hairy. It can be found on many plants.

* The aptly named *Troilus luridus*, with a luridly coloured, metallic blue and red nymph, was found for the first time in 2001 at Summerseat Nature Reserve, Ramsbottom.

Sand dune systems support a particularly rich heteropteran fauna and the Sefton coast dunes, which are a nationally important habitat for invertebrates generally, support about 140 species, including all of the modern records for nationally scarce bugs in Lancashire. This is the one Lancashire location where bugs have been reasonably well studied and, for this reason, its fauna is featured in this account.

Sloe Bug.
(Bob Marsh)

First modern records:

* *Rhacognathus punctatus*, a species of wet heathland, where it feeds on the larvae of the destructive Heather Beetle (*Lochmaea suturalis*), was recorded in 1991 from Winmarleigh Moss.

* The attractive green shieldbug *Palomena prasina* was found inside a greenhouse at the Liverpool Garden Festival in 1983.

* Until recently, the Juniper Shieldbug (*Cythostethus tristriatus*) was only known in Britain from Common Juniper in southern England, apart from a disputed 1935 record from Witherslack Wood in Furness (historic Lancashire). Extensive searching of native Juniper in 1985 revealed a single specimen just over the county border at Arnside Knott, and it may have always occurred on the Morecambe Bay limestones. In recent years, however, it has transferred to garden cypresses and cultivated junipers in southern England and has been rapidly extending its range northwards. It was first recorded close to Liverpool city centre in 1991, and is probably now widely established in Lancashire.

The colourful nymph of *Troilus luridus*.
(Mike Atkinson)

What next?

* Surprisingly, some of the commonest British shieldbugs have not been recorded in Lancashire, such as the black and white Pied Shieldbug (*Sehirus bicolor*), which mainly feeds on White Dead Nettle (*Lamium album*).

* Look out for the appropriately named Bishop's Mitre (*Aelia acuminata*), a species that has recently colonized sand dunes in Flintshire, and which might soon be found on Lancashire dune grassland.

* A prize awaits the discoverer of *Chlorochroa juniperina*, another Juniper feeding shieldbug. This species was surprisingly recorded from near Heywood, Lancashire in 1925, one of only three confirmed British records. It is now thought to be extinct in Britain – but is it?

Land Invertebrates:
Bugs

Unlike most British shieldbugs, *Picromerus bidens* is a predator, here feeding on a Cinnabar Moth caterpillar. *(Phil Smith)*

Sporadic searching for bugs on the Sefton coast over the last fifteen years has produced some interesting finds, including first Lancashire records for two nationally scarce species which are predominantly restricted in their British distribution to southern and eastern England. The first of these, the plant bug *Systellonotus triguttatus*, could at first glance be confused with an ant. It was recorded in 1987 from short turf at Altcar Rifle Range (Judd 1999). The second species, the seedbug *Graptopeltus lynceus*, was pitfall-trapped from Ravenmeols Sand Dunes LNR in 1993 (Haughton and Bell, 1996). It requires open sunny spaces and is probably associated here with Hound's-tongue.

A further four nationally scarce species, three plant bugs and a water bug, all of which are associated with dune slacks, are recorded from the Sefton coast dunes. *Monosynamma sabulicola* and *Globiceps cruciatus* are both found on Creeping Willow whilst *Polymerus palustris* occurs on Marsh Bedstraw. The pond skater *Gerris lateralis*, a predominantly northern species in Britain, also occurs here.

Some coastal specialists, such as the distinctive, nationally scarce, Spurgebug (*Dicranocephalus agilis*) and the striking, red and black rhopalid bug *Corizus hyoscyami* were recorded in an old checklist for Lancashire (Whittaker 1906, 1908), but have not been seen since and have probably been extinct within the county for many years. They both occur on the west coast of Wales. The latter species is one to look out for, as it has recently been recorded for the first time on the Flintshire coast.

About 75% of heteropteran bugs recorded from the Sefton coast are common nationally. However, many common, widely distributed bug species in southern and central England, such as the Nettle feeding seedbug *Heterogaster urticae*, become coastal towards the extremes of their range in Britain and are extremely local in their occurrence in Lancashire.

The targeting of poorly studied habitats within the Sefton dune system has been productive for bugs, and a 1997–98 Liverpool Museum survey of dune heath recorded 16 new species for this coastline. Unfortunately, very little is known of the distribution and abundance of heteropteran bugs elsewhere in Lancashire.

Moths, by Steve Palmer

Moths are the major part of the order Lepidoptera, an insect group which also includes butterflies (Box 11.11). British moths have a

Box 11.11 Butterflies and Moths

Insects as a whole are not liked by the general public, but an exception are the butterflies with their dancing flight and attractive colours. Butterflies and moths belong to the insect order Lepidoptera of which there are nearly 150,000 species world-wide, most of them moths. However, there is no single characteristic that distinguishes these two groups and it seems that butterflies have evolved from moths several times quite independently. So what distinguishes butterflies from moths? Moths fly at night, hold the wings angled over the body when at rest, link the wings together with a hook (or frenulum) on the hind wing when flying and do not have clubbed antennae, but there are exceptions to all of these statements. In contrast butterflies are active by day, have clubbed antennae, lack a frenulum and usually hold the wings vertically over the body when at rest.

Moths are tasty morsels for birds, and it may be for this reason that they evolved a nocturnal habit and typically brownish colours, resting by day camouflaged on trees and other vegetation. Some, however, developed chemical defences and bright warning colours (like the Garden Tiger), and a few of these are active by day, e.g. the red and greenish black Cinnabar and Six-spot Burnet (*Tyria jacobaeae* and *Zygaena filipendulae*). It was from some of these foul-tasting day-flying moths that the various groups of butterflies evolved. This does not, however, mean that all butterflies are protected from predators. In the evolutionary arms race many predators have evolved the ability to digest insect defensive chemicals, or to avoid eating wings and other parts of the body where these are concentrated, while even the nocturnal moths have acquired specialist predators such as Nightjars and bats. In response to bats many moths have evolved 'ears' sensitive to the high frequency sounds of bats, so when they hear a bat they can take evasive action. For the naturalist both butterflies and moths are fascinating animals.

Malcolm Edmunds

Six-spot Burnet, one of only a few species of moth that fly during the day.
(*Laura Sivell*)

top Silver Y, equally well camouflaged on tree bark and among dead leaves.
(Mike Atkinson)

bottom Adult Garden Tigers have warning colouration with black and white forewings and black and red hindwings.
(Peter Smith)

wingspan varying from a few millimetres to over 10 cm, and they have a range of foodplants enabling them to occupy a wide variety of habitats. From the Formby shoreline to the highest point in the Forest of Bowland and the smallest backyard in urban Manchester, the determined naturalist can find signs of these fascinating creatures. Approximately 2,500 different moths are found in Britain, of which at least 1,460 occur in Lancashire, including about 890 micromoths and 570 macromoths.

Moths to look out for

Silver Y (*Autographa gamma*). This attractive moth with a white y mark on the forewing is commonly seen resting on flowers in late summer. Most are immigrants from Europe supplemented by a few home bred moths.

Large Yellow Underwing (*Noctua pronuba*). The numbers of this moth vary considerably from year to year, but it is usually abundant. Adults normally rest hidden among vegetation, but when disturbed by gardeners they are easy to follow in flight because of the bright yellow hind wings. When they land the yellow is hidden and the insects vanish.

Garden Tiger (*Arctia caja*). As a child, most of us would have been familiar with the woolly bear caterpillar wandering around in late spring looking for a suitable pupation site. Nowadays you are quite fortunate if you encounter one. This attractive moth flies from late June to early August and appears to be restricted to areas below about 150 m, although this may be due to the smaller number of moth recorders living in upland areas.

Magpie Moth (*Abraxas grossulariata*). Until the mid-twentieth century, gardeners would have been very familiar with this moth as the distinctive caterpillar was regularly found feeding on currant and gooseberry bushes as well as hedgerow shrubs. It belongs to the Geometridae family, its black, white and yellow warning colours deterring predation by

birds. It still occurs in many lowland Lancashire gardens, but is much less common than formerly.

Emperor Moth (*Saturnia pavonia*). There is an intriguing report (possibly in the mid 1950s) of a gentleman driving his car on a road through an area of moorland north-east of Manchester and encountering large numbers of Emperor Moths in flight on a sunny spring morning. The day-flying males were searching for females, being attracted by a scent (or pheromone) emitted by the waiting females. The mature large green caterpillars with their pink warts are perhaps

left The female Emperor Moth is much larger and lighter coloured than the male.
(Laura Sivell)

right The woolly bear caterpillar of the Garden Tiger has hairs which can be very painful irritants on our skin.
(Peter Smith)

Caterpillar of the Emperor Moth. When first emerged the caterpillar is black, changing to this distinctive green after it sheds its first skin.
(Phil Smith)

225

Elephant Hawkmoth. In spite of its large size, this moth is rarely found except when attracted to light.
(Peter Smith)

as well known as the moth itself. The Emperor Moth is still a distinctive species of the heather moors, but is rarely encountered in such numbers and appears to be absent from some uplands where heather has become uncommon.

Hawkmoths. As with the Emperor Moth, large hawkmoths with narrow wings and rapid flight are exciting insects to find, and two of the commonest in Lancashire are the Poplar and the Elephant Hawkmoths (*Laothoe populi* and *Deilephila elpenor*). Full grown caterpillars are 7–8 cm long with a pointed tail, and occur in August, the Poplar Hawk on willows and poplars where they are superbly camouflaged (Box 11.12). Elephant Hawk caterpillars feed on willowherbs, Bogbean (*Menyanthes trifoliata*) and occasionally on garden fuchsias. The full grown dramatic brown caterpillars with grey-blue eyespots crawl away to pupate.

Recording of moths

The moth fauna of Lancashire has been studied for over 150 years, so the list of the larger moths is quite comprehensive. However, the smaller moths and those species expanding or shifting their ranges are much less well known (Boxes 11.13 and 11.14). It is important to have an extensive network of recorders using their gardens and surrounding areas to track these population changes. With such a group important discoveries can be made (Box 11.15). A recording scheme, established in 1998, now has over eighty participants but more are needed, particularly in the east of the county.

Box 11.12 *Hawkmoth caterpillars*

Most hawkmoth caterpillars are large and do not contain any toxic chemicals, so they provide excellent meals for birds. Heavy predation by birds has led to the evolution of superb camouflage in these insects. Caterpillars of the poplar hawkmoth are common on willows and poplars throughout our area. On Crack Willow (*Salix fragilis*) large caterpillars are yellow-green like the leaves, on other willows they may be dark green, again matching the leaves, while on White Poplar (*Populus alba*) they are almost pure white resting on the white underside of the leaves. Research in Lancashire has shown that this colour matching is achieved by the young caterpillars on green leaves absorbing the plant pigment lutein in the gut and depositing it below the skin to give a green colour, while those on white leaves deposit hardly any lutein and so remain white.

Experiments at Cuerden Valley Park, Bamber Bridge, showed that when yellow-green and white caterpillars were placed on Crack Willow and on White Poplar the greens survived better on the willow and the whites survived better on the poplar, presumably because birds found the more conspicuous caterpillars more easily. Eyed Hawkmoth caterpillars (*Smerinthus ocellata*) show similar variation, those found at Lytham St Annes on Grey Willow were mostly yellow-green while those on White Willow (*Salix alba*) were grey-green, once again both forms being wonderfully camouflaged.

Malcolm Edmunds

top left Poplar Hawkmoth caterpillars on White Poplar are usually white.
(Malcolm Edmunds)

top right Poplar Hawkmoth caterpillars on Crack Willow are usually yellow-green.
(Malcolm Edmunds)

left Adult Poplar Hawkmoths at rest resemble dead leaves.
(Malcolm Edmunds)

227

Land Invertebrates:
Moths

Barred Tooth-striped
resting camouflaged
on a tree.
(Ken Blamire)

Box 11.13 *Lancashire moths of national importance*

In the past Lancashire held populations of several nationally scarce moths, but, as elsewhere in the UK, many of these have been lost due to habitat loss and modern intensive agricultural methods. The two most significant species still occurring in Lancashire are both apparently confined to the limestone areas of the North West and have very restricted distributions nationally.

The Barred Tooth-striped (*Trichopteryx polycommata*), a member of the Geometridae family, occurs at Gait Barrows NNR, limestone areas of Leighton Moss RSPB reserve and at Warton Crag nature reserve. The larval foodplants in these areas are not known, but probably include both Ash and Wild Privet (*Ligustrum vulgare*). The moth flies very early in the year and is often attracted to light in April, sometimes flying in temperatures only a few degrees above freezing.

The Least Minor (*Photedes captiuncula* ssp. *expolita*) is an unusually small member of the Noctuidae family and, when seen in flight, can easily be mistaken for a micromoth. It is also one of only a few day-flying noctuids. It occurs at the same three locations as the Barred Tooth-striped, but its stronghold appears to be Warton Crag where it flies during sunny periods from mid June to mid July. The larva feeds on the inner parts of Glaucous Sedge (*Carex flacca*).

Box 11.14 *Declining and expanding species*

The Argent and Sable (*Rheumaptera hastata*), Sword-grass (*Xylena exsoleta*) and Sandhill Rustic (*Luperina nickerlii*) are all species becoming scarce nationally which have been recorded in Lancashire during the latter half of the twentieth century. The first was a moth of birch woodland requiring younger trees to complete its life-cycle, the Sword-grass was found on moorland and open woodland, and the Sandhill Rustic inhabited coastal sand dunes. There are no recent records from their former haunts in Lancashire for the first two species, but the last still hangs on at one site.

However, all is not doom and gloom: Blair's Shoulder-knot (*Lithophane leautieri*), Freyer's Pug (*Eupithecia intricata*), *Caloptilia rufipennella* (a micromoth lacking an English name) and the Firethorn Leaf-miner (*Phyllonorycter leucographella*), have all arrived in Lancashire over the last decade or so. The last two have larvae that mine the leaves of Sycamore and *Pyracantha* respectively while Blair's Shoulder-knot, first recorded in Britain in 1951, and Freyer's Pug both utilise some of the cypresses, particularly Monterey Cypress (*Cupressus macrocarpa*), planted in gardens.

*Wildlife of
Lancashire*

Box 11.15 Belted Beauty (Lycia zonaria)

The Belted Beauty moth was first recorded in Lancashire around 1900 in Crosby, near Liverpool, with further records from Longton Marsh, near Preston, in 1918 and in Lytham and Blackpool during the 1960s and 1970s. It was very much a coastal species and declined rapidly with the development of coastal areas for housing and leisure. However, during the period 1975 to 1993 there were three reports of a single moth or caterpillar in the Sunderland Point area, south-west of Lancaster, but the lack of any further sightings suggested that the moth had become extinct in the county.

During April 2002 a group of moth enthusiasts together with Butterfly Conservation organised a series of searches of the Sunderland Point area with dramatic results. Significant numbers of both males and wingless females were found scattered over several kilometres of salt marsh. This was the first time salt marsh had been recorded as a breeding site for the Belted Beauty, and it is only the second recent colony of the moth in England.

Further visits to the area by members of the LWT North Lancashire Naturalists during the summer of 2002 produced vital information on the plants being used by the attractive yellow-striped caterpillar, at least one not previously recorded as a foodplant in Britain. Perhaps the most dramatic discovery was that the overwintering pupa and the eggs can withstand regular immersion in sea-water for at least a couple of hours during the many winter and spring high tides.

top Male Belted Beauty.
(Mike Atkinson)

above The female Belted Beauty has no trace of wings and can only crawl short distances. This means that it is very difficult for this rare moth to colonise new areas.
(Mike Atkinson)

Butterflies, by Laura Sivell

Of Britain's 58 butterfly species, 33 occur in the old county of Lancashire, and 31 have been found on the Wildlife Trust's reserves. The commoner species can find suitable breeding conditions in many areas so they may be found anywhere from nature reserves to gardens (Box 11.16).

229

Box 11.16 *Garden Butterflies*

Common garden butterflies are all adaptable and mobile species – if the garden is not quite right, they will fly off and find somewhere more suitable. Their caterpillars use common foodplants: the Small Tortoiseshell (*Aglais urticae*), Peacock (*Inachis io*), Comma (*Polygonia c-album*), Red Admiral (*Vanessa atalanta*) and Painted Lady (*Cynthia cardui*) all eat Nettle (*Urtica dioica*), but the Painted Lady seems to prefer thistle.

The Small Tortoiseshell, Peacock and Comma hibernate as adults in outbuildings, holes in trees or amongst dense ivy or other creepers. In upland areas, Peacocks hibernate in the gaps in drystone walls. When these butterflies come into the house you can help them survive by gently moving them into a shed or garage, as the warm dry conditions with central heating will usually kill them. Like other hibernating animals, they have to put on enough fat to survive the winter. It may seem strange to think of butterflies getting fat, but that is what they are doing when they feed for hours on Buddleia or Sedum in late summer.

Instead of hibernating properly, Red Admirals have to emerge every week or two to feed, so most do not survive the British winter. Although they are very common here, they migrate each year from southern Europe, and they have also been tracked flying south in the autumn. The Painted Lady is another migrant that we see in most years. It breeds all year round in North Africa, and in the spring they move north, stopping to breed as they go. If there is a strong wind, huge numbers can arrive. This happened in 1996, when whole fields of Nettles and thistles were stripped bare by their caterpillars. Painted Ladies do not hibernate, and those that do not return south will rarely survive.

The Large White (*Pieris brassicae*) and Small White (*Pieris rapae*) eat wild and cultivated plants of the

Wildlife of Lancashire

cabbage family including Cabbages, Aubretia, Honesty, Wallflowers and Rocket, and they will also eat Nasturtiums. Because the adult butterflies do not have to go far to find these plants, they are very widespread. They are seen around gardens more frequently than their close relatives, the Green-veined White (*Pieris napi*) and Orange Tip (*Anthocharis cardamines*), which are happier in a woodland edge habitat. Orange Tips are only found in the spring, but all the other whites have a series of broods from spring to autumn. The Large White caterpillar concentrates foul-tasting chemicals in its body, and its yellow and black bands warn predators. The green caterpillars of the Small White cannot do this, so they rely on camouflage to escape from birds.

As the countryside has become more intensively farmed, gardens have become more important for these adaptable butterflies.

However, those butterflies with specialised requirements are much more restricted in range. For instance, the fritillary family has four species in Lancashire. Two of these, the High Brown Fritillary and the Pearl-bordered Fritillary, need freshly coppiced woodland where their caterpillars bask on bare ground between meals of Dog-violet leaves. As Lancashire is sparsely wooded, and few woods are managed by coppicing, it must come as no surprise that these species are rare. We are very lucky, though, to have good colonies of both these endangered butterflies on the Wildlife Trust's Warton Crag reserve (Box 11.17). Trees grow slowly on the thin limestone soils round Morecambe Bay, and naturalists now understand exactly what conditions the butterflies need. They are now working towards maintaining these conditions, whilst in other areas more rapid tree growth has shaded the butterflies into extinction.

top left The Painted Lady is a welcome immigrant from southern Europe, but it seldom survives our cold winters.
(Laura Sivell)

The caterpillar of the Large White sits conspicuously on cabbage leaves and contains noxious chemicals so that most birds avoid eating it.
(Peter Smith)

Land Invertebrates:
Butterflies

Box 11.17 *Butterflies of the Morecambe Bay limestones*

Some of Britain's rarest butterflies can be found on the limestone hills around Morecambe Bay.

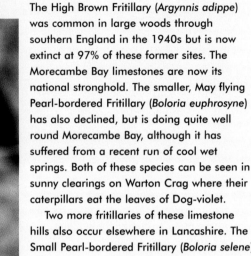

The High Brown Fritillary (*Argynnis adippe*) was common in large woods through southern England in the 1940s but is now extinct at 97% of these former sites. The Morecambe Bay limestones are now its national stronghold. The smaller, May flying Pearl-bordered Fritillary (*Boloria euphrosyne*) has also declined, but is doing quite well round Morecambe Bay, although it has suffered from a recent run of cool wet springs. Both of these species can be seen in sunny clearings on Warton Crag where their caterpillars eat the leaves of Dog-violet.

Two more fritillaries of these limestone hills also occur elsewhere in Lancashire. The Small Pearl-bordered Fritillary (*Boloria selene*) flies in June and July, and also occurs in low numbers on some damp moorlands where its caterpillars eat Marsh Violet. The Dark Green Fritillary (*Argynnis aglaja*) flies in July and August with the very similar High Brown, but it is also quite common on the Sefton coast near Southport. All these fritillaries have a checkerboard pattern of orange with black lines and splotches, and all are fast fliers, so accurate identification takes a lot of experience!

Also at Warton Crag is the Northern Brown Argus (*Aricia artaxerxes*), whose caterpillars feed on Common Rock-rose. It belongs to the same family as the blues, but the wings are brown above with orange spots along the edges. However, the pattern of the underside is similar to the Common Blue and the family relationship becomes clear. It is one of our smallest butterflies and flies from mid June to late July.

As well as the Wildlife Trusts for Lancashire and Cumbria, English Nature, the National Trust, the Royal Society for the Protection of Birds, Butterfly Conservation, Forest Enterprise and some private landowners are all working together to ensure the continued survival of these special butterflies.

Wildlife of
Lancashire

Another butterfly dependent on trees is the little White-letter Hairstreak (*Strymondia w-album*) that spends most of its life living high in the canopy of mature elms. Although always rare in Lancashire, in the late 1970s hundreds could be seen at Red Scar and Tun Brook woods (now a Trust reserve) near Preston, but since the ravages of Dutch Elm Disease, numbers have been much reduced. It was feared that the butterfly could be lost from the site, but work to encourage young elm suckers and removal of diseased timber to slow spread of the disease has been successful in preserving a small colony in the adjacent Boilton Wood. Recent news of a disease resistant elm is good news for this species. The related Green Hairstreak (*Callophrys rubi*) (Britain's only green butterfly) is much more widespread in Lancashire.

Two of Britain's blue butterflies, the Common Blue (*Polyommatus icarus*) and the Holly Blue (*Celastrina argiolus*) are found in Lancashire. The Common Blue occurs on sunny grassland and good colonies are found at many reserves, e.g. Seaforth, Heysham, Moses Gate Country Park and Red Moss. The Holly Blue prefers woods and gardens with

White-letter
Hairstreak.
(Phil Smith)

Green Hairstreaks
mating.
(Laura Sivell)

233

trees, and may be found at any wood that contains both Holly and Ivy (H*edera helix*), the caterpillar's foodplants. Both butterflies occur on the Morecambe Bay limestones together with the Northern Brown Argus (see Box 11.17).

The Gatekeeper (*Pyronia tithonus*) is mainly found in south and west Lancashire, Merseyside and west Manchester where it flies from July to mid August. It is spreading slowly and in most years a few are found to have colonised new areas. The best places to see them are the Trust's Mere Sands Wood reserve, where dozens feed on Fleabane (*Pulicaria dysenterica*), and Seaforth.

Another member of the 'brown' family is the Wall (*Lasiommata megera*), a butterfly that is surprisingly difficult to approach closely. There has been some concern over this normally common butterfly, as it has been disappearing from South East England in the last few years, but nobody really knows why. In Lancashire it is still quite common on sunny grassland reserves, and Seaforth supports a very strong colony.

Two other butterflies that have changed their distributions in recent years are the Speckled Wood and the Small Skipper (Boxes 11.18 and 11.19)

Speckled Wood.
(Laura Sivell)

Box 11.18 *The Speckled Wood* (Pararge aegeria) *at Warton Crag*

The Speckled Wood was only recorded from a few sites in Lancashire until the early 1980s, all in the west. Since then there has since been a massive expansion across most of Lancashire apart from the Bowland fells. In 1993 the first one was recorded at the Trust's Warton Crag reserve, and just five years later it had become the commonest butterfly on the site. We do not know why this butterfly has done so well, but the milder winters may have been a factor.

This graph shows how rapidly the population of the Speckled Wood butterfly has expanded over the course of just seven years at Warton Crag. The population in 2000 had reached more than 300.

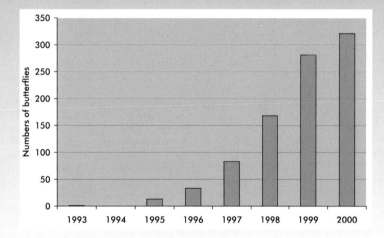

All the Trust's reserves have butterflies either as resident breeding species or as casual visitors. So even if you're visiting a site to see birds or plants, keep your eyes open for these colourful insects. With their fascinating behaviour and their intricate lifestyles, they deserve a closer look.

Land Invertebrates:
Butterflies

Map 11.
**Distribution of
Small Skipper
Records in the
Wildlife Trust Area.**
(Nik Bruce)

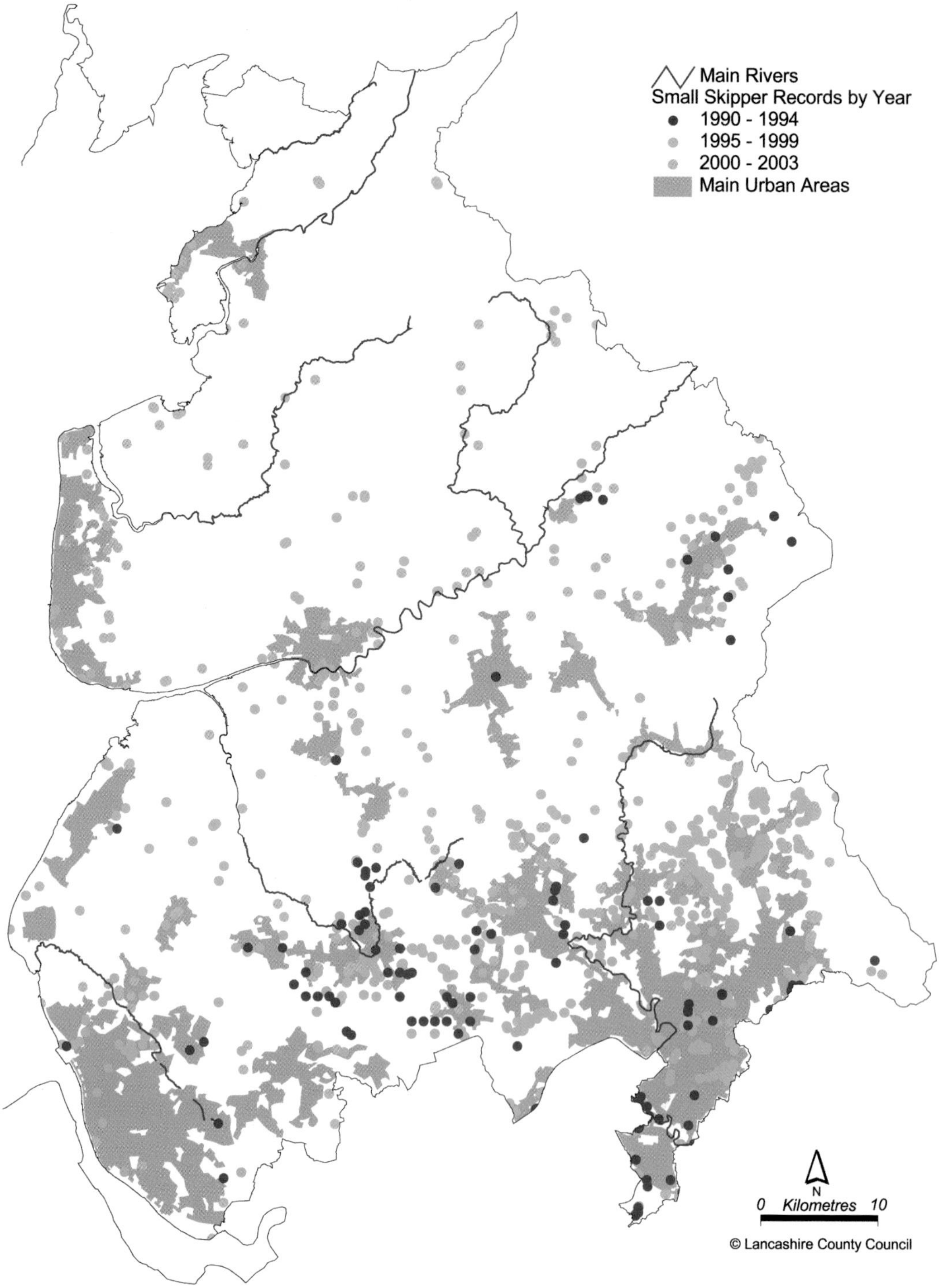

Main Rivers
Small Skipper Records by Year
● 1990 - 1994
● 1995 - 1999
● 2000 - 2003
Main Urban Areas

0 Kilometres 10

N

© Lancashire County Council

The Small Skipper became extinct in the Lancashire/Cumbria border area before 1970, and until the early 1980s it was only found around the southern borders of Manchester and Merseyside. Through the 1990s there was a dramatic spread north across Lancashire and this little golden-brown butterfly has now, in 2004, spread into Cumbria. It lays its round white eggs in the curled leaves around the stem of the grass Yorkshire-fog, where the tiny caterpillars spend the winter. In spring they start eating the young growth. Uncut roadsides and motorway verges are a possible route for spread, and the financial constraints on many councils which have resulted in grass being cut less frequently may have unwittingly aided colonisation northwards.

The map on the facing page shows how the Small Skipper has spread northwards from the Manchester and Merseyside region, but does not include 2004 records.

top Small Skipper.
(*Laura Sivell*)

above Eggs of the Small Skipper in a curled leaf of Yorkshire Fog.
(*Laura Sivell*)

Flies, by Simon Hayhow

Many insects have the word 'fly' in their common names but are not 'true flies': dragonflies, mayflies, stoneflies, caddisflies and scorpion-flies all belong to different Orders. 'True flies' belonging to the Order Diptera have just one pair of wings for flying; their second pair have been modified through evolution into a pair of small knobbed organs, the halteres, which act as gyroscopic stabilisers during flight. The exception to the rule is a small number of totally wingless parasitic flies. Flies feed on liquids ranging from nectar to blood and the juices of insects.

Flies are among the most familiar of insects. We notice them when they are a nuisance: bluebottles and other blow-flies taint our food,

flies swarm around us and our animals during the summer; some bite, some buzz and some just disgust us with their habits of living in dung, sewage, carrion and even living flesh. This impression does not do justice to a fascinating group which is very diverse, ranging from stout-bodied horseflies and bluebottles, to colourful hoverflies and soldierflies, to slender, long-legged craneflies and mosquitoes. Their body length ranges from 1 to 28 mm, and the structure of their antennae is very important in their classification. There are at least 5,200 species in Britain but no complete Lancashire checklist has yet been published.

The most primitive flies, the Nematocera, have long antennae and include the familiar 'daddy long-legs' or craneflies, of which there are some 300 species. Some of the soil-living larvae are the notorious 'leatherjackets', e.g. *Tipula paludosa*, which can be very common and cause serious damage to crops. The largest cranefly, *Tipula maxima*, has a wingspan of 65 mm. A study of Holden Clough (Kidd and Fitton 1971) near Oldham produced an impressive list of craneflies showing

*Wildlife of
Lancashire*

that our damp northern woods and valleys are rich in species. One rarity is *Lipsothrix nigristigma*, only known in Britain from a single specimen found in 1924 near Blackburn until discovered on the Welsh border in 1995.

As far as humans are concerned, the most important of the nematocerous families is the Culicidae. This family contains the familiar mosquitoes which are nearly all blood-sucking and, world-wide, they are responsible for the spread of serious diseases including malaria and yellow fever. In Britain there are only 33 species. Both sexes have a slender proboscis but only the females pierce skin and suck blood. *Culex pipiens* is common around buildings in Lancashire. Mosquito larvae live in water and hang at an angle from the surface film.

Other related families, like the Dixidae and Chironomidae, contain non-biting midges but the tiny, humped Ceratopogonidae, less than 5 mm long, include a few species which bite humans and can be extremely irritating on summer evenings.

The Brachycera include several distinctive groups with short, stout antennae. Soldierflies are rather flattened with bright and often metallic colours. Many are indicators of good quality wetlands. The White-barred Soldier (*Oxycera morrissii*) and Pygmy Soldier (*Oxycera pygmaea*) are characteristic of calcareous seepages, such as at White Coppice or Lundsfield Quarry, while the Barred Snout (*Nemotelus uliginosus*) requires saline wetlands such as around the salt marshes of Morecambe Bay. Terrestrial species include the metallic Broad Centurion (*Chloromyia formosa*), often seen in parks and gardens.

left The common large mosquito *Culiseta annulata*.
(Richard Revels/Woodfall Wild Images)

right *Oxycera rara* is one of several attractive species of soldierflies that occur in damp pastures.
(© Harry Fox/OSF/ Photolibrary.com)

239

Land Invertebrates:
Flies

The Dark-edged Bee-fly is a common visitor to flowers in gardens. (Lance Gorman)

Some bee-flies resemble bumblebees and the Dark-edged Bee-fly (*Bombylius major*) is the best known. It is seen in spring hovering and plunging its long proboscis into tubular flowers or flicking its eggs towards the nests of solitary bees where its larvae seek a host. The tiny Flea Bee-fly (*Phthiria pulicaria*) feeds at yellow hawkweed flowers on our sand dunes at Ainsdale and Lytham St Annes.

Robber-flies, sturdy, slender insects with powerful bristly legs, are predators that catch their prey in mid-air and suck out the juices. The Dune Robber-fly (*Philonicus albiceps*) is a common species of our sand dunes, while the handsome Orange-legged Robber-fly (*Dioctria oelandica*), shiny black with darkened wings and bright orange legs, is found in oak woodlands near Silverdale.

left One of our commonest droneflies is *Eristalis pertinax,* which many people mistake for a Honeybee. (Lance Gorman)

right Another common visitor to flowers is *Helophilus pendulus*. (Malcolm Edmunds)

The Dolichopodidae, known as 'Dolis', include over 250 British species, most of them small and metallic or bronze. The male genitalia are usually prominent and the legs are ornamented with swellings and tufts of hairs. Many species, such as *Poecilobothrus nobilitatus* with black and white wing markings, hunt over water and around the muddy margins of ponds and ditches, often waving their wings in display.

The Cyclorrhapha are flies with antennae of three segments and with barrel-shaped puparia. Hoverflies are a good group to begin the study of Diptera because many have bright colours, and some are remarkable mimics of bees and wasps (see Box 11.20). The very common dronefly *Eristalis tenax* mimics the Honeybee while the different colour forms of *Volucella bombylans* mimic different species of bumblebee. The most familiar yellow and black garden species include *Syrphus* spp., *Eupeodes* spp. and *Episyrphus balteatus* whose larvae feed on aphids, and *Helophilus* spp. whose larvae live in stagnant water.

Box 11.20 *Hoverflies*

Just over 200 of Britain's 270 species of hoverfly are known in Lancashire, many of which are brightly coloured and attractive. Some of them hover in our gardens in the sunshine and are not recognized for what they are because they mimic bees and wasps in both appearance and behaviour. Hoverflies, however, do not bite or sting. They feed on pollen and nectar, and the larvae of many of the commoner species feed on aphids which is good news for gardeners.

Hoverflies are mostly relatively easy to identify with the aid of a hand lens and an excellent illustrated key (Stubbs and Falk 1983). In Lancashire we are lucky to have good populations of some of the more spectacular species, including the bee-like *Microdon mutabilis* whose larvae scavenge in ant nests, and four superb bumblebee mimics *Criorhina ranunculi*, *C. berberina*, *Arctophila superbiens* and *Volucella bombylans*. *Doros profuges* is a much rarer black and yellow wasp-like species.

Some hoverflies are indicators of ancient woodland because they

top *Microdon mutabilis* has longer antennae than most of our hoverflies.
(Lance Gorman)

centre The typical colour form of *Criorhina berberina* mimics a black and yellow bumblebee.
(Lance Gorman)

bottom The oxyacanthae form of *Criorhina berberina* mimics the Common Carder Bee.
(Lance Gorman)

241

Land Invertebrates:
Flies

breed in rotting wood. Good hoverfly sites with ancient dead wood and rot holes are Brock Valley, Red Scar and Tun Brook Woods and Gait Barrows NNR. These have produced rare species including the red and black *Brachypalpoides lentus*, and two more superb bee-mimics *Brachypalpus laphriformis* and *Mallota cimbiciformis*. The larvae of other species scavenge in the nests of bees, wasps and ants or live in compost heaps or stagnant water, and a few eat plants.

Hoverflies can be observed in most habitats as their habits are so diverse. They are on the wing from late February until late October and can in rare cases be seen in well sheltered warm spots during winter. Several groups study and record hoverflies in Lancashire, so if you have an interest in these insects contact your local museum or natural history society for information.

Lance Gorman

top Two different colour forms of *Volucella bombylans* mating, the female mimicking a black and yellow bumblebee, the male, which is a very rare colour form, mimicking the rusty-tailed Early Bumblebee.
(Malcolm Edmunds)

above The slender wasp-like *Doros profuges* occurs at a single site in our area.
(Lance Gorman)

The conopids are also good wasp mimics. They pounce and lay their eggs on bees and wasps as the larvae are internal parasites. *Conops quadrifasciatus* is the most frequent species along woodland edges whilst the orange *Sicus ferrugineus* is fairly common amongst bees and wasps on the coast. There are many groups of small flies with patterned wings, the 'picture-winged' flies. *Urophora cardui* is a common species whose larvae live in the stems of creeping thistle. The sciomyzids are mostly wetland species whose larvae feed on snails.

right The conopid fly *Conops quadrifasciatus* mimics a solitary wasp.
(Malcolm Edmunds)

Wildlife of Lancashire

The common dung-fly *Scathophaga stercoraria* mating on a cow-pat. *(Peter Perfect/ Woodfall Wild Images)*

There are several families of stout, bristly flies which can be tricky to identify. They include familiar groups like the bluebottles, greenbottles, fleshflies and dungflies. A few species are well known because they are so common like the House-fly (*Musca domestica*), the blow-fly *Calliphora vomitoria* and the yellow dungfly *Scathophaga stercoraria* which swarms on fresh cow-pats. Many other species are more specialised in their requirements. The louse-flies are amongst the strangest flies, with wings reduced or absent, and they suck blood as parasites of birds and mammals.

Much valuable recording work was carried out on Lancashire Diptera between 1920 and 1970 by Harry Britten, Leonard Kidd, Alan Brindle, Peter Skidmore and others. A few dipterists are continuing their pioneering work in pursuit of Lancashire flies, but only a few groups are being studied in any detail at present. Recent new identification guides and keys as well as a national organisation, the Dipterists' Forum, now make the 'true flies' more accessible than they have ever been. There is a wealth of fascinating species in the county, many of which are useful indicators of high-quality woodland and wetland habitats. There are still many interesting discoveries to be made and much to learn about the Diptera.

Bees, Wasps and Ants (aculeate Hymenoptera), by Neil Robinson

Bees, wasps and flying ants have two pairs of wings married together by rows of hooks so that they function as a single pair, and females (except for some ants) have stings. For bees these are purely defensive, whereas wasps use their stings to subdue their prey. This relates to one of the basic differences between bees and wasps: bees collect nectar and pollen to provision their young, but wasps provide animal protein in the form of stung and paralysed invertebrates. Their ingenious behaviour makes bees, wasps and ants fascinating insects to study. They can be found in gardens, parks and anywhere with lots of flowers; sand dunes, old sand quarries and derelict industrial sites are particularly good places.

Most people are familiar with the social bees: Hive Bees (or Honeybees, *Apis mellifera*) and bumblebees (which used to be called humble bees). Social bees live in colonies with a queen which does the egg-laying, accompanied by a large number of workers (infertile females) which do most of the work of constructing and provisioning the nest, and some drones (males), whose only function is to inseminate the next generation of queens. Hive Bee colonies can live over winter, but in a bumblebee colony the old queen and all the workers die in the autumn leaving only the new queens to hibernate and start new colonies from scratch in spring. There are six species of bumblebees which commonly visit gardens in Lancashire as well as being widespread in the countryside (Box 11.21).

Less well known are the solitary bees of which about 200 species occur in Britain, and over 80 of these are known to be present in Lancashire, Merseyside and Manchester. They range in size from that of a Honeybee to some so small that they are not easily recognisable as bees at all. Each female makes a simple nest consisting of only a few cells. The cells of leaf-cutting bees are arranged in line in a tunnel in soft wood. If you find neat circular and oblong pieces cut out of the rose leaves in your garden this will be the work of leaf-cutting bees, which use the oblong pieces for the sides of their cells and the round pieces to plug the ends. Each cell is lined with a waterproof secretion and provisioned with a paste of nectar and pollen.

Mason bees make their cells of mud in a cavity. In mining bees they are grouped like a bunch of grapes at the end of a tunnel excavated in the ground. An egg is laid, then the cell is sealed and left for the egg to hatch, and the larva to develop, pupate and emerge as an adult – often in the following year, by which time the previous adults have

Box 11.21 Bumblebees

Bumblebees which are common in Lancashire are:

* White-tailed Bumblebee (*Bombus lucorum*) with one yellow band on the thorax, another on the abdomen and a white tail.
* Buff-tailed Bumblebee (*B. terrestris*) is similar, but with a brown tail in the queen.
* Garden Bumblebee (*B. hortorum*) is similar, but the yellow abdominal band extends onto the thorax, with a white tail.
* Early Bumblebee (*B. pratorum*) with two yellow bands and a red tail.
* Red-tailed Bumblebee (*B. lapidarius*) is all black with a red tail.
* Common Carder Bee (*B. pascuorum*) is sandy coloured.

In hilly areas where there is bilberry and heather you may see the much less common Mountain Bumblebee (*B. monticola*), which has a yellow band across the thorax but the abdomen is covered by bright orange hairs.

top Garden Bumblebee. (Malcolm Edmunds)

above Common Carder Bee on Marjoram. (Richard Revels/ Woodfall Wild Images)

died. Sometimes, however, a cleptoparasitic nomad bee sneaks in to lay its own egg, which will hatch first so that its larva can eat the hosts egg and then develop on its food. Nomad bees (*Nomada* spp.), which look very like wasps, have few hairs, make no nests and collect no pollen. Throughout the world of bees, wasps and ants we find species which work hard to provide for their offspring and others which do no work but cash in on their labours.

The Tawny Mining Bee (*Andrena fulva*), with foxy-red hair on its thorax and abdomen, is commonly found in gardens in spring where it throws up mini–volcanoes of soil around its nest entrances in flower beds and sandy lawns. A recent study (Paxton and Pohl 1999) found that about 20% of the bees which emerged from the nests next year were the nomad bees which particularly afflict this species. *Andrena haemorrhoa*, which has blood-red hair on the thorax and a shiny black

245

This bee's body is covered with bright red hair. The female often visits garden flowers and collects pollen on a brush of hairs underneath her body. She makes her cells out of mud which sets hard (hence her name), in any sort of cylindrical tunnel which she can find, such as nail holes in wood or walls. In recent years, with a decline in bee-keeping in many areas due to the *Varroa* mite, interest has developed in encouraging this bee as a pollinator. It is easy to encourage it to nest in gardens, as is described in a book by Christopher O'Toole.

Red Mason Bee.
(Oxford Bee
Company)

abdomen, is also common in gardens in spring, and has its own nomad bee *Nomada ruficornis. Andrena scotica* is another common spring species which resembles a brown Honeybee and often comes into houses in May-June. It mines its tunnels behind unmortared retaining walls around rockeries, etc., and its habit of flying up and down walls

below Female Wall Mason Bee on Bird's-foot Trefoil.
(Neil Robinson)

Box 11.23 *The Wall Mason Bee* (Osmia parietina)

This rare solitary bee was first described in 1828 flying around walls near Ambleside, which led its discoverer to give it the scientific name of *parietina* meaning 'wall'). It is classed as Nationally Rare: Red Data Book 3 (Falk 1991). It is mainly black, with red-brown hair on the thorax. The abdomen has a blue metallic glint and the female has a black pollen brush underneath. Adult bees appear to be dependent on flowers of Common Bird's-foot-trefoil, from which it collects pollen and nectar (Robinson 1996). In Lancashire its habitat is open, sheltered areas in scrubby woodland on limestone, with reflective rock and patches of Common Bird's-foot-trefoil. The only records of this bee within the last five years are of three populations in Lancashire, four in Cumbria and two at coastal sites on the Lleyn Peninsula in Wales. The Lancashire/Cumbria sites represent the largest concentration of populations currently known in Britain, and thus are of major importance nationally.

looking for gaps causes it to fly in through transom windows. If you find what looks like a Hive Bee on the inside of a window at this time of year it will probably be this species. Its parasite is the equally common *Nomada marshamella*, a nomad bee very like a black and yellow wasp with orange legs.

A different kind of solitary bee which often visits garden flowers is the Red Mason Bee (Box 11.22), while Lancashire also has nationally important populations of the Wall Mason Bee, one of Britain's rarest bees (Box 11.23).

The picture for wasps is similar to that for bees. There are 6 species which are social (or anti-social, depending on your viewpoint!) – their pestering habits and nests delicately constructed of *papier maché* are well known. There are also about 200 solitary species in Britain, of which over 70 are known in our area (Garland and Appleton 1994), ranging from black and yellow species as big as social wasps to tiny black insects. One of the commonest is the Field Digger Wasp (*Mellinus arvensis*) which captures large flies and brings them back to its holes in south-facing sandy banks on roadsides, riversides and sand dunes etc. right through to September. The Sand Wasp (*Ammophila sabulosa*) with its amazingly slender red and black body can also often be seen on sand dunes. Some new species of wasps have recently arrived in North West England (Box 11.24).

Field Digger Wasp beside her burrow.
(Neil Robinson)

Box 11.24 *Wasps recently arrived in the North West*

The Bee-wolf (*Philanthus triangulum*) is a large black and yellow European wasp that preys exclusively on Hive Bees, which it stings and carries slung underneath it to its burrows in sandy places. After first becoming widely established on the south coast in the 1980s it has spread rapidly northwards and is now established on the Sefton coast.

Another wasp that has moved north to reach Lancashire since the 1980s is the social wasp *Dolichovespula media*, known, for want of a better name, as the Median Wasp – singularly inappropriate as it is larger than the other social wasps and is armed with a correspondingly more powerful sting.

Among the dozen or so species of ants which occur in Lancashire the commonest is probably the tiny black *Lasius niger* which nests under stones in countryside, gardens and cities – it might well be called the pavement ant. More conspicuous are the mounds of grass-covered soil on undisturbed grassland built by the Yellow Meadow Ant (*Lasius flavus*), but it also nests under stones. The largest species is the Red Wood Ant (*Formica rufa*) whose huge mound nests of twigs and leaves can be seen beside paths in Eaves Wood and Gait Barrows NNR in Silverdale. It also occurs on Arnside Knott, which is about its northern limit in England (Robinson 2001). Even ants are not immune from scroungers. The tiny ant *Formicoxenus nitidulus* lives in their nests, stealing food from its hosts but not being harmed by them (Robinson 1998, 1999).

Bee-wolf about to take prey into her burrow.
(Neil Robinson)

Mound of Red Wood Ant near Silverdale.
(Jennifer Newton)

Lancashire Beetles, by Steve Cross

Introduction

When the geneticist and biologist J. B. S. Haldane was asked by a theologian what could be inferred about the work of the Creator from a study of His works, the classic reply was that He seemed to have 'an inordinate fondness for beetles'. Indeed one in four species of animal in the world is a beetle, with over 360,000 known species, and probably several million more not known. There are over 4,000 species in Britain and over half of these occur in Lancashire. Indeed Lancashire is the northernmost outpost for many southern species and the southernmost county for some northern species.

In Britain beetles range in size from less than a millimetre for the featherwing beetles found locally in decaying timber, fungus and leaf litter to over 8 cm for the Stag Beetle (*Lucanus cervus*) of southern England. Although most species are herbivores, there are also predators, carrion and dung feeders, fungivores, and even parasites. They inhabit every terrestrial and freshwater ecosystem. One of the main reasons for their success is the protection for the soft, vulnerable hindwings by the hardened forewings, giving some a tank-like toughness.

The diversity of beetles

Some of our most familiar beetles are the predatory ground beetles (Box 11.25). Many of the rove beetles (Staphylinidae), with their shortened elytra (or wing cases), are also predators: when threatened the fierce looking Devil's Coach Horse *Staphylinus olens* mimics a scorpion by arching its back as though it was about to sting. This is all bluff, but

249

Box 11.25 *Ground beetles (family Carabidae)*

The familiar, mainly black ground beetles (though some have dazzling bright metallic colours) are fierce predators and can act as biological pest controls. With nearly two hundred species to be found in the county, ground beetles are to be found everywhere, but they usually hide away under stones, logs or leaf litter during the day. Their sharp jaws and fast movements make short work of their invertebrate prey. Some are so terrestrial that their wings are fused together and they are incapable of flight. This is the case with *Cychrus caraboides*, making it a good indicator of ancient woodland, such as at the Trust's Red Scar Woods Nature Reserve and Brock Valley woods, where it feeds on snails.

The Violet Ground Beetle (*Carabus violaceus*) is common and conspicuous in gardens and fields,

The Green Tiger Beetle is surely our most beautiful ground beetle. (Mike Atkinson)

black with a violet sheen on the edge of the wing case. The adult is surprisingly long-lived for a beetle, surviving for up to nine months.

The Green Tiger Beetle (*Cicindela campestris*), a lovely green beetle with yellow spots and a bronzy metallic sheen, is local, though widespread in Lancashire on sandy soils from Ainsdale to Longridge Fell and Little Hawes Water. A much rarer tiger beetle is described in Box 11.26.

the sharp fangs are not, and they can deliver a nasty bite that could break the skin.

Carrion feeders include the familiar black or black and orange burying and sexton beetles (*Nicrophorus* spp. and related genera, family Silphidae) that bury the carcasses of small mammals and birds to be fed on by their larvae.

Box 11.26 The Northern Dune Tiger Beetle (Cicindela hybrida)

This long-legged, fast-running, conspicuous, brown beetle with creamy-yellow stripes and tinges of red, green and purple iridescence is found on the sandy areas of the dunes from Birkdale to Altcar Rifle Range on the Sefton coast. Although locally abundant, it is found on only two dune systems in Britain, Sefton and the Drigg-Eskmeals Dunes of Cumbria, but it was found on dunes in North Wales at the beginning of the twentieth century. However it is commoner on the continent: Britain is at the north-western limit of the range of this heat-loving insect.

Beetles are active from April to October on the open sand along paths and other dry open sand areas of the dunes. It is a fierce, active predator that will take any small insect (especially ants) or other invertebrate as food and chew it with its large 'fangs'. Breeding occurs in early summer and the larvae live in burrows in the sand, catching any unwary ant or other insect within range of their powerful jaws as they sit at the mouth of their burrow. Larvae and overwintering adults spend the winter buried in the sand. The conservation of this species involves finding the right balance of enough open sand for it to live in, without going too far and opening the dunes to just bare sand and losing the binding vegetation.

Northern Dune Tiger Beetle.
(Phil Smith)

Two colourful species of burying beetle, Nicrophorus investigator and Oiceoptoma thoracica.
(Peter Smith, left, and Ken Blamire)

Land Invertebrates:
Beetles

The Cockchafer flies
in May and June,
but its large larva
living underground
provides good food
for Blackbirds and
Starlings.
(Mike Atkinson)

The Scarabaeidae – scarabs and chafers – are dung and plant feeders; they include the large, conspicuous Cockchafer or Maybug (*Melolontha melolontha*), which can be a pest of grasslands and can often fly straight in to a lighted window at night with a frighteningly loud thud. Another member of the family that you sometimes come across is the Rose Chafer (*Cetonia aurata*) with striking green colouration and an iridescent golden sheen, found in the summer on large flowers.

Click beetles (family Elateridae) are named for their ability to right themselves if they fall over on their backs, the spring like mechanism makes the distinctive clicking sound. The wireworm larva of *Agriotes lineatus* is a familiar garden and agricultural pest, and a favourite food of Starlings and Rooks. The military-like soldier and sailor beetles of

Oil Beetle.
(Jennifer Newton)

252

Ladybirds are well known to all, even to very young children, though not as many know that there are 42 species in Britain. The lady they are named after is the Virgin Mary and amongst the many tales, myths and rhymes for these aphid predators is an old Lancashire name of God's Horses.

Found from coast to hilltop, the most familiar and numerous are the Two-spot Ladybird (*Adalia bipunctata*), Seven-spot Ladybird (*Coccinella septempunctata*) and 22-spot Ladybird (*Psyllobora vigintiduopunctata*), the latter unusual in feeding on mildew, not aphids. Some species are very variable in colour and pattern, with the 10-spot Ladybird (*Adalia decempunctata*) having over 120 different named pattern forms. The bright colours acts as warning of alkaloids and they will also reflex-bleed nasty smelling yellow blood from their leg joints.

1976 was the year of the ladybird plague, when numbers exploded and everywhere was literally crawling with them, and they even bit people too, not normal behaviour.

top The Eyed Ladybird (*Anatis ocellata*) is one of our largest and most beautiful ladybirds.
(*Ken Blamire*)

above The Orange Ladybird (*Halyzia 16-guttata*) is one of a few species of ladybird that feed on mildews rather than aphids.
(*Ken Blamire*)

the family Cantharidae include a common species *Rhagonycha fulva*, sometimes called the 'Bonking Beetle' due to its seemingly never ending mating on umbel flowers during the summer. The Oil Beetle (*Meloe proscarabeus*), with its shortened wing cases and oily secretions when disturbed, is a parasite of solitary bees and an occasional find in Lancashire.

Much smaller are the ladybirds, many of which eat aphids and so are the gardener's friend (Box 11.27). The ladybird-like plant feeding leaf, flea and tortoise beetles (family Chrysomelidae) include the black and yellow striped, potato feeding Colorado Beetle (*Leptinotarsa decemlineata*), probably best known from the 'wanted posters' of the 1950s and 1960s. However, the majority of species are restricted to a single (or small range) of flowering plant species. The slug like larvae can be found on most plants you search.

Land Invertebrates:
Beetles

The long-nosed weevils are a massive family of over 600 species with elbow-angled antennae (the Curculionidae and Apionidae). They include the black Vine Weevil (*Otiorhynchus sulcatus*), which people with potplants or greenhouses may know: in this species there are usually no males, only females! The genera *Apion*, *Sitona* and *Phyllobius* provide a host of colourful weevils that can be commonly seen on a wide range of flowering plants. Some weevils are pests of stored foods, and there are a variety of other beetles that damage food and fabrics, many of which are now cosmopolitan (Box 11.28).

above Larder Beetle (*Dermestes lardarius*). (Stephen Dalton/ NHPA)

right Australian Spider Beetle. (Stephen Dalton/ NHPA)

Box 11.28 *Stored Product Beetles*

Animal skins and woollen items can be decimated by the larvae of carpet and museum beetles (*Attagenus* and *Anthrenus* spp.) and hide beetles (*Dermestes* spp.). The larvae are hairy and known as 'woolly bears'. They leave their cast skins on their food, and moult six times before they are ready to pupate.

Food in the larder is the target of the Larder and bacon beetles (*Dermestes* spp.), Biscuit or Drugstore Beetles (*Stegobium paniceum*), and spider beetles (*Ptinus* and *Niptus* spp., family Ptinidae). The Australian Spider Beetle (*Ptinus tectus*) did not reach this country until 1900, but is now widespread throughout feeding on dried animal or plant products, in bird nests, on carrion and even strong spices. They are spider like in shape and the larvae produce silk.

Stored grain and grain derivatives can be decimated by Grain and Rice Weevils (*Sitophilus granarius* and *S. oryzae*), Mealworm Beetles (*Tenebrio molitor*), flour beetles (*Tribolium* spp.) and grain beetles (*Oryzaephilus* spp.).

Timber is the food of the striking and large longhorn beetles (family Cerambycidae) which include the wasp-mimicking Wasp Beetle (*Clytus arietis*) and the spectacular black and yellow *Saperda scalaris* found in the Lune Valley woods (Newton 1998). The large green Musk Beetle (*Aromia moschata*) with its musky emissions can commonly be found around willows. Other wood and bark feeders include the bark beetles (Scolytidae), best known for the Elm Bark Beetle *Scolytus scolytus*, the infamous spreader of Dutch Elm Disease Fungus *Ophiostoma ulmi*. The Woodworm or Furniture Beetle (*Anobium punctatum*) may destroy your furniture, but the Deathwatch Beetle (*Xestobium rufovillosum*) needs very large oak beams such as in churches, halls and barns to feed on. In such places, listen out for the tapping of the male as it head-bangs to call to females. Even timber on the strandline of the beach or harbourside wharves can be a food-source for the Wharfborer (*Nacerdes melanura*). Many exotic beetles from different parts of the world have been imported into Lancashire amongst timber and other products, especially bark beetles and longhorn beetles.

Rare Lancashire beetles include the pselaphid beetle *Plectophloeus erichsoni*, only known in Britain from a 1981 specimen found in Botany Bay Wood near Worsley. The subterranean, endangered dung beetles *Aegialia rufa* and *Aphodius brevis* are currently only known in Britain from the Sefton coast dunes.

Although some beetles are large, conspicuous and easy to identify, the majority are small, hard to find and difficult to name without a microscope and specialist literature. However, everywhere you go in Lancashire you will find beetles.

above The longhorn beetle *Rhagium mordax*. (Jennifer Neston)

top Wasp Beetle. (Mike Atkinson)

255

Land Invertebrates:
Beetles

Other Insects, *by Simon Hayhow and Malcolm Edmunds*

With over 20,000 species of insect in Britain this book has only been able to mention a small percentage of those that occur in Lancashire. More specialist identification guides and keys, recording schemes, journal and distribution atlases are available which enable anyone to find out more.

Many of the insects not covered in the main sections are very small, difficult to identify and often secretive. Despite their size, however, some will be familiar from domestic situations in our homes or as serious agricultural pests.

Bristletails (order Thysanura) are less than 20 mm long with thread-like antennae and three tail filaments. The Silverfish (*Lepisma saccharina*) is often seen scurrying away from a neglected corner of a kitchen or bathroom cupboard where it has been scavenging on starchy remains like flour, paper or glue. The majority of bristletails live in the soil, under bark and in other dark and humid places, as do the two-tailed bristletails (Diplura) and proturans (Protura). These are all primitive wingless insects, as are the very much more numerous collembolans or springtails (Collembola). Springtails have a large forked organ at

Silverfish.
(Stephen Dalton/ NHPA)

Mass of springtails (*Lipura maritima*) or the surface of a tidal pool. Related species occur on freshwater pools, but most springtails live in soil.
(Bob Gibbons/ Woodfall Wild Images)

the tip of the abdomen folded beneath their body, and this can be flipped so that they can jump several centimetres into the air to escape from predators. Springtails occur under rockery plants and in soil or leaf-litter, but the ones from deeper in the soil lack the jumping organ and instead of being brown and camouflaged they are white.

Booklice (Psocoptera) are soft-bodied and rarely exceed 6 mm in length. Most eat pollen grains, algae or minute fungi and live outside buildings including in birds' nests. The indoor species are mostly wingless and live among paper, where they feed on minute traces of mould on infrequently used books. They can do considerable damage to old and often valuable books and papers.

The biting lice (Mallophaga) contain many species but they are poorly known and little-studied in Lancashire (or elsewhere). Most are less than 5 mm long and are primarily parasites on birds and mammals, feeding on skin, fur, feathers and blood. The Shaft Louse (*Menopon gallinae*) is an important pest of poultry.

The sucking lice (Anoplura) are exclusively parasitic on mammals whose blood they suck through highly-specialised mouthparts. The Human Louse (*Pediculus humanus*) is familiar to us. There are two sub-species, which may actually be separate species: the occurrence of the Body Louse is related to poor hygiene, but Head Lice can stand any amount of washing. These are the 'nits' which occur in infestations in the hair of school children. The Crab Louse (*Pthirus pubis*) is largely confined to pubic hair but may turn up on eyebrows and eyelashes.

Thrips (Thysanoptera) are minute, slender, usually black or brown and are commonly found on flowers. They sometimes occur in

Male scorpion-fly *Panorpa communis* with its swollen genital appendage resembling a scorpion sting. *(Peter Perfect/ Woodfall Wild Images)*

The delicate green lacewings have predatory larvae that eat aphids. This one is probably *Chrysoperla carnea*.
(Malcolm Edmunds)

Larvae of the braconid wasp *Apanteles glomeratus* emerging from a Large White caterpillar and pupating beside the now empty skin.
(Ken Blamire)

incredible numbers and several species, like the Pea Thrip (*Kakothrips robustus*), can be agricultural pests.

Fleas (Siphonaptera) are wingless and the adults suck blood. Different species of flea can be found on Moles, dogs, cats, Rabbits and many other mammals. Some are host-specific but others will feed on the blood of a variety of hosts. The Human Flea is primarily a parasite of Foxes, Badgers and other hole-dwelling mammals and was not introduced to humans until they began to live in caves.

Other small insect orders in our area include the attractive scorpion-flies (Mecoptera), rather sinister looking earwigs (Dermaptera), both quite widespread, stylopids (Strepsiptera) which are scarce, and cockroaches (Dictyoptera) which are surprisingly frequent in catering establishments, though you may need to search for them at night-time. More welcome in the house and garden are green lacewings (Planipennia e.g. *Chrysopa* spp.) with delicate lace-like wing veins whose larvae are rapacious devourers of aphids.

Ants, bees and wasps are dealt with in their own section, but the insect order Hymenoptera also includes the Parasitica – ichneumons, chalcids, gall wasps and other parasitic wasps which parasitise the young stages of other insects. There are over 3,000 British species but little work has been carried out in Lancashire. Most ichneumons and braconids pierce the host with their egg-laying ovipositor and lay their egg(s) inside the body. The hatching larvae concentrate on eating away the non-essential organs at first before killing it when fully grown. Through this life-history they can kill huge numbers of pest insects. For example caterpillars of the Large White Butterfly are often parasitised by the small braconid wasp *Apanteles glomeratus* which to some extent controls its population. Some ichneumons are large and impressive.

The Yellow Ophion (*Ophion luteus*) is one of the commonest large ichneumons.
(Mike Atkinson)

Alder Sawfly caterpillars (*Poecilosoma pulveratum*) with warning colouration implying that they have an unpleasant taste.
(Malcolm Edmunds)

Rhyssa persuasoria has an ovipositor 40 mm long to reach wood-boring larvae, but they present no threat to humans.

The sawflies (Symphyta) are also Hymenoptera but differ by the lack of a narrow 'waist'. The 'saw' in the name refers to the shape of the egg-laying ovipositor. The larvae resemble moth caterpillars and can cause considerable horticultural damage, like the Gooseberry Sawfly (*Nematus ribesii*). Stem-boring species can damage cereals and other crops. The largest species is the impressive yellow and black Wood Wasp or Horntail (*Urocerus gigas*).

The fearsome looking Wood Wasp is actually quite harmless.
(Malcolm Edmunds)

Millipedes, Centipedes and Woodlice, *by Steve Garland*

Introduction

Millipedes, centipedes and woodlice (Box 11.29) tend to be poorly studied and often overlooked, but there have been several experts resident in the North West which has resulted in quite a good knowledge of the Lancashire fauna. They occur in a variety of habitats, including heated greenhouses, where many exotic, introduced species have been discovered across Britain in recent years, e.g. the large flat-back millipede *Oxidus gracilis*, which has been found in many such places in Lancashire.

Millipedes

Millipedes come in many different forms, snake millipedes, flat-backed millipedes, pill millipedes and the curious, tiny bristly and rarely found *Polyxenus lagurus*. They all feed on decomposing organic material and fungi. When digging in garden soil, tiny blind snake millipedes *Blaniulus guttulatus* can often be found. They are pale and

The common snake millipede *Tachypodoiulus niger*.
(Lance Gorman)

below The pink-striped *Omatoiulus sabulosus* lives on sand dunes.
(Malcolm Edmunds)

blind with red spots along their sides. These are openings of repugnatorial glands, which discharge unpleasant chemicals to deter potential predators. After handling larger species of millipede, a sniff of the fingers will reveal a pungent smell from these repellent chemicals. Larger snake millipedes, such as as *Cylindroiulus punctatus*, *C. britannicus*, *Tachypodoiulus niger*, *Iulius scandinavius* and *Ophyiulus pilosus* are very numerous in woodland throughout Lancashire, amongst leaf litter and under loose bark. The tiny brown-spotted *Proteroiulus fuscus* is also very common under loose bark. Also in woodland are found the flat-backed millipedes, which are blind and adapted to forcing their way through layers of leaf-litter. *Polydesmus angustus* and *Brachydesmus superus* are the most numerous (also found in gardens), but others such as *Polydesmus denticulatus* and P. *inconstans* may be found. Similar, but with eyes is *Nanogona polydesmoides*, *Melagona scutellare* and the rather localised species *Craspedosoma rawlinsi*. The rare flat-back *Brachychaetuma bradeae* was first discovered and described from a park in Darwen in 1917. In the sand dunes of the south Lancashire coast the snake millipede *Cylindroiulus latestriatus* is frequent.

Centipedes

Centipedes are largely predatory, with the genus *Lithobius* being particularly energetic, fast-running species with 15 pairs of legs. They have large, curved jaws which inject poison into their prey. The largest species of *Lithobius* can nip delicate skin, but the bite is not dangerous, unlike the large *Scolopendra* spp. in the tropics, which can occasionally be fatal! In most gardens across the region the large, fast-running

The common large centipede *Lithobius forficatus*.
(David Chapman/ Woodfall Wild Images

Lithobius forficatus is common under stones and amongst dead leaves. It is the only species that seems to regularly enter houses, usually at night, and it is only common in cellars. Related to the bigger tropical *Scolopendra*, with 21 pairs of legs, is *Cryptops hortensis* which is widespread in Lancashire gardens. While digging the soil one may find several species of very long slender centipedes including *Necrophloeophagus flavus*, *Geophilus imsculptus* and *Geophilus carpophagus*, which hunt tiny soil creatures. *G. carpophagus* is also one of the commonest centipedes on moorland in Bowland and the Pennines.

In woodland there are several other *Lithobius* species with *L. crassipes* the most numerous. Rotting logs and loose bark in woodland provide favourite habitats for the tiny long centipede *Brachygeophilus truncorum* and the large banded *Lithobius variegatus*.

Rocky coastal habitats are restricted to the northern part of Lancashire, near Silverdale, and here amongst the rocks the coastal centipede *Strigamia maritima* can be found.

left The woodlouse *Philoscia muscorum*. (N. A. Callow/NHPA)

right The woodlouse *Oniscus asellus*, sometimes called the Slater or Common Woodlouse. (N. A. Callow/NHPA)

Woodlice

Several species of woodlouse are widespread in gardens throughout the North West including *Oniscus asellus* (often called the Slater) and *Porcellio scaber*, both abundant under stones and logs. A close look at the contents of a compost heap may reveal a small pink woodlouse with a double yellow line down its back, *Androniscus dentiger*. This species is also common in limestone areas in northern Lancashire. Woodlice are especially diverse in limestone areas, being small terrestrial relatives of shrimps and crabs with exoskeletons containing calcium, but they are completely absent in very acidic areas such as peat bogs and mosses. Other common species on the north Lancashire limestone are *Philoscia muscorum* and *Porcellio spinicornis*. A close look at ant nests under stones in this area of the county, especially nests of the Yellow Meadow Ant, will reveal the tiny, colourless, blind *Platyarthrus hoffmanseggi*. It gains protection from the ants and feeds harmlessly on detritus in the nest. The rocky shore at Silverdale provides a home for our largest woodlouse, the coastal *Ligia oceanica*.

The pill woodlouse *Armadillidium pictum*.
(Bob Marsh)

Woodlands are particularly rich in woodlice, where sieving leaf litter can help find the smaller species, the tiniest being *Trichoniscus pygmaeus* at only 2.5 mm long. These small species are rarely recorded because they are often overlooked, although each sample of leaf litter will contain thousands of the extremely abundant *Trichoniscus pusillus*.

Four species of pill woodlouse, so named because they can roll up into a ball, are found in Lancashire. The largest and commonest species, *Armadillidium vulgare*, occurs in large numbers along the Lancashire coast and in the limestone grasslands and rocks of the Silverdale area, where the small but attractively variegated *A. pulchellum* is also fairly common. The rare *Armadillidium album* occurs only between the strand line and the dunes along the south Lancashire coast and in similar dune systems elsewhere in England. One early record for the very rare Red Data Book species *A. pictum* was from Gait Barrows NNR, but more recently it has also been found in North Lancashire on the gritstone

Box 11.30 *Our rarest woodlouse*

Warton Crag in North Lancashire has the distinction of being the site of the first discovery in Britain of a tiny woodlouse with a very long name, *Trichoniscoides saeroeensis*. This is a whitish woodlouse up to 4 mm long, with the diagnostic single pair of orange eyes visible only under a microscope. It was first found in 1964 in a piece of permanently wet timber in a disused mine on the Crag. Since then it has been found in tidal debris and shingle in scattered sites round the coast of Britain, with one other inland site in timber in a disused Victorian mine on the Isle of Man.

Jennifer Newton

screes of Clougha, and in the damp shady woodlands of Roeburndale. It seems to require very humid conditions, and in hot dry weather will burrow some distance down, even to 2 m in woodland soil, where it is very difficult to find.

Land Invertebrates:
Millipedes, Centipedes and Woodlice

Spiders in Lancashire, by Jennifer Newton

Mention spiders and the reaction is very likely to be one of horror, disgust and fear. And yet there is no British spider which is any real threat to humans, and many are very prettily marked when viewed close-up inside a glass container. The jumping spiders in particular have an engaging way of turning their heads to view the observer with two large and two small forward-facing eyes (and another four further back on the head). Spiders undoubtedly play a very important role in nature, controlling numbers of small invertebrates (including many pests) and providing food for many birds, amphibians and small mammals. They are found in practically all terrestrial habitats, from the deepest caves to mountain tops, from densely populated urban areas to undisturbed wilderness sites (Box 11.31), although only one species in the world, the Water Spider (*Argyroneta aquatica*), is able to spend its life underwater. A good place to start looking for spiders is in your house and garden (Box 11.32)

All spiders are predators feeding on a variety of small invertebrates including flies, midges, woodlice, ants and springtails. Unlike cater-

pillars which just munch their way through the food where their parents deposited them as eggs, spiders have to work to catch their food, by ensnaring in webs, chasing (wolf spiders), pouncing (jumping spiders), or lying in ambush (crab spiders). Although all spiders produce silk, they use it in many ways, to trap prey, protect their eggs, or line a retreat, but relatively few spiders produce the well-known orb webs, with the beautiful symmetry of a spiral thread with connecting radials. More common are the small sheet webs produced in thousands by the tiny money spiders which land on lawns and fields from their dispersal flights on a thread of gossamer. Money spiders (family Linyphiidae) account for about two-fifths of British spiders, with a higher proportion in northern counties. Better known are the messy cobwebs produced by House Spiders, where the spider sits on top of the web at the entrance to a retreat. A relative of the House Spider is the Funnel Web Spider (*Agelena labyrinthica*), found on the

Box 11.31 Where to look for spiders

Spiders are found everywhere:

* Houses and gardens are a good place to start
* Brownfield sites, disused quarries, railway sidings e.g. Heysham Nature Reserve, Summerseat Nature Reserve, Nob End
* Sand dunes, salt marshes and other coastal habitats e.g. Sefton coast, Fylde coast, Morecambe Bay
* Woodlands, limestone grassland with rock outcrops, other semi-natural habitats

Box 11.32 *Spiders commonly found in houses and gardens*

Houses and gardens can be very productive habitats for spiders, with 60 to 80 species recorded even from suburban homes with gardens of no great size. Among the spiders found inside houses are the well-known House Spider (which in fact covers two or three closely related species of *Tegenaria* which may hybridise), and the very distinctive Daddy-long-legs Spider (*Pholcus phalangioides*) with its slender body and very long legs. This is a relatively recent arrival in Lancashire, but now seems well established in many places. Although apparently a delicate spider it is actually quite aggressive and will attack and eat the much larger and heavier house spider. Its long legs enable it to wrap the house spider in silk, while keeping its body well away from the fangs. More common on the outside of houses are the Zebra Spider (*Salticus scenicus*), a small black and white jumping spider, and the Lace-web Spider (*Amaurobius similis*), a larger dark brown spider with cream markings, which hides in crevices in walls and fences. The surroundings of the crevices are covered in an untidy open web with a bluish tinge. The spider is very sensitive to vibrations and will rush out to attack a vibrating tuning fork held against the web.

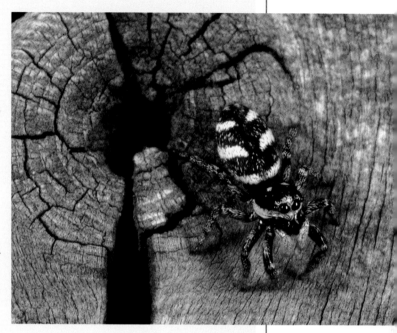

above The Zebra Spider is common on fences and walls. (*Ken Blamire*)

Sefton coast and in some numbers at Heysham Nature Reserve, where its cobwebs can cover considerable areas of the ground or low shrubs. It sits at the opening of the tunnel retreat and waits for grasshoppers and other insects to jump onto the sheet. Later in the summer the females construct complicated labyrinth webs in gorse bushes, in which the eggs are laid. The species can be common in some parts of southern England and Wales, but it is very rare this far north.

opposite The Garden Spider is widespread throughout the Trust area in urban and rural places. (*Mike Atkinson*)

More elaborate are the three-dimensional scaffolding webs of the comb-footed spiders (family Theridiidae), small spiders, many with attractive patterns on their abdomens. A good example is *Theridion sisyphium* which typically spins its web in gorse, heather or thistles. At the top of the web the female constructs a complicated retreat in which she lays her eggs, and later guards and feeds the tiny spiderlings. The remains of meals, wings, legs, and outer cases of insects cover the surface of the retreat.

265

Land Invertebrates:
Spiders

One of the most unusual webs is that of the Purse Web Spider (Atypus affinis), present in some numbers on the Trust's Warton Crag Nature Reserve and other sites in Silverdale. The web forms a tube like the finger of a glove, with an inch or two projecting above ground, and perhaps four times as much below ground. The spider lies in wait

inside the tube and when an insect walks across the tube, rushes up, its fangs piercing through the tube to catch and kill the insect from inside. It then repairs the tube and consumes its prey at leisure. *Atypus* is a surprisingly long-lived spider, taking four years to reach maturity and females surviving for perhaps another 3 or 4 years after that.

Since spiders are able to eat a variety of animal prey, in general what matters is the structure of the vegetation, rather than actual plants present. The impressive Nursery Web Spider (*Pisaura mirabilis*), present in good numbers at Summerseat Nature Reserve, and the bigger orb-web spiders like the Garden Spider (*Araneus diadematus*), *Araneus quadratus*, and *Larinioides cornutus*, all require reasonably substantial plants to fasten their webs to (like thistles, Hogweed,

The beautiful orb web of *Araneus quadratus* shows up well in September dew. (Malcolm Edmunds)

Box 11.33 *Spiders of sand dunes on the Sefton and Fylde coasts*

Sand dunes provide a very specialized habitat with a unique set of problems. Certain spiders are practically confined to sand dunes. *Arctosa perita* and *Philodromus fallax* are two rare spiders found only on sand. Both burrow into bare, mobile sand, and their mottled colouration of pinks, greys, and browns makes them very hard to spot even when not completely buried. *Sitticus saltator* is a tiny jumping spider, also confined to sand dunes and rarely seen, but recorded from both the Sefton coast and the Lytham dunes. The wolf spider *Xerolycosa miniata* prefers more vegetated sand and is less inclined to burrow but also has good camouflage colouring. *Tibellus oblongus* aligns its long narrow body with outstretched legs along a stem of marram grass, and waits for passing prey. It is found elsewhere in other rank vegetation, including reed beds, but in Lancashire is commonest along the coast. Other spiders of rank vegetation including Marram grass, brambles and rushes are the Nursery Web Spider and the orb-weavers *Araneus diadematus*, *Araneus quadratus*, *Larinioides cornutus* and the rare *Agelenatea redii*.

Box 11.34
A *Lancashire rarity*:
Arctosa cinerea

***Arctosa cinerea* is an impressively large wolf spider, up to 17mm body length, which inhabits shingle beds by fast-flowing rivers. It hides in burrows under stones, lying in wait for passing insects, and survives immersion under water for several days, as well as the** turbulence of a river in flood. It has been recorded from several shingle beds along the River Lune, so far its most southerly sites in England.

Arctosa cinerea.
(Bob Marsh)

rushes and reeds) and to provide hiding places. Bramble or Meadow-sweet leaves are favoured by *Clubiona* spp. and *Enoplognatha ovata* for protection of eggs. The leaves are folded over and fastened with silk to provide a sheltered retreat for the egg-sac and mother who stands guard until the spiderlings hatch out. All over Lancashire derelict areas and brownfield sites with rank vegetation will be much more productive for spiders than carefully manicured parks or gardens. The coastal sand dunes are especially interesting for spiders (Box 11.33).

Another very important factor is the presence of damp hiding places, under stones, logs or bark, and cracks in walls or fences. Spiders are much more prone to drying out than many insects, and are more likely to die of dehydration than lack of food. Wolf spiders often hunt their prey across bare ground, short turf, or rocks, but must have hiding places nearby. Mosses and leaf litter provide an important retreat for many ground dwelling species, and in winter this is one of the most productive habitats to search for spiders. A rare Lancashire wolf spider is described in Box 11.34).

At present 645 species of spiders have been recorded from Britain, with one or two new species added each year, and around 340 have been recorded from Lancashire, again with new additions in most years. There is still much to be found out about spiders in Lancashire and anyone prepared to spend some time on the group is very likely to be rewarded with new discoveries, perhaps even a new species for the county.

Further reading

General

Chinery, M. (1973). A *Field Guide to the Insects of Britain and Northern Europe*. Collins, London.

Chinery, M. (1986). *Collins Guide to the Insects of Britain and Western Europe*. Collins, London.

Earthworms

Edwards, C. A. and Bohlen, P. J. (1996). *Biology and Ecology of Earthworms* (3rd edn). Chapman & Hall, London.

Sims, R. W. and Gerard, B. M. (1999). *Earthworms*. Synopses of the British Fauna No. 31 (revised), Linnean Society, London.

Snails and Slugs

Kerney, M. P. and Cameron, R. A. D. (1979). *Land Snails of Britain and North-West Europe*. Collins, London.

Kerney, M. P. (1999). *Atlas of the Land and Freshwater Molluscs of Britain and Ireland*. Harley Books, Colchester.

Dragonflies

Brooks, S. and Lewington, R. (1997). *Field Guide to the Dragonflies and Damselflies of Great Britain and Ireland*. British Wildlife Publishing, Hants.

Grasshoppers

Marshall, J. A. and Haes, E. C. M. (1988). *Grasshoppers and Allied Insects of Great Britain and Ireland*. Harley Books, Colchester.

Haes, E. C. M., and Harding, P. T. (1997). *Atlas of grasshoppers, crickets and allied insects in Britain and Ireland*. JNCC & CEH, the Stationery Office, London.

Bugs

Southwood, T. R. E. and Leston, D. (1959). *Land and Water Bugs of the British Isles*. Warne, London. This is also available as a recently issued CD-ROM.

Butterflies and Moths

Asher, J., Warren, M. and Fox, R. (2001). *The Millennium Atlas of Butterflies in Britain and Ireland*. Oxford University Press, Oxford.

Porter, J. (1997). *The Colour Identification Guide to Caterpillars of the British Isles*. Viking, London.

Skinner, B. (1984). *Colour Identification Guide to Moths of the British Isles*. Viking, London.

Thomas, J. A. (1989). *Hamlyn Guide to the Butterflies of the British Isles*. Hamlyn, London.

Thomas, J. and Lewington, R. (1991). *The Butterflies of Britain and Ireland*. National Trust, London.

Wildlife of
Lancashire

County-wide organisations:

Butterfly Conservation (Lancashire and Merseyside Branch): contact Ms. L. Sivell 01524 752247

Lancashire and Cheshire Entomological Society: contact Mr D Barlow at Liverpool Museum

Lancashire Moth Group: contact Mr. S. Palmer on 01772 861570

Flies

Colyer, C.N. and Hammond, C.O. (1968). *Flies of the British Isles*. Warne, London.

Gilbert, F. S. (1986). *Hoverflies*. Naturalists' Handbooks 5. C.U.P., Cambridge.

Stubbs, A. E. and Falk, S. J. (1983). *British Hoverflies*. British Entomological and Natural History Society, London.

Bees, Wasps and Ants

O'Toole, C. and Raw, A. (1991). *Bees of the World*. Blandford, London.

Andrewes, C. (1969). *The Lives of Wasps and Bees*. Chatto & Windus, London.

Benton, E. (2000). *The Bumblebees of Essex*. Lopinga Books, Wimbish, Essex.

Prys-Jones, O. and Corbet, S. A. (1987). *Bumblebees*. Naturalists' Handbooks 6. C.U.P., Cambridge.

Yeo, P. F. and Corbet, S. A. (1983). *Solitary Wasps*. Naturalists' Handbooks 3. C.U.P., Cambridge.

Skinner, G. J. and Allen, G. W. (1996). *Ants*. Naturalists' Handbooks 24. Richmond, Slough.

O'Toole, C. (2000). *The Red Mason Bee: Taking the Sting out of Bee-keeping*. Osmia Publications, Banbury.

The Bees, Wasps and Ants Recording Society (BWARS) produces a newsletter, Starter Pack and Provisional Atlases. For information about BWARS, and how to join, visit its website at http://www.bwars.com

Beetles

Harde, K. W. (1998). *A Field Guide in Colour to Beetles*. Blitz Editions, Leicester.

Centipedes, Millipedes and Woodlice

Hopkin, S. P. (1991). *A key to the Woodlice of Britain and Ireland*. Aidgap Key, Field Studies Council Publications.

Blower, J. G. (1985). *Millipedes*. Linnean Society Synopses of the British Fauna (New Series), Number 35. Brill/Backhuys, London.

Eason, E. H. (1964). *Centipedes of the British Isles*. Warne, London.

The British Myriapod and Isopod Group gives information on identification and distribution. Contact the Biological Records Centre, Monks Wood, Huntingdon PE27 6TU or visit their website on http://www.bmig.org.uk/

Spiders

Bristowe, W. S. (1958). *The World of Spiders*. Collins New Naturalist, London.

Jones, D. (1983). *The Country Life Guide to Spiders of Britain and Northern Europe*. Country Life Books, Feltham.

Preston-Mafham, K. and Preston-Mafham, R. (1996). *The Natural History of Spiders*. Crowood Press, Ramsbury, Marlborough.

Roberts, M. J. (1995). *Collins Field Guide: Spiders of Britain and Northern Europe*. Harper-Collins, London.

Chapter 12

Lancashire – Conservation and the Future

Tim Mitcham

opposite Corn
Marigold growing
near Rufford.
(Jon Hickling)

'Future generations are unlikely to condone our lack of
concern for the natural world that supports all life.'

Rachel Carson, *Silent Spring*

In spite of tremendous pressures from industry, agriculture and
housing, Lancashire, Manchester and North Merseyside still retain a
rich wildlife heritage. Many species of international importance live
here or use it as a migratory service station. However, we should not
take this richness for granted: conflicting pressures from humans
could enhance our wildlife richness (our biodiversity), but they could
equally lead to its further impoverishment.

Between 1968 and 2000 far more species of bird have been added
to the breeding list of Lancashire than have been lost, indeed there
are more species breeding now than in historical times (Pyefinch and
Golborn 2001). Studies into our flora show a similar story with many
introductions of non-native species swelling the variety of plants that
can be seen (Greenwood 2003). But this apparently rosy picture hides
the fact that large numbers of both common and rare native species
have suffered severe declines in recent decades, including Yellow
Wagtail, Lapwing, Song Thrush, Meadow Brown butterfly (*Maniola
jurtina*), Red Squirrel, Corn Marigold and Cowslip (*Primula veris*).

The scale of habitat loss

Change in our wildlife habitats is not new. Since the last major glaciation over 10,000 years ago, our plant and animal communities have been in a state of continual change. Human activity has been just one of the many forces causing change, but the scale and intensity of human activity in recent times means that change has accelerated enormously. Decisions today will have profound effects upon habitats and the species that depend upon them. The loss of land to urbanisation, agricultural improvement, pollution, industry and transport networks over the last one hundred and fifty years has resulted in wildlife habitats being highly modified or reduced to isolated fragments.

Over the last two hundred years, Lancashire has lost about 40 native vascular plant species (i.e. flowering plants, conifers and ferns) (Greenwood 2003). Many of the key losses occurred between 1850 and 1914, a period of huge industrial and urban growth (Savidge *et al.* 1963), but collecting of plants and animals and persecution of some

Steam navvies were used to pull down the high dune crests into the hollows and make the ground suitable for development. This 1893 photograph of Fairhaven between Lytham and St Anne's shows the destruction of a once very extensive habitat.
(*From* Lytham St Anne's. A Pictorial History, *by* R. A. Haley, 1995)

species were also significant factors. Lancashire's dunes illustrate the story of habitat and species loss:

above Rabbiting in Lytham Sandhills in 1878 by Richard Ansdell (1815–85) gives the wilderness feel of the once extensive Lytham dunes.
(Fylde Borough Council)

> Up to about the year 1875 the coast from Blackpool to Lytham was truly a botanist's paradise and presented a plant association scarcely to be met with elsewhere in England, except on the similar and perhaps even richer coast of South Lancashire between Southport and Formby. The sand dunes were practically undisturbed and in the neighbourhood of where St Annes now stands, extended a considerable distance inland … On the land side of these dunes were flat stretches of boggy and sandy marsh, whilst inland again were more sandhills and marshes succeeding one another and intermixed. The boggy hollows formed beautiful natural gardens, filled during the summer with a wealth of flowers delightful to behold; and in them grew many rare plants and mosses, unnoticed by the ordinary passer-by but of fascinating interest to the botanist.
> (Wheldon and Wilson 1907)

These authors witnessed the destruction of the dunes through urbanisation and conversion into golf links.

'God's grace and Pilling Moss are endless' is a Fylde saying which gives the impression of the large areas of relatively untouched wilderness that once existed. The floras of the nineteenth-century record mossland plants including Bog-rosemary, Bog Asphodel, Bog-myrtle, White Beak-sedge (*Rhynchospora alba*) and all three species of

below Round-leaved Sundew was once a common plant on the mosses of Manchester; here it is digesting an ant.
(Tim Mitcham)

275

Marsh Gentian.
(Malcolm Edmunds)

sundew (*Drosera* spp.), as 'common on all the mosses around Manchester' (Savidge *et. al.* 1963). Extensive drainage schemes in the nineteenth century reclaimed a great deal of the bog-land which was fertilised with 'night-soil', so many of these typical plant associations were lost and replaced by rich farmland. Such changes were applauded even by naturalists (see Box 12.1).

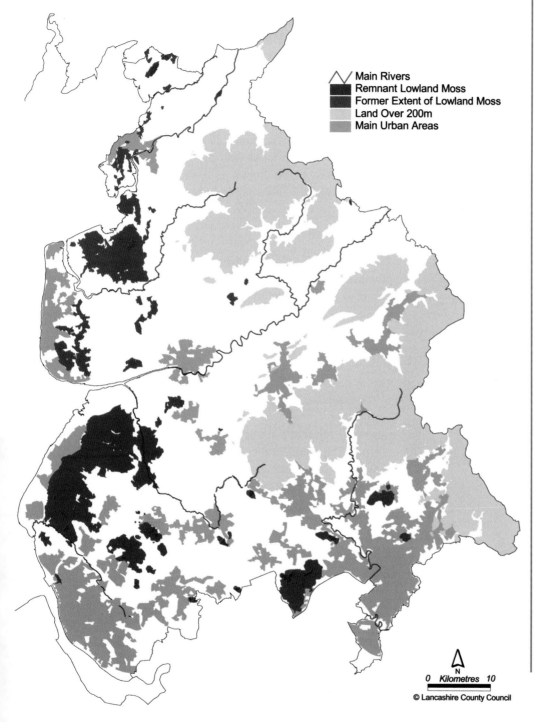

Legend:

- Main Rivers
- Remnant Lowland Moss
- Former Extent of Lowland Moss
- Land Over 200m
- Main Urban Areas

N

0   *Kilometres*   10

© Lancashire County Council

Map 12
Decline of Lowland Mossland in the Wildlife Trust Area.

The former extent of lowland mossland has been derived from a variety of sources including geological drift maps of various dates. In present day Lancashire an attempt was made to determine the pre-1600 mossland boundary as part of the Historic Landscape Characterisation Programme.
(Nik Bruce)

opposite The rewetting of the impoverished Astley Moss has resulted in dramatic improvements to plant communities.
(Graham Standring)

*Lancashire –
Conservation and the Future*

Great Crested Grebes breed in many lakes and gravel pits throughout the Trust area.
(Peter Smith)

The scale of this loss can be illustrated by Chat Moss to the north of Manchester. In the middle of the nineteenth century this was one of the most extensive lowland raised bogs in England covering 2,650 hectares. By 1989 it had been reduced by 92% to 233 hectares (Greater Manchester Countryside Unit 1989), and the remaining mossland was in a very poor state. With many characteristic species missing, it has a lowered water table and has been invaded by Purple Moor-grass, heath and woodland. It is remarkable that any mossland at all survived, however, by a quirk of historical fortune, a proportion of this land was earmarked for waste tipping by the Coal Board but never developed. This area, known as Astley Moss, was bought from the Coal Board in 1988 and is now a Wildlife Trust Nature Reserve.

Changing attitudes

This massive change in land use and associated loss of species prompted a change in attitudes to the way landscape should be managed. The late Victorian era saw an increase in popularity of nature study and many natural history societies and field clubs were established in Lancashire. These societies recorded and raised awareness of the wildlife in their areas, and some became actively involved in campaigning for change – the beginnings of nature conservation.

The Selborne Society, established in 1885, was the first national organisation primarily concerned with safeguarding wildlife, but many naturalists felt that a society specifically concerned with bird protection was required. To fill the vacuum, Mrs Robert W. Williamson of Didsbury, Manchester, formed a new society in 1889 to counter the growing trade in feathers of grebes, herons, egrets and other tropical birds. Such was the demand that by 1860 the Great Crested Grebe was almost extinct in Britain. Originally called the Society for the Protection of Birds, it gained its royal charter in 1904 to become the Royal Society for the Protection of Birds (RSPB) and now has over a million members.

In spite of the many excellent natural history societies in Lancashire and the national RSPB, wildlife habitats in our area continued to deteriorate throughout the twentieth century. This led to the formation of the Wildlife Trust whose primary aim is to protect and enhance the wildlife of our area (see Box 12.2).

Wildlife of Lancashire

The Wildlife Trust was founded in 1962 by a group of naturalists who called it The Lancashire Naturalists' Trust. Initially a group of active amateurs, It has now metamorphosed into the Wildlife Trust for Lancashire, Manchester and North Merseyside. Today it blends the aspirations and experience of amateur enthusiasts with the drive and expertise of professionals as it continues to campaign and safeguard wildlife of this region with an annual budget of more than a million pounds.

The Wildlife Trust works closely with other local and national organisations in its campaign for a change in the way we look at our environment. The important message is that a rich and diverse wildlife is essential for environmental well-being, a healthy economy and high quality of life. Wildlife should play a central part in decisions on how our landscape is managed.

Trust Volunteers working at Fox Hill Bank Local Nature Reserve, Oswaldtwistle.
(Tim Mitcham)

A new agricultural revolution

Since the Second World War the landscape has changed as a consequence of the following farming practices:

* land drainage,
* increasing the nutrient status of land with fertilisers,
* application of herbicides and pesticides,
* loss of hedgerows,
* the move to winter sowing of cereals and resultant loss of stubble,
* the productivity of silage systems,
* the loss of hay production,
* increased stocking densities.

All have taken their toll on wildlife. There has been a dramatic loss of semi-natural grassland, and most of those that remain are still without statutory protection. It has taken 40 years for the dark side of the post-war agricultural revolution to become fully apparent. In addition to damaging the environment, it has also eroded farmers' status in society, caused collapse of farm incomes, and encouraged the wastefulness of centralised food retail systems. Many of these ills have been brought about by a policy based on post-war recovery, food security, new technology, increased efficiency and low cost to the

Intensive agriculture has pushed wildlife populations to the limits of survival.
(Tim Mitcham)

consumer, all championed by the European Union's Common Agri-cultural Policy (CAP).

To their credit, many landowners have resisted inducements to 'improve' every piece of marginal land. Many of Lancashire's remaining ancient woodlands, moorlands and species-rich grasslands owe their continued existence to landowners with a commitment to the principles of custodianship. The importance of game shooting as an economic and leisure activity has maintained valuable habitats since medieval times, particularly in the uplands. However, losses continue and current agri-environment schemes provide inadequate payment incentive to encourage large numbers of farmers to sign up to agreements. Despite repeated efforts on the part of local bodies, none of Lancashire has benefited from landscape designations that enhance environmental payments to land managers such as the Environmentally Sensitive Area Scheme that has operated in Cumbria and elsewhere.

The end of 2001 heralded the all clear on a devastating epidemic of foot and mouth disease. The epidemic stimulated a major debate on the future of farming, its role in the food chain and its impact upon rural communities, cherished landscapes and wildlife habitats. The results of this debate will hopefully lead to a new holistic vision of the countryside that comes with the resources to sustain a transformation.

Initial signs are positive with the Government's Policy Commission report on *The Future of Farming and Food* (2002), chaired by Sir Donald Curry. The Commission has mapped out a shift in policy as profound as that which inspired the 1947 Agriculture Act with its commitment to raising domestic crop yields.

The closing of the footpath network and loss of access for contracting work due to foot and mouth disease showed how the countryside was vital to industries other than food production. The importance of landscape quality in attracting tourists and as a resource for recreation, forestry and craft was very evident, and in some areas of the North West tourism easily outstripped agriculture as the main economic driver. However, most of our landscape is still managed by the farming community, so their role in caring for wildlife habitats in rural areas over the next few decades will be crucial.

Traditional hay meadow management at Daisy Nook, Oldham c.1890. Lancashire is rapidly losing its last few remnants of hay meadow, a sustainable system appropriate to the moorland fringe. (*Oldham Local Studies and Archives*)

Lancashire –
Conservation and the Future

Box 12.3 *The Environmental Economy of North West England* (2000)

This report, commissioned by the Regional Biodiversity Steering Group for North West England, brought together information about the environmental sector and its value to the economy of the North West. It found that companies, local authorities and charities spent almost £3 billion per annum, much of it on provision of environmental goods and services, and environmental work linked to agriculture, with indirect benefits of a clean attractive environment for tourism and inward investment. The sector employs over 100,000 people – that's 5.6% of all employment in the region. A case study of the RSPB's Leighton Moss Reserve showed that it generated visitor spending of £1.65m per year supporting at least 47 full time equivalent jobs in the local economy.

The report demonstrated for the first time that the environmental sector is not just about selling a bit of locally made charcoal, but is a significant force for the future improvement of the North West. It aimed to raise awareness of the scale of work and investment in our natural environment and the need for further investment for the benefit of the economy and the quality of life of the region's citizens.

Wildlife of
Lancashire

The 'Curry Report' highlights the need to maintain countryside skills and local traditions. It suggests a move towards a more diverse rural economy with wildlife and landscape quality of prime importance. CAP reform could pave the way towards a new agricultural revolution. It could support farmers for regimes that encourage quality products, local processing and marketing, and also pay realistic fees for stewardship of wildlife and countryside. These changes could have a profoundly positive impact upon wildlife in the wider countryside and give real hope to many threatened habitats and species.

Wildlife and the economy

The move towards regional government has inspired a host of new policy documents that have developed the idea of sustainable development. The Northwest Development Agency's *England's North West – a strategy towards* 2020 (1999) outlined policies which interlinked the economy, society and environment. It recommended that progress should be made on all three fronts without jeopardising future options. Similar policies are now being developed at a local level where they take into account local situations and appropriate actions. This move towards holistic policy and planning gives cause for optimism that wildlife and environmental quality are no longer the poor relation of economic gain, and their importance to quality of life is accepted. The environmental sector has grown significantly and is now a major driving force in the North West's economy (see Box 12.3).

The 'Bowland Initiative' of 1999–2001 is a good example of local agencies, including English Nature and the Wildlife Trust, working together with the Ministry of Agriculture Fisheries and Food to find local solutions in the Forest of Bowland Area of Outstanding Natural Beauty (AONB). In the light of declining farm incomes it explored new ways of supporting sustainable farming so that the natural environment and local communities also benefited. The Initiative greatly simplified procedures for farmers wishing to access financial help and advice, and achieved notable economic, environmental and social gains.

Living landscapes

There are now signs of new policies and initiatives based upon the landscape as a working ecological system rather than the previous focus on parts of the landscape in isolation. They involve partnerships, for example

* The Mersey Basin Campaign (see Box 12.4)

opposite The RSPB's Leighton Moss Nature Reserve has shown that wildlife conservation can be a major contributor to the local economy as well as a haven for wildlife. *(David Mower)*

283

Multi-agency
working in the
Forest of Bowland
has highlighted the
importance of
planning for
sustainability if we
are to safeguard
important
landscapes.
(Jon Hickling)

* ELWOOD (East Lancashire Woodlands) initiative which encourages the restoration and creation of new green corridors and the development of nature conservation sites and sustainable access routes.
* In the Forest of Bowland both the Environment Agency and English Nature are working with landowners to create new habitat for upland species by allowing water to remain within the soil, thereby also helping to prevent flooding in low lying areas. By preventing bank erosion they are promoting healthy fisheries and encouraging the leisure industry.
* Nature reserves are now seen as a source of local genetic material and are being used as a seed source to develop new habitat and to restore post-industrial sites.
* On the Sefton coast active policies to encourage sand dune development are providing protection from the sea in the face of a changing climate in place of unsustainable concrete defences.

Who will pay for all these changes, you might ask? We will, of course

Box 12.4 *The Mersey Basin Campaign:*
Partnership Leads the Way

This is a 20 year, international award winning campaign that has pioneered joint working between government agencies, industry and the voluntary sector, including the Wildlife Trust, to achieve a remarkable turn-around in the condition of the River Mersey. It has transformed the Mersey and its tributaries from some of the most badly polluted waters in Europe to rivers where Salmon are now once again being caught. The Commonwealth Games, hosted in Manchester during 2002, staged the triathlon swimming event in the rehabilitated waterways of Salford Quays – a symbol of the confidence in the region's regeneration and better quality of life.

Commonwealth Games Triathlon.
(Tim Mitcham)

– but then we already pay the considerable bill for unsustainable land and water management. The floods that occurred in 2000 across the UK led to insurance claims of £3 billion – equivalent to the UK's annual CAP grant from Europe (Baines 2002). Of course much more needs to be done to secure a sustainable living landscape. But a start has been made, and key to this are policies based upon longer-term objectives with a greater sensitivity to the important role of natural systems.

An urban renaissance – putting people first

Recent research has shown that urban parks and naturalistic greenspace improve the quality of human life. Results indicate that 'these environments are important places of refuge for people to step aside from stress and fatigue and regain inner composure' (Price and Stoneman 2001). Communities that have naturalistic greenspaces are generally more content and healthy than those in hard landscaped, concrete dominated environments. Good design principles can create landscapes that encourage a sense of security and a feeling of satisfaction with the community and the environment.

The Urban Green Space Task Force (DTLR 2002) reported that, despite their popularity, there has been a major decline in the extent and quality of greenspace through reduced funding, the selling of

285

Creative use of annual cornfield flowers produced a high quality environment on an area of demolished housing in Bolton. (David Woodfall)

below Song Thrush, a welcome guest in 'wildlife friendly' suburban gardens. (Malcolm Edmunds)

playing fields and the use of derelict and underused sites for development. Since most people live and work in towns and cities, major improvements in quality of life can be achieved through investing in greenspace. Good landscape design will benefit individuals and the community by reduced absenteeism from work due to ill health and reduced vandalism. It will generate a happier community and also make a significant contribution to the economy.

It is now recognised that conservation is just as important in towns as it is in the countryside, and a surprising variety of wildlife, including some national rarities, can be found in our urban areas. The Song Thrush is now more likely to be seen in suburban gardens and parkland where earthworms and snails are abundant than in agricultural land where intensive cropping and poaching of the surface has reduced their food.

One of the main challenges to increasing urban wildlife is how to elevate it from being an issue relevant only to the image of an area to being a fundamental part of mainstream social and economic agendas (Paterson 2001). The physical environment and greenspace are normally looked after by local authority planning or parks departments, but there is now clear evidence that they should be a cross department responsibility of importance to health, education, regeneration and social services departments as well.

Greening initiatives with the aim of improving appearance often fail to take on board the community's aspirations and energies. Supporting community self-help projects in the environment often appear more expensive than paying contractors to provide a quick fix. However, these projects should be about reconnecting people and their local environment and rebuilding a sense of place, opportunity and choice. Who would have thought, ten years ago, that the Wildlife Trust would be encouraging urban families to grow their own food to benefit both themselves and wildlife? People are more likely to care for an environment they have helped to create than one that has been imposed on them.

Community allotments, like this one in Bolton with secure family orientated plots, are providing a renaissance in urban food growing. (Wildlife Trust)

New opportunities for urban wildlife

Our region's industrial heritage has left behind many wildlife rich areas: post-industrial sites, canals and derelict lodges have all been colonised by a variety of wildlife some of which may not have occurred in the area before. At Nob End in Moses Gate Country Park, Farnworth, Fragrant Orchid and marsh orchids abound on a site reclaimed from a former chemical works in a landscape surrounded by housing and industry. Formed on alkaline nineteenth-century Leblanc process waste, its basic soil is without significant available nitrogen and phosphorus and has gained a species rich calcareous flora many miles from the nearest natural calcareous habitats (Ash 1998).

The Wigan Flashes, formed by mining subsidence, now support major reed beds and booming Bitterns – one of the UK's scarcest habitats and rarest breeding species. Accessible to many thousands of people by foot and bicycle, the Flashes have been colonised by wildlife naturally without deliberate introductions, and they indicate nature's ability to take advantage of new opportunities.

Wigan Flashes reed bed.
(Wildlife Trust)

There is huge scope for creating new wildlife areas and thereby adding greatly to our present wildlife's ability to cope with future change. English Nature has recommended targets and guidelines for providing adequate accessible natural greenspace in urban areas. They suggest residents should be able to enter a natural greenspace of at least 2 hectares within 0.5 km of their home. They also recommend that provision should be made for Local Nature Reserves in every urban area at the minimum level of 1 hectare per thousand population (English Nature 1995). These targets are being actively pursued by many of the local authorities in our area. In some cases, derelict sites within or adjacent to urban areas are being considered for natural greenspace rather than redevelopment for commercial or residential uses. These encouraging trends may lead to an increase of wildlife sites across the region instead of the present continuing attrition of greenspace.

Planning conservation for the future

The British Government signed up to the Biodiversity Convention at the United Nations Conference on Environment and Development (Earth Summit) at Rio de Janeiro in 1992. This resulted in the Government producing *Biodiversity: the UK Action Plan* (HMG 1994c), which aimed to 'conserve and enhance biological diversity within the UK and to contribute to Global diversity through all appropriate mechanisms'.

For the first time a plan took account of what was valuable about our wildlife. It produced a programme of Biodiversity Action Plans (BAPs) to actively safeguard not only the rare and endangered but the commonplace and local. This document was a major step forward in wildlife conservation. It has resulted in the production of local BAPs and major initiatives to conserve the wild habitats and species of Lancashire, Manchester and North Merseyside. The local BAPs have highlighted that we have internationally important habitats, such as Bluebell woods, mosslands, sand dunes and estuaries. They have also

Lancashire's sand dunes are home to several UK endemic plants including Isle of Man Cabbage. *(Phil Smith)*

highlighted that we have important populations of species with very limited world distributions such as the Great Crested Newt and Isle of Man Cabbage, while the nemertean worm *Prostoma jenningsi*, is, as far as we know, unique to Lancashire.

The local BAPs are a partnership initiative in which the Wildlife Trust has taken a major role. Local BAPs have detailed plans identifying action priorities for each species and habitat, and who should co-ordinate and carry out the work. Taking the plans forward will not be easy as resources for proactive nature conservation are still very limited. This partial success in changing the minds of politicians and decision makers about the importance of the natural environment is only the beginning: the major task ahead is to encourage the resources to fund it.

The Government's main agent for biodiversity conservation, English Nature, is mainly funded to support European (Special Areas of Conservation, SACs) and nationally important sites (Sites of Special Scientific Interest, SSSIs). There are very few Governmental resources available for wider countryside and urban wildlife projects. Protecting SACs and SSSIs alone will not give our wildlife a sustainable future. The impact of climate change on our wildlife is still largely unknown and without a joined up network of wildlife habitats, it is much harder

Mere Sands Wood.
(Tim Mitcham)

Box 12.5 Mere Sands Wood: An Example of Planned Wildlife Development

Mere Sands Wood Nature Reserve, Rufford was created at the beginning of the 1980s out of a worked out sand quarry. The Wildlife Trust realised the importance of not only creating new opportunities for wildlife but also of building into the site facilities for people to observe the wildlife at close hand. Over twenty years the landscape has been remodelled to create a series of deep and shallow lakes, grassland, heath and new woodland. There is also a visitor centre, excellent bird hides and a network of paths. Wildlife has flourished and it is now an excellent site to see over-wintering Teal, Pochard and Pintail as well as summer breeding birds including Great Crested Grebe, Little Grebe (*Tachybaptus ruficollis*), Tufted Duck and Gadwall. Recent projects have encouraged the growth of reed beds along the lake margins which has encouraged use by breeding warblers and many dragonfly species. Mere Sands is an excellent example of how 'creative' conservation work can make a tremendous contribution to our wildlife resource.

Box 12.6 Barn Owl Recovery in South West Lancashire

Barn Owls hunt in open habitats of rough grasslands and field margins for their diet of small mammals. Barn owl populations suffered a severe decline from the mid-twentieth century due to changes in agricultural practices and loss of habitat and suitable nesting sites. Their Lancashire population declined by 62% in the twenty year period from the mid-1970s (Pyefinch 2001).

The South West Lancashire Ringing Group began to try to reverse this decline by working closely with local landowners to erect nest boxes near suitable foraging habitat. Nestlings have been ringed annually to monitor population trends. In the early years of the box scheme only 20 pairs of Barn Owls were using boxes, but by the turn of the century 40 to 50 pairs were breeding in the area. Over 1,000 young birds have been ringed with adults recorded as far away as Essex (Duckles 2002).

A wildlife success story: The healthy breeding population of Barn Owls in West Lancashire is thanks to the partnership between active volunteers and receptive landowners.
(Peter Smith)

for species to adapt to change. Implementation of a landscape-based approach and roll-out of the Biodiversity Action Plans is the only realistic option for Lancashire's wildlife, but more resources are needed for the co-ordination and implementation of the plans. Meanwhile enthusiasm and some resources can make considerable progress, for example, the work to save Barn Owls in South West Lancashire (see Boxes 12.5 and 12.6) – a major contribution to local BAPs.

Against the trend in many parts of the country, Barn Owls are once again flourishing in South West Lancashire thanks to sympathetic local voluntary conservation action. The introduction of agri-environment schemes has also had a beneficial impact upon owls and many other forms of wildlife. Planning authorities have recognised the importance of old barns for owls and bats and now request surveys and sensitive construction work to safeguard this resource.

Key partners in the road ahead are the amateur naturalists and committed professionals who are the unsung heroes of wildlife conservation. It is they who have monitored the decline of our once rich heritage and campaigned tirelessly for improved policy and resources. But safeguarding wildlife for wildlife's sake is not a persuasive tool in the present political climate. Conservationists have learned that wildlife has to be seen to be contributing to the economy and to our quality of life, and then many more will support us.

It is this major awareness raising process that we must address if

We all have a duty to pass on to future generations an awareness of the wonders of the natural world.
(Tim Mitcham)

policy and resources are to be forthcoming to implement the BAPs on the ground. The Biodiversity Action Plan will succeed only if the whole of society puts its energy into safeguarding our heritage and making wildlife conservation a cornerstone of our way of life.

It is easy to think that we are powerless to prevent the continuing deterioration of our environment and loss of still more rare animals and plants against the forces of big business and agriculture; but at the local level if we work with organisations such as the Wildlife Trust we can actually do a very great deal to change our environment for the better.

Everybody needs beauty as well as bread, places to play in and pray in, where nature may heal and give strength to body and soul alike.
John Muir (1838–1914). *The Yosemite* (1912).

Further Reading

Greenwood, E. F. (1999). *Ecology and Landscape Development: A History of the Mersey Basin.* Liverpool University Press.

Regional Biodiversity Steering Group for the North West (1999). *A Biodiversity Audit of North West England.*

Greater Manchester Ecology Unit (2000). *Greater Manchester Biodiversity Action Plan.*

Lancashire's Biodiversity Partnership (2001). *Lancashire's Biodiversity Action Plan.*

Merseyside Biodiversity Group (2001). *Biodiversity Action Plan for North Merseyside.*

Wildlife of
Lancashire

Glossary

Word or term	Meaning
accreting	of sand or mud: accumulating in the course of time
acidic	sour, sharp-tasting
aestivate	to rest quiescent during the summer
afforestation	newly planted forest
alkaline	having properties of an alkali, not an acid; in water or soil it usually means rich in calcium carbonate
alkaloid	a group of organic chemicals found in many plants which often make them unpalatable
alluvial	fine sediment carried by river water and deposited as the flow decreases
amphibian	animal belonging to the vertebrate class Amphibia which includes frogs and newts, many of which spend part of their lives on land and part in water
amphipod	animal belonging to the crustacean order Amphipoda, including freshwater shrimps and sand-hoppers
anecdotal	a short account, not necessarily verified scientifically
antecedent	ancestor
apomixis	in a plant: production of seeds without a sexual process
apothecary	old word for pharmacist, chemist
arachnid	animal belonging to the subphylum Arachnida including spiders, scorpions and ticks
arthropod	phylum of animals with an exoskeleton and jointed limbs e.g. insects, spiders
artisan	skilled workman
atoll	a raised mound or circle of coral
benthic	of animals and plants: living on the bottom of the sea or freshwater
biomass	the weight of living material
bivalve	mollusc with a pair of shells belonging to the class Bivalvia (or Lamellibranchia), e.g. mussels
brackish	water that is more salty than fresh water but less salty than sea water
braconid	belonging to a family of parasitic wasps, the Braconidae
bryophyte	moss or liverwort plant
bryozoan	encrusting colonial animal with tentacles around the mouth belonging to the phylum Bryozoa
bulbil	small bulb or tuber arising from a flower or leaf axis
calcareous	containing the chemical element calcium
calico	cotton cloth, originally from India
carboniferous	refers to rocks laid down about 340 to 280 million years ago

carr	woodland growing in a marsh
cetacean	whales, dolphins and porpoises
chalcid	belonging to a family of parasitic wasps, the Chalcidae
chironomid	belonging to the midge family, the Chironomidae
chitin	a polysaccharide (related to sugars but with additional nitrogen) which is the main component of the covering of insects and which also occurs in fungi
chlorophyll	green pigment in plants responsible for photosynthesis
chromosome	hereditary structures in the nucleus of each cell composed of DNA and protein
clint	ridge of eroded limestone separated from neighbouring ridges by deep clefts or grikes
clough	a ravine or valley
coppice	small wood managed by cutting on (typically) a 20 year rotation
curriculum	course of study
cyst	a bladder or bag-like structure which may be normal or pathological
deciduous	of trees: those that shed their leaves in autumn
delta	part of river entering the sea through many channels
desiccation	drying up
detritivores	animals that feed on detritus (the decaying organic matter at the bottom of fresh waters and the sea)
diatom	microscopic planktonic plant enclosed in two valves made of silica
dinoflagellate	microscopic planktonic plant with one flagellum round its equator and one trailing
diurnal	active during the day not at night
drumlin	low hill of variable material formed underneath an ice sheet
dune	ridge formed of wind-blown sand
ecosystem	an interacting group of organisms in their physical enviroment which is more or less clearly separated from organisms in neighbouring environments e.g a pond, a meadow, a wood
elytra	the hardened forewings of beetles which are protective and not used in flight
embryo	early stage of development
endemic	only occurring naturally in a particular area
entomology	the study of insects
entrepreneur	someone who undertakes a novel activity often at financial risk
Eurasian	pertaining to both Europe and Asia
eutrophic	nutrient rich water, often but not necessarily resulting from organic pollution; eutrophication is the progressive enrichment of water
exoskeleton	a hard external covering to the body as in beetles
exuviae	shed skin of an insect
feral	domestic animal that has gone wild
fireclay	clay deficient in lime and iron, suitable for making fire bricks
floristically	relating to flowers, e.g. floristically rich means many different flowers
forage	search for food
frenulum	hook that links forewings and hindwings of moths

fungivore	feeding on fungi
fustian	coarse fabric for making clothes
gadoid	fish belonging to the family Gadidae including cod
geology	the study of the Earth's crust and its rocks
glaciation	in geology: covered with ice
gorge	steep-sided valley
gryke	(or grike) cleft in eroded limestone separated from neighbouring clefts by narrow ridges or clints
habitat	the normal place where an organism lives
hallucinogenic	causing the sensation of something which is illusory
herbalist	person who studies or collects plants believed to have curative properties
herbarium	collection of flattened and preserved plants mounted on paper
herbivore	feeding on plants
hermaphrodite	having both male and female sex organs
heteropterans	bugs of the insect order Hemiptera distinguished from homopterans by wings and mouthparts (see Box 11.8)
homopterans	bugs of the insect order Hemiptera distinguished from heteropterans by wings and mouthparts (see Box 11.8)
horticulturalist	someone who spends much time gardening
hummock	small hill
hybrid	offspring from a mating between two different species or varieties
hydatid	cyst containing a tapeworm larva
hydroid	solitary or branching colonial animal with a mouth surrounded by tentacles belonging to the phylum Coelenterata, class Hydrozoa
hyphae	threads of a fungus that absorb nutients from their surroundings
ichneumon	belonging to a family of parasitic wasps, the Ichneumonidae
indigenous	occurring naturally in the area; native
inflorescence	a group of flowers close together on a plant
infralittoral	shallow seabed, slightly deeper water than sublittoral
insectivore	animal or plant that eats insects
intertidal	the seashore between the highest and lowest water levels reached by a spring tide
invertebrate	animal lacking a backbone
isopod	animal belonging to the crustacean order Isopoda, including woodlice
karst	rough limestone country
lichenologist	person who studies lichens
limestone	sedimentary rock rich in calcium carbonate
link sand dunes	ground between the hills and hollows of the dunes and the boggy ground inland
littoral	the strip of seashore between low and high tide marks
LNR	Local Nature Reserve
marl	lime-rich clay
meanders	of a river: an ox-bow lake or marsh formed when a slow-flowing meandering river

Glossary

	cuts through one of its loops so that the old course (oxbow or meander) is left to gradually silt up and dry out
melanic	black form (e.g. of a moth)
menagerie	collection of wild animals
mesotrophic	water with some nutrients, intermediate between eutrophic and oligotrophic
metamorphosis	of animals: the drastic change in appearance as some animals grow, e.g. a caterpillar changing into a butterfly
monoculture	a habitat occupied by a single species of plant e.g. a field of wheat
monograph	book on a specific topic
montane	of a plant: living on mountains
mosaic	of an environment: patches of different habitats e.g. fields, woods, plantations
moult	shedding body covering of fur, feathers or (in arthropods) cuticle
mudstone	sedimentary rock formed by compression of mud
musci britannica	Latin phrase meaning British mosses
mustelid	carnivorous mammals including weasels, stoats, otters and badgers
mycorrhiza	fungus that lives symbiotically in the roots of many plants: the fungus gets sugars from the plant, the plant gets salts from the fungus
nanoplankton	minute planktonic plants so small that they are not visible with a normal microscope, about one millionth of a millimetre in diameter
nematocerous	flies of the group known as the Nematocera with long antennae
nemertean	unsegmented worms with a characteristic proboscis belonging to the phylum Nemertea
night-soil	the human faeces and urine that in Victorian times was collected from houses daily for disposal
NNR	National Nature Reserve
noctuid	moth belonging to the family Noctuidae
nymphal	refers to the juvenile stage of many insects
odonate	a dragonfly or damselfly (belonging to the insect order Odonata)
oligochaete	annelid (i.e. segmented) worms belonging to the class Oligochaeta e.g. earthworms
oligotrophic	water very poor in nutrients as in many ancient lakes
oraches	plants belonging to the genus *Atriplex*
organochlorine	organic chemical insecticides containing chlorine e.g. DDT
ovipositor	the egg-laying apparatus of some insects e.g. parasitic wasps
palaeontology	the study of fossils
palmate	of a leaf: with lobes radiating from a point
parasite	organism that obtains food by living in or on another organism which is thereby harmed
pathogen	organism that causes illness or disease in another organism
paucity	scarce
pedunculate	in a plant: stalked inflorescence
pelagic	living in the surface or middle waters, but not at the bottom
percussive	like a percussion musical instrument

permian	refers to rocks laid down about 280 to 230 million years ago
photosynthesis	process by which green plants convert carbon dioxide and water to sugars and oxygen with the aid of sunlight
phylum	a major group of animals or plants e.g. Mollusca for snails, mussels and squids or Chordata for fish, birds and mammals
phytoplankton	microscopic plants of the plankton
piscivorous	feeding on fish
plankton	small animals and plants living in the surface and middle waters (above the bottom) and drifting at the mercy of currents
plateaux	more or less flat land that is higher than adjacent land
pleistocene	from about 2.5 million until about 10,000 years ago
polychaete	annelid (i.e. segmented) worms belonging to the class Polychaeta e.g. ragworms, lugworms
polypore	type of fungus with underside comprising numerous holes or pores
proboscis	long tubular, sucking mouthparts
Protozoa	phylum including all animals composed of just one cell
pselaphid	belonging to a family of beetles, the Pselaphidae
Red Data Book	A list of rare and endangered organisms world-wide originally devised by the International Union for the Conservation of Nature. The British Red Data species are documented by the Joint Nature Conservation Committee in a series of Red Data Books
repugnatorial	(of a gland or secretion) unpleasant or repellent to a predator
riverine	associated with rivers
rodenticide	chemical designed to kill rodents
saline	salty
sandstone	sedimentary rock formed of compressed sand
saprophyte	plant or fungus that obtains sugars from dead and decaying organic matter
sessile	in a plant: with no stalk
shale	clay rock that splits or breaks into thin pieces
skears	local word for cobble-like stones found in shallow water in parts of Morecambe Bay
smoltification	the change from the young salmon, or parr, into the next stage called a smolt
species	a group of organisms that can interbreed freely with each other and can be distinguished from other organisms by their characteristics
sporadic	occasional
sublittoral	shallow seabed never exposed to air at low tide
substrate	surface or material on which an organism lives
subtidal	shallow sea-bed close to the seashore that is always covered by water even at the lowest tides
sward	grassy surface; turf
symbionts	two organisms that live together so that both benefit from the association
symbiotic	living together in close association such that both partners benefit from the relationship
taxonomist	person who describes and classifies organisms

Glossary

terrace	of a river: flat platform where the river once ran before it cut down to its present course
tetrad	in ecology: a 2 x 2 km square of land in Britain derived from the National Grid lines on Ordnance Survey maps
thallose	flattish, like a thallus
thallus	flattish plant structure not differentiated into stem and leaves
till	sediment deposited from ice, formerly called boulder clay
topography	the characteristic features of the landscape
transect	in ecology: a usually random line along which samples are taken
transition	boundary between two distinct regions
triassic	refers to rocks laid down about 230 to 200 million years ago
turves	mat of plant or animal material
tussock	a tuft or clump of, for example, grass
ubiquitous	occurring almost everywhere
vascular	(of plants) those plants with conducting tissues, i.e. ferns, conifers and flowering plants
yeoman	countryman or small farmer from 15th to 20th century above the rank of labourer but below that of gentleman
zooplankton	minute animals in the plankton
zygopteran	damselfly

Sites of Wildlife Interest

compiled by Geoff Saul

The following sites are referred to in the text, and to help readers who may wish to visit them details are given here of their location and access. Each site is numbered so as to correspond with the numbers on the map.

Map No.	Name/ grid reference	Location	Description	Access details
1	Abbeystead SD 559542	South east of Lancaster. Village signed from A6 at Bay Horse (south from junction 33 M6)	Reservoir site	Private – permission needed
2	Abram Flashes SD 612006	See Pennington and Wigan Flashes	Lake/reed beds/ marsh habitat	Can be viewed from Leeds and Liverpool canal
3	Ainsdale NNR SD 285105	South of Southport on main coast road (A565)	Sand dunes	Public footpath; contact English Nature on 01942 820342 for wider access
4	Alston Reservoir SD 610364	Longridge. Take footpath by side of St Paul's church on Lower Lane	Reservoir	Can be viewed from public paths
5	Altcar SD 324063	West Lancashire, south west of Ormskirk. Waterloo cup – Hare coursing in area	Marsh habitat	Some public paths
6	Anglezarke SD 619161	East of Chorley. Follow signs from Chorley town centre. Plenty of public parking	Reservoir	Public access
7	Astley Moss SJ 692975	Four miles south of Leigh, off A580(T) on Rindle Road	One of last remaining fragments of Chat Moss (Primeval moss land)	Contact Wildlife Trust on 01772 324129 for permit
8	Banks Marsh SD 405240	Southern bank of Ribble. Public access through Marsh Farm	Salt Marsh	Can be viewed from sea defence path. Contact English Nature on 01942 820342
9	Birkacre Country Park SD 570153	Chorley	Country park	Part of Yarrow Valley Country Park. Good access

Appendix:
Sites of Wildlife Interest

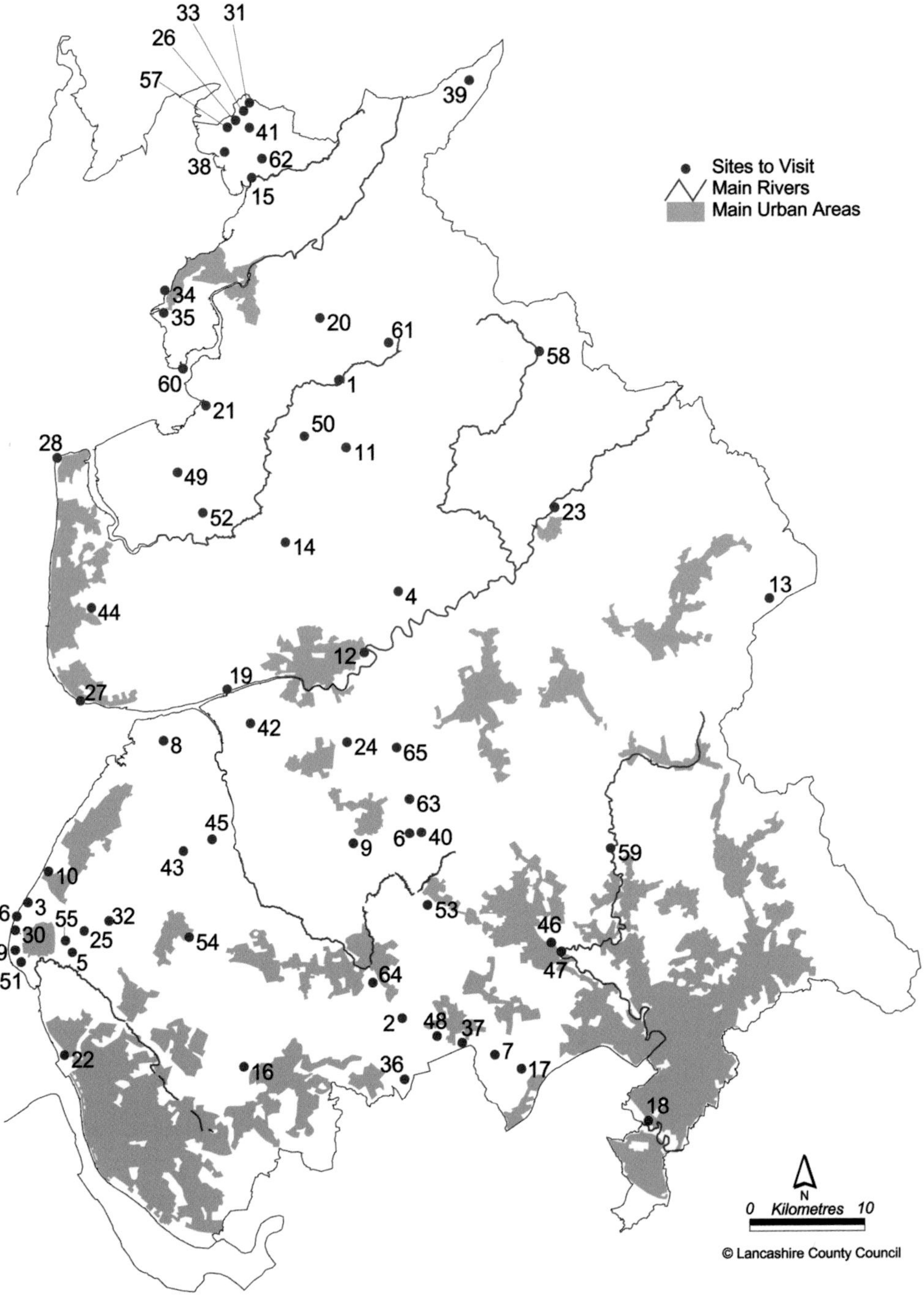

Map 13.
Sites to visit
referenced in the
text.
(Nik Bruce)

Sites to Visit
Main Rivers
Main Urban Areas

0   Kilometres   10

© Lancashire County Council

Wildlife of
Lancashire

Map No.	Name/ grid reference	Location	Description	Access details
10	Birkdale SD 303131	Southport – see Ainsdale	Sand dunes	Park on beach, near holiday centre
11	Bleasdale SD 565485	Take Garstang signed road from Chipping (north of Longridge)	Moorland habitat – see signs at access points for access details	Access under review
12	Boilton Wood SD 580313	Red Scar, Preston. Access from Grange Park (road bridge over M6)	Woodland	Public and permissive paths
13	Boulsworth Hill SD 930357	East of Nelson	Moorland	Access land. Good public access
14	Brock Valley SD 549431	Car park on Brock Mill Lane, opposite Higher Brock Mill	River Valley with mixed habitat. Fields, woodland and old re-populated mill ruins	Public footpath follows river
15	Carnforth SD 484712	Road out of Carnforth towards Warton. Marshes on North Lancs Cycleway	Marsh	No restrictions
16	Catchdale Moss SJ 474966	St Helens	Mossland	View from Green Lane off B5203
17	Chat Moss SJ 715963	Large mossland complex west of Manchester	Moss, most of which has been drained and lost – see Astley Moss	Some public paths
18	Chorlton Water Park SJ 824919	South Manchester	Water park	Good public access
19	Clifton Marsh SD 461283	Off A593 road West of Preston. Turn left, off dual carriageway, at L.C.C. depot traffic lights (towards refuse tip)	Salt Marshes on north bank of Ribble opposite Banks Marsh	Limited access
20	Clougha SD 543594	Signed from road leading from Lancaster to Trough of Bowland. See also Tarnbrook Fell	Moorland habitat	Access land
21	Cockerham Moss SD 443521	Take Pilling road out of village access by side of River Cocker bridge	Salt Marshes	Access along sea defence
22	Crosby Marine Park SJ 317977	West of Waterloo Park, Liverpool. Off A565	Artificial lake	Good public access
23	Cross Hills SD 745434	Waddington Road out of Clitheroe. At river bridge, follow Ribble Way footpath upstream (east), site within ½ mile	Old limestone workings and spoil heaps. Recolonisation very advanced. Eastern quarry used for landfill in 1970s creating today's landscape	Nature Reserve. Public and permissive paths
24	Cuerden Valley Park SD 565238	Off A49 south of Bamber Bridge. Car park just beyond M6 bridge (going south) or turn into Shady Lane, 3rd left into Berkeley Drive	Woodland, grassland, lakes	Good path network. No restrictions
25	Downholland Moss SD 335081	South West of Ormskirk, close to Altcar	Mossland	Can be viewed from the Cheshire Lines path

Appendix:
Sites of Wildlife Interest

Map No.	Name/ grid reference	Location	Description	Access details
26	Eaves Wood SD 470760	Just off A6 between Carnforth and Milnthorpe. See also Silverdale	Woodland with Limestone outcrops	Public footpaths. Parking on road side
27	Fairhaven SD 332274	Lytham St. Annes. Take coast road, parking on road just past Lake	Coastal sand dunes – some experimental work ongoing re stabilisation	Good public access
28	Fleetwood SD 312478	Walk along promenade from main resort towards Rossall (west). Ample parking in town, either on road or various car parks (fee)	Sand dunes	Public access. Parking fee
29	Formby Point SD 274065	Follow signs from A565(T) Southport to Liverpool road. See also Ainsdale and Birkdale	Sand dunes	Good access, National Trust. Car parking fee
30	Freshfields SD 274082	From Southport follow A565 south. Follow station signs (Freshfield) parking beyond station at National Trust car park	Woodland, and sand dunes. See also Ainsdale, Birkdale and Formby Point	National Trust. Car parking fee
31	Gait Barrows NNR SD 482775	3 km south west of Beetham (A6) on lane to Waterslack	Ancient woodland and limestone outcrops. Managed by English Nature	Public footpath; contact English Nature on 01942 820342 for further access
32	Haskayne SD 357089	On the western edge of Barton village	Disused railway line; carr, fen and swamp	Contact Wildlife Trust on 01772 324129
33	Hawes Water SD 477768	See Gait Barrows NNR, lake is adjacent	Lake habitat similar to Leighton Moss	See Gait Barrows NNR
34	Heysham Head SD 408618	Follow signs south from Morecambe along A589	Sea cliffs (sandstone)	Car park fee
35	Heysham Reserve SD 407599	Off A589 from Morecambe, just before Heysham harbour, on Money Close Lane, adjacent to power stations	Pond, marsh, reed bed, stream habitats	Permissive paths
36	Highfield Moss SJ 614955	Golbourne, Warrington	Mossland	Public paths
37	Hope Carr Nature Reserve SJ 664985	Leigh. To west of A574, approx. 1 mile north of junction with A580	Wetlands, scrub	Public and permissive paths
38	Jenny Brown's Point SD 460734	Silverdale	Seashore outcrops of limestone	National Trust. Cul-de-sac. Parking can be difficult
40	Lead Mines Clough SD 629162	Use same car park as Anglezarke	Upland river valley leading onto Anglezarke moor	Public footpaths
39	Leck Fell SD 672793	Highest point in Lancashire. South east from Kirby Lonsdale on A65(T) for 2 miles, cul de sac on left	Uplands habitat	Public paths

302

Map No.	Name/ grid reference	Location	Description	Access details
41	Leighton Moss SD 482754	Junction 35 on M6. Follow signs to A6 and turn right towards Kendal. Reserve is south east of Silverdale. Follow signs from A6. (approx. 5 miles from M6)	RSPB managed reserve. Lake/wetland with reed beds etc.	Free to RSPB members. Charge to public. Shop, toilets
42	Longton Brickcroft SD 481254	Longton, south of Preston on A59. Follow signs to Longton village, Brickcroft well signed in village	Lake habitat with reed beds and undergrowth round edges	Open to public. Warden on site in visitor centre
43	Martin Mere SD 422147	Follow signs from A59 Burscough, or A565 Mere Brow	Large system of lakes	Wildfowl and Wetlands Trust. Entrance fee
44	Marton Mere SD 342352	From junction 4 on M55, take A583 towards Blackpool town centre. Turn right at second set of traffic lights signed Staining. Reserve 1 mile on left	Lake habitat	Public and permissive paths
45	Mere Sands Wood SD 447157	Take B5246 from Rufford, look for sign to cattery on left within ½ mile. Turn down unmade lane, site beyond cattery	Large mixed reserve. Woodlands, lakes and heath	Wildlife Trust Reserve. Visitor centre with toilets on site. Members free
46	Moses Gate Country Park SD 741069	Take Hall Lane (A6053) from Little Lever towards Farnworth. Country park main entrance and car parks on road	River (Croal and Irwell), canal and lodge habitats, plus industrial remains	Open to public
47	Nob End SD 750062	Part of Moses Gate Country Park	Industrial archaeology and remains regenerated	Public access
48	Pennington Flash SJ 642991	Well signed from A580 East Lancs Road. See Abram and Wigan Flashes	Lake/Reed beds type habitat	Country park with good access
49	Pilling Moss SD 418465	South from Pilling along Bradshaw Lane	Mostly now farmed	Little access
50	Quernmore SD 529495	On road from Caton to Trough of Bowland. Pinic site and car park on Littledale road from Quernmore church	Upland/open fell	Public access and free car park
51	Ravenmeols SD 279055	Off A565(T) just south of Formby	Sand dunes. See also Ainsdale, Birkdale, Formby Point, and Freshfields	Public access
52	Rawcliffe Moss SD 440431	On road between Out Rawcliffe and Garstang	Moss, mostly now farmed	Public path
53	Red Moss SD 634101	West of Horwich next to M61	Mossland	Public footpaths
54	Ruff Wood SD 427075	Ormskirk. Off Ruff Lane on the eastern edge Ormskirk	Broadleaved woodland	Public access

Appendix:
Sites of Wildlife Interest

Map No.	Name/ grid reference	Location	Description	Access details
55	Seaforth SD 318073	Within Port of Liverpool	Coastal lagoons	Wildlife Trust Reserve. Prebooked groups only; contact Trust on 0151 9203769 or lwildlife@cix.co.uk
56	Sefton Coast SD 276094	See Ravenmeols	Sand Dunes. See also Ainsdale	Public access except Ainsdale
57	Silverdale SD 463755	Just off A6 between Carnforth and Milnthorpe Turn left at Wildlife centre. Wood on right. See also Eaves Wood	Ancient woodland with Limestone outcrops. See also Gait Barrows.	Public footpaths Parking on road side
58	Stocks Reservoir SD 732565	North of Slaidburn. Various points of access. Parking available on road through Gisburn forest	Large lakes complex with reed beds and marsh areas	Public access and hides from Gisburn Forest
59	Summerseat Nature Reserve SD 792148	Entrance close to Summerseat station on East Lancashire railway	Former sewage works, has been developed into a complex of wood/scrub with reed beds	Wildlife Trust Reserve. Contact 01204 361847
60	Sunderland Point SD 423552	Access only at low water as tides can cover road. Follow signs from Lancaster/Morecambe main road	Sea coast with outcrops and pebbles on shoreline	Public path with access to shore
61	Tarnbrook Fell SD 602573	Open fell above village of Tarnbrook. See Clougha for approach	Upland habitat	Some public footpaths; further access under review
62	Warton Crag SD 493728	Junction 35 M6. A6 turn south; at traffic lights in Carnforth turn right to Warton. Turn left in village and take steep lane. Reserve on right	Ancient woodland and grassland. Limestone ledges and pavement	Public and permissive paths
63	White Coppice SD 619190	Take A674 towards Blackburn from M61 junction at Chorley. Turn right within 1 mile at sign for White Coppice. Follow lane and signs. Parking can be limited if cricket match day	Regenerated industrial sites with geological trail up Dean Black Clough. Lodges and open moor also	Public access
64	Wigan Flashes SD 587036	Series of lakes south east of Wigan. See also Abram flashes and Pennington Flash	Lakes/reed beds marshes	Public and permissive paths. Leeds and Liverpool canal towpath offers good vantage point
65	Withnell Fold SD 608233	Northern side of Leeds Liverpool canal. Access via canal bridge in Withnell Fold village, Chorley	Local Nature reserve. Canal/reed beds habitat	Limited parking within Withnell Fold village

Wildlife of
Lancashire

References

Chapter 1

British Association (1962). *Manchester and its Region.* University Press, Manchester.

Buck, A. (1993). *An Inventory of UK Estuaries. Vol. 3 North West Britain.* JNCC, Peterborough.

Burd, F. (1989). *The Saltmarsh Survey of Great Britain.* Research Survey Report No. 17. Nature Conservancy Council, Peterborough.

Countryside Commission (1992). *The Forest of Bowland Landscape* (CCP 399). The Countryside Commission, Cheltenham.

Countryside Commission (1997). *The Arnside and Silverdale Landscape* (CCP 528). The Countryside Commission, Cheltenham.

Countryside Commission (1998). *Countryside Character Vol. 2: The North West* (CCP 536). The Countryside Commission, Cheltenham.

Drewitt, A. L. and Manley, V. J. (1997). *The Vegetation of the Mountains and Moorlands of England.* English Nature Research Survey Report No. 218, Peterborough.

Edmundson, S. E., Gateley, P. S. and Nissenbaum, D. A. (1989). *National Sand Dune Vegetation Survey: Sefton Coast, Merseyside.* Unpublished Report for the Nature Conservancy Council.

Edwards, W. and Trotter, F. M. (1954). *The Pennines and Adjacent Areas.* HMSO.

English Nature (1994). *Inventory of Ancient Woodland (Provisional) – Lancashire.* English Nature, Peterborough.

English Nature (1995). *Grassland Inventory – Lancashire.* English Nature, Peterborough.

English Nature (1996) *Grassland Inventory – Merseyside.* English Nature, Peterborough.

English Nature et al. (1999). *Morecambe Bay: The Secrets of the Sands.* Morecambe Bay Partnership.

Hall, B. R. and Folland, C. J. (1970). *Soils of Lancashire.* Harpenden.

Heath, M. (1989). *Limestone Pavement Survey of Cumbria and Lancashire 1986/87.* North West Region. Nature Conservancy Council.

Kelly, P. G. and Harwood, T. R. (1993). *Wildlife Habitats in Lancashire, a Report on the habitat Survey of Lancashire 1988–1992.* English Nature, North West Region, Bowness and Lancashire County Council Planning Department, Preston.

Lancashire Biodiversity Partnership (2001). *Lancashire's Biodiversity Action Plan.* The Wildlife Trust for Lancashire, Manchester and north Merseyside.

Meteorological Office (1977). *Average Annual Rainfall. International Standard Period Map 1941–1970 Map.* Meteorological Office.

Nature Conservancy Council (1988). *Inventory of Ancient Woodlands: Greater Manchester and Merseyside.* Nature Conservancy Council, Peterborough.

Regional Biodiversity Steering Group for North West England (1999). *A Biodiversity Audit of North West England.*

Smith, P. H. (1999). *The Sands of Time: an Introduction to the Sand Dunes of the Sefton Coast.* The National Museums and Galleries on Merseyside with Sefton Borough Council, Liverpool.

Smith, B. P. and Laffoley, D. (1992). *A Directory of Saline Lagoons and Lagoon like Inundations in England.* English Nature Science Report No. 6, Peterborough.

Trueman, A. E. (1971). *Geology and Scenery in England and Wales.* Pelican.

Chapter 2
(Key ones marked *)
*Allen, D. E. (1976). *The Naturalist in Britain.* Allen Lane, London.

*Buxton, R. (1849). *A botanical guide to the flowering plants, ferns, mosses, and algae, found indigenous within sixteen miles of Manchester ... together with a sketch of the author's life.* London.

*Cash, J. (1873). *Where there's a will there's a way! Or, science in the cottage: an account of the labours of naturalists in humble life.* London.

Crosfield, G. (1810). *Calendar of flora composed during the year 1809 at Warrington, Lt. 53 30'.* J. Haddock, London.

Desmond, R. (1977). *A dictionary of British and Irish botanists and horticulturists.* Taylor & Francis Ltd., London.

*Fisher, C. (Ed.) (2002). *A passion for natural history. The life and legacy of the 13th Earl of Derby.* Board of Trustees of the National Museums and Galleries on Merseyside, Liverpool.

Grindon, L. H. (1858). *Manchester walks and wild flowers: an introduction to the botany and rural beauty of the district, with biographical notices of the Lancashire botanists, and an account of their societies; select lists of the birds and other living creatures of the neighbourhood.* London.

Hall, T. B. (1839). *A flora of Liverpool.* Whitaker & Co., London.

Holt, J. (1795). *General view of the agriculture of the County of Lancaster.* Reprinted by David & Charles, Newton Abbot (1969).

Percy, J. (1991). Scientists in humble life: the artisan naturalists of south Lancashire. *Manchester Region History Review* V, 3–10.

Secord, A. (1994a). Corresponding interests: artisans and gentlemen in nineteenth century natural history. *British Journal for the History of Science*, 27, 383–408.

*Secord, A. (1994b). Science in the pub: artisan botanists in early nineteenth-century Lancashire. *History of Science*, 32, 269–315.

Wystrach, V. P. (1977). Anna Blackburne (1726–1793) – a neglected patroness of natural history. *Journal of the Society for the Bibliography of natural history*, 8, 148–168.

Chapter 3

Buck, A. L. (1998). *An Inventory of UK Estuaries. Vol. 3 North-West Britain.* Joint Nature Conservation Committee, Peterborough.

Davies, L. M. (1991). *Littoral survey of the coast from Crosby to Fleetwood.* Nature Conservancy Council, CSD Report, No 1217 (Marine Nature Conservation Review Report, MNCR/SR/017).

Davies, J. (1992). *Littoral survey of the Ribble, Duddon and Ravenglass estuary systems, east basin of the Irish Sea.* JNCC Report, No. 37 (Marine Nature Conservation Review Report, MNCR/SR/21).

Emblow, C. S. (1992). *Survey of the sublittoral hard substrata from Morecambe Bay to Whitehaven.* JNCC Report No: 28 (Marine Nature Conservation Review Report, MNCR/SR/19).

Potts, G. W. and Swaby, S. E. (1993). *Review of the status of estuarine fishes.* English Nature Research Reports 34. Marine Biological Association/English Nature, Plymouth.

Robinson, N. A. and Pringle, A. W. (1987). *Morecambe Bay: an assessment of present ecological knowledge.* Centre for North-West Regional Studies and Morecambe Bay Study Group, University of Lancaster, Lancaster.

Rostron, D. R. (1992). *Sublittoral benthic sediment communities of Morecambe Bay.* JNCC Report, No 47 (Marine Nature Conservation Review Report, MNCR/SR/22).

Chapter 4

(Key ones marked *)

*Ash, H. J. (1999). Man-made habitats of the Mersey Basin: what is new. *Ecology and Landscape development: a history of the Mersey Basin* (Ed. E. F. Greenwood), 73–80. Liverpool University Press, National Museums and Galleries on Merseyside, Liverpool.

Ashfield, C. J. (1864). A list of Silverdale plants. *Botanists' Chronicle*, 10, 73–75.

Boothby, J. (Ed.) (2000). *A landscape worth saving. Final report of the Pond diversity survey of North west England.* The Pond Life Project, Liverpool.

Hubbard, J. C. E. and Stebbings, R. E. (1967). Distribution, dates of origin and acreage of *Spartina townsendii* (s. l.) marshes in Great Britain. *Proceedings of the Botanical Society of the British Isles*, 7, 1–7.

Jenkinson, J. (1775). *A generic and specific description of British plants, translated from the Genera et Species Plantarum of the celebrated Linnaeus ... with notes and observations by James Jenkinson.* London, Kendal & Lancaster.

Mabey, R. (1996). *Flora Britannica.* Sinclair-Stevenson, London.

Marren, P. (1999). *Britain's rare flowers*. T. & A. D. Poyser, London.

Meikle, R. D. (1984). *Willows and poplars of Great Britain and Ireland*. BSBI Handbook No. 4. Botanical Society of the British Isles, London.

Preston, C. D., Pearman, A. D. and Dines, T. D. (Eds) (2002). *New Atlas of the British and Irish flora*. Oxford University Press, Oxford.

*Savidge, J., Heywood, V. H. and Gordon, V. (1963). *Travis's Flora of South Lancashire*. Liverpool Botanical Society, Liverpool.

*Smith, P. H. (1999). *The sands of time. An introduction to the sand dunes of the Sefton coast*. National Museums and Galleries on Merseyside with Sefton Metropolitan Borough Council, Liverpool.

Preston, C. D. and Croft, J. M. (1997). *Aquatic plants in Britain and Ireland*. Harley books, Colchester.

Stewart, A., Pearman, D. A. and Preston C. D. (Eds) (1994). *Scarce plants in Britain*. JNCC, Peterborough.

*Wheldon, J. A. and Wilson, A. (1907). *The flora of West Lancashire*. Henry Young & Sons, Liverpool.

Wigginton, M. J. (Ed.) (1999). *British Red Data Books. 1 Vascular Plants*. 3rd edn, Joint Nature Conservation Committee, Peterborough.

Chapter 5

Bishop, J. A., Cook, L. M., Muggleton, J. and Seaward, M. R. D. (1975). Moths, lichens and air pollution along a transect from Manchester to North Wales. *Journal of Applied Ecology*, 12, 83–98.

Cook, L. M., Rigby, K. D. and Seaward, M. R. D. (1990). Melanic moths and changes in epiphytic vegetation in north-west England and north Wales. *Biological Journal of the Linnean Society*, 39, 343–354.

Dillenius, J. J. (1741). *Historia muscorum*. Sheldonian Theatre, Oxford.

Grindon, L. H. (1859). *The Manchester flora*. W. White, London.

Hawksworth, D. L. and Seaward, M. R. D. (1977). *Lichenology in the British Isles 1568–1975. An historical and bibliographical survey*. Richmond Publishing, Richmond.

Marrat, F. P. (1860). On the hepatics and lichens of Liverpool and its vicinity. *Proceedings of the Literary and Philosophical Society of Liverpool*, 14 suppl., 1–14.

Ray, J. (1677). *Catalogus plantarum angliae et insularum adjacentium*. 2nd edn, London.

Salisbury, G. (1953). A new species of *Arthopyrenia* with blue-green algal cells. *Naturalist*, 78, 17–18.

Salisbury, G. (1953a). The genus *Thelocarpon* in Britain. *North-Western Naturalist*, 24, 66–76.

Salisbury, G. (1966). A monograph of the lichen genus *Thelocarpon* Nyl. *Lichenologist*, 3, 175–196.

Savidge, J., Heywood, V. H. and Gordon, V. (1963). *Travis's Flora of South Lancashire*. Liverpool Botanical Society, Liverpool.

Stansfield, A. and Nowell, J. (1911). *The flora of Todmorden*. Manchester.

Wheldon, J. A. and Travis, W. G. (1915). The lichens of south Lancashire. *Journal of the Linnean Society (Botany)*, 43, 87–136.

Wheldon, J. A. and Wilson, A. (1907). *The flora of West Lancashire*. Henry Young & Sons, Liverpool.

Dobson, F. S. (2000). *Lichens. An illustrated guide to the British and Irish species*. Richmond Publishing, Slough.

Purvis, O. W., Coppins, B. J., Hawksworth, D. L., James, P. W. and Moore, D. M. (ed.) (1992). *The lichen flora of Great Britain and Ireland*. British Lichen Society, London.

Seaward, M. R. D., ed. (1995–2001). *Lichen atlas of the British Isles*. Fascicles 1–6. British Lichen Society, London.

Chapter 6

Breitenbach, J. and Kranzlin, F. (1984–1995). *Fungi of Switzerland Vols 1–4*.

Butin, H. (1995). *Tree Diseases and Disorders, Causes, Biology, and Control in Forest and Amenity Trees*.

Hawksworth, D.L., Kirk, P.M., Sutton, B.C. and Pegler, D.N. (1995). *Ainsworth and Bisby's Dictionary of the Fungi. Eighth edn*.

Webster, J. (1970). *Introduction to Fungi*.

Chapter 7

Bunn, D. S. (1970). Is the Hedgehog changing its habits? *Nature in Lancashire*, 1, 27.

Coward, T. A. (1910). *The Vertebrate Fauna of Cheshire and Liverpool Bay*. Witherby, London.

Ellison, N. F. (1959). *Vertebrate Fauna of Lancashire and Cheshire*. Lancs. and Cheshire Fauna Society, T. Buncle, Arbroath.

References

Evans, G. E. and Thomson, D. (1972). *The Leaping Hare*. Faber & Faber, London.

Evans, P. G. H. (1990). Cetaceans. *1990 North Sea Report*. Marine Forum for Environmental Issues, London.

Harris, S. (1986). *Urban Foxes*. Whittet Books, London.

Harris, S. (1994). *The Red Fox*. Mammal Society, London.

Harris, S. (1996). A Race for Survival. *Countrylife*, 190 (No. 22), IPC Magazines, London.

Harris, S. and McLaren, G. (1998). *Brown Hare in Britain*. University of Bristol. Bristol.

Hayhow, S. J. (2000). The Brown Hare. *Lancashire's Biodiversity Action Plan*. (Ed. T. Serjeant), Lancashire Biodiversity Partnership, Preston.

Lloyd, H. G. (1983). *Past and present distribution of red and grey squirrels*. Mammal Society, London.

Northridge, S. (1990). Mammals in the Irish Sea. *The Irish Sea: An Environmental Review*. Irish Sea Study Group, Liverpool University Press, Liverpool.

Papastavrou, V. (1991). British Whales and Dolphins – Threats, Research and Conservation. *British Wildlife*, 2 (No. 4), 197–205.

Skelcher, G. (2003). A *Survey of Water Vole in Lancashire and North Merseyside River Catchments 1999 – 2003, First Draft*. A report for The Wildlife Trust for Lancashire, Manchester and North Merseyside and the Environment Agency.

Yalden, D. (1999). *The History of British Mammals*. Poyser, London.

Chapter 8

Cramp, S. and Simmons, K. E. L. (1983). *Handbook of the Birds of Europe, the Middle East and North Africa. The Birds of the Western Palearctic Vol. 3*. Oxford University Press, Oxford.

Gibbons, D. W., Avery, M. I., Baillie, S. R., Gregory, R. D., Kirby, J., Porter, R. F., Tucker, G. M. and Williams, G. (1996). Bird species of conservation concern in the United Kingdom, Channel Islands and Isle of Man: revising the Red Data List. RSPB *Conservation Review*, 10, 7–18.

Ogilvie, M. and the Rare Breeding Birds Panel (2001). Rare breeding birds in the United Kingdom in 1999. *British Birds*, 94, 358–393.

Also several volumes in recent years of the following:

Lancashire Bird Reports. Lancashire and Cheshire Fauna Society.

Birds in Greater Manchester. County Report. Greater Manchester Bird Club.

The Wetland Bird Survey. Wildfowl and Wader Counts. WWT/BTO/JNCC/RSPB.

Chapter 9

British Herpetological Society Conservation Committee (undated). *Save Our Reptiles*. British Herpetological Society.

British Herpetological Society Conservation Committee (1996). *Surveying for Amphibians*. British Herpetological Society.

British Herpetological Society Conservation Committee (undated). *Garden Ponds as Amphibian Sanctuaries*. British Herpetological Society.

Froglife (2001). *Advice Sheet 2, Surveying for (Great Crested) Newt Conservation*. Froglife, Suffolk.

Chapter 10

Internet sites

www.benthos.org/ The site of the North American Benthological Society, an international organisation that promotes aquatic ecology.

www.environment-agency.gov.uk/ A massive site with both local and more general environmental information e.g. Local Environmental Action Plans, fishery details, pollution information and conservation and ecology data and links.

www.fba.org.uk/ The Freshwater Biological Association is based in Ambleside and has many resident expert freshwater ecologists.

www.lancsenvironment.com/ecology/ Lancashire County Council's Environment and Countryside site. This gives useful information including details of local nature reserves, Public Rights of Way, events and educational materials.

www.lbap.org.uk/ Lancashire's Biodiversity Action Plan gives details on rare and endangered species together with information on important habitats.

www.waterpolicyteam.org/ The Wildlife Trusts wetland site gives information for practising conservationists. It includes information on water policy and also gives useful practical and educational fact sheets.

There are many excellent identification keys published by the Freshwater Biological Association, The Ferry House, Ambleside, Cumbria LA22 0LP

Chapter 11

Earthworms
Butt, K. R. (2000). Earthworms of the Malham Tarn Estate (Yorkshire Dales National Park). *Field Studies*, 9, 701–710.

Dragonflies
Hall, R. A. and Smith, P. H. (1991). Dragonflies of the Sefton Coast Sand-dune System, Merseyside. *Lancashire Wildlife Journal*, 1, 22–34.

Riley, J. and Haycock, K. Some notes on the Dragonflies of Red Moss. *Lancashire Wildlife Journal*, 2/3, 61–62 …

Smith, P. H. (1997). The Ruddy Darter *Sympetrum sanguineum* (Muller) in South Lancashire. *Journal of the British Dragonfly Society*, 13, 27–29.

Smith P. H. (1998). Dispersion or migration of *Sympetrum danae* (Sulzer) in South Lancashire. *Journal of the British Dragonfly Society*, 14, 12–14.

Smith P. H. (1999). The Dragonflies of Lancashire and North Merseyside: An introduction to their distribution and status. *Lancashire Bird Report 1998*, 74–76.

Butterflies and Moths
Edmunds, M. and Grayson, J. (1991). Camouflage and selective predation in caterpillars of the poplar and eyed hawkmoths (*Laothoe populi* and *Smerinthus ocellata*). *Biological Journal of the Linnean Society* 42: 467–480.

Flies
Falk, S. (1991). *A review of scarce and threatened bees, wasps and ants of Great Britain*. NCC, Peterborough.

Kidd, L. N. and Fitton, M. G. (Eds) (1971). *Holden Clough – the natural history of a small Lancashire valley*. Oldham Museum and Libraries, Oldham.

Bees, Wasps and Ants
Garland, S. and Appleton, T. (1994). Solitary Wasps and Ants (Sphecidae and Formicidae) of Lancashire and Cheshire. *Lancashire Wildlife Journal*, 4, 1–25.

Paxton, R. J. and Pohl, H. (1999). The tawny mining bee, *Andrena fulva* Muller (Hymenoptera, Andreninae) at a South Wales field site and its associated organisms: Hymenoptera, Diptera, Nematoda and Strepsiptera. *British Journal of Entomology and Natural History*, 12, 57–67.

Robinson, N. A. (1996). Observations on *Osmia parietina* (Hym. Megachilidae) in Lancashire. *Entomologist's Monthly Magazine*,132, 31–32.

Robinson, N. A. (1998). Observations on the guest ant *Formicoxenus nitidulus* (Nylander) in nests of the red wood ant *Formica rufa* L in 1997. *British Journal of Entomology and Natural History*, 11, 125–128.

Robinson, N. A. (1999). Observations on the guest ant *Formicoxenus nitidulus* Nylander in nests of the wood ants *Formica rufa* L. and *F. lugubris* Zetterstedt in 1998. *British Journal of Entomology and Natural History*, 12, 138–140.

Robinson, N. A. (2001). Changes in the status of the red wood ant *Formica rufa* L. (Hymenoptera: Formicidae) in north west England during the 20th century. *British Journal of Entomology and Natural History*, 14, 29–38.

Beetles
Britten, H. (1930). *Coleoptera. Checklist of the Fauna of Lancashire and Cheshire*. Part 1. pp. 26–65. T. Buncle & Co., Arbroath.

Dempsey, M. J. (1993). Kidney-spot Ladybirds in Lancashire and adjoining counties 1991–1992. *Lancashire Wildlife Journal*, 2/3, 17–22.

Ellis, J. W. (1889). The Coleopterous Fauna of the Liverpool District. *Proceedings of the Liverpool Biological Society*, 2, 182–220.

Newton, J. (1998). Reserves Round Up, Endangered Beetles in Burton Wood and Warton Crag. *Lapwing* Summer 1998, 10.

Sharp, W. E. (1908). *The Coleoptera of Lancashire and Cheshire*. Lancashire and Cheshire Entomological Society, St Albans.

Spiders

Harvey, P. R., Nellist, D. R. and Telfer, M. (2002). *Provisional Atlas of British Spiders* Volumes 1 and 2. JNCC & CEH, Biological Records Centre, Huntingdon.

Jones-Walters, L. (1989). *Key to the Families of British Spiders*. Field Studies Council AIDGAP key, Preston Montford, Shrewsbury.

Chapter 12

Ash, H. J. (1999). Man-made habitats of the Mersey Basin: what is new? In: *Ecology and Landscape Development: A History of the Mersey Basin*. Liverpool University Press.

Baines, C. (2002). Nature of the Future. BBC Wildlife, 20 (June), 36–44.

Carson, R. (1962). *Silent Spring*. Houghton Mifflin.

Department of Transport, Local Government and the Regions (2002). *Green Spaces, Better Places*. Final report of the Urban Green Spaces Task Force. DTLR, London.

Duckles, T. (2002). The Barn Owl in South West Lancashire. *Coast Lines, The Sefton Coast Newsletter* (Summer edition). Sefton Coast and Countryside Management Service, Formby.

English Nature (1995). *Accessible natural greenspace in towns and cities: A review of appropriate size and distance criteria*. English Nature Research Reports No. 153.

Greater Manchester Countryside Unit (1989). *The Mosslands Strategy: A Strategy for the Future of Chat Moss, Greater Manchester*. Greater Manchester Countryside Unit, Manchester.

Greenwood, E. F. (2003). Understanding change: a Lancashire perspective. *Watsonia* 24, 337–350.

Muir, J. (1912). *The Yosemite*.

Northwest Development Agency (2002). *England's North West – a strategy towards 2020*. Northwest Development Agency, Warrington.

Paterson, K. (2001). Experiencing Deeply. Ecos 22 (3/4), 14–19.

Price, P. and Stoneman, J. (2001). *Making Connections: A Guide to Accessible Greenspace*. The Sensory Trust.

Pyefinch, R. and Golborn, P. (2001). *The Atlas of Breeding Birds in Lancashire and North Merseyside*. Hobby Publications, Liverpool.

Regional Biodiversity Steering Group for North West England (2000). *The Environmental Economy of the North West – a driver for economic and social progress*. Regional Biodiversity Steering Group for North West England, Wigan.

Savidge, J., Heywood, V. H. and Gordon, V. (1963). *Travis's Flora of South Lancashire*. Liverpool Botanical Society, Liverpool.

Index

Where animal and plant names have two words they are listed under the second name e.g. Sparrow, House; but hyphenated names are listed under the first word e.g. Enchanter's-nightshade. Scientific names are cross-referenced to their common name where there is one. If there is no common name the group to which it belongs is given in brackets.

Wildlife of
Lancashire

Index

315

Index

Cerambycidae (beetles), 255

Cerastium diffusum. See Mouse-ear, Sea

Cerastium semidecandrum. See Mouse-ear, Little

Cerastoderma edule. See Cockle, Edible

Ceratophyllum (hornwort), 92

Ceratopogonidae (flies), 239

Cernuella virgata. See Snail, Striped

Cervus elaphus. See Deer, Red

Cervus nippon. See Deer, Sika

cetacean, 130–133

Cetonia aurata. See Chafer, Rose

Cettia cetti. See Warbler, Cetti's

Chaerophyllum temulum. See Chervil, Rough

chafers, 252

Chafer, Rose, 252

Chaffinch, 169

chalcid (parasitic wasp), 258

Challan Hall Allotment, 40

Chamerion angustifolium. See Willowherb, Rosebay

Charadrius dubius. See Plover, Little Ringed

Charadrius hiaticula. See Plover, Ringed

Charadrius morinellus. See Dotterel

chaser (dragonfly), 212

Chaser, Broad-bodied, 12, 208, 212, 213

Chaser, Four-spotted, 208, 212

Chat Moss, 84, 155, 278, 301

Chenopodium album. See

Fat-hen

Cherry, Bird, 60, 61

Cherry, Wild, 60, 61

Chervil, Bur, 99

Chervil, Rough, 79

Chickweed, Common, 93, 94

Chickweed, Lesser, 55

Chiffchaff, 166

Chironomidae (midges), 239

Chironomus (midge), 182, 186

Chlorochroa juniperina (shieldbug), 221

Chloromyia formosa. See Centurion, Broad

Chorley, 7, 9, 103, 118, 120, 128, 166, 184, 210

Chorlton Water Park, 150, 301

Chorthippus brunneus. See Grasshopper, Field

Chorthippus parallelus. See Grasshopper, Meadow

Chrysanthemum segetum. See Marigold, Corn

Chrysomelidae (flea beetles), 253

Chrysopa (lacewing), 258

Chrysoperla carnea (lacewing), 258

Chrysosplenium alternifolium. See Golden-saxifrage, Alternate-leaved

Chrysosplenium oppositifolium. See Golden-saxifrage, Opposite-leaved

Chthonius (false scorpion), 200

Chthonius ischnochelus, 200

Chub, 192, 193, 194, 195

Churchtown, 210

churchyards, 106

Cicindela campestris. See Beetle, Green Tiger

Cicindela hybrida. See

Beetle, Northern Dune Tiger

Cinclus cinclus. See Dipper

Cinquefoil, Spring, 70

Circaea alpina. See Enchanter's-nightshade, Alpine

Circaea lutetiana. See Enchanter's-nightshade

Circaea x *intermedia* (hybrid enchanter's nightshade), 65

Circus aeruginosus. See Harrier, Marsh

Circus cyaneus. See Harrier, Hen

Cirsium arvense. See Thistle, Creeping

Cirsium heterophyllum. See Thistle, Melancholy

Cirsium vulgare. See Thistle, Spear

Cladium mariscus. See Fen-sedge, Great

Clausilia bidentata. See Snail, Common Door

clay pits, 3, 92, 97

Claytonia sibirica. See Purslane, Pink

Clayton-le-Woods, 200, 203, 210

Clean Air Acts, 106

Clearbeck, 75

Clethrionomys glareolus. See Vole, Bank

Clifton Marsh, 124, 301

climate, 3

clints, 7

Clitheroe, 5, 7, 194

Clock, Town-hall. See Moschatel

Cloudberry, 8, 86

Clougha, 82, 263, 301

cloughs, 8, 9, 15, 40, 103, 104, 160

Clover, Hare's-foot, 54

Clover, Strawberry, 48, 58

Clover, White, 78

Clubiona (spider), 269

clubmosses, 41, 42

Clubmoss, Alpine, 42

Clubmoss, Fir, 42, 67

Clubmoss, Lesser, 42, 87

Clubmoss, Marsh, 42

Clubmoss, Stag's-horn, 42

Club-rush, Grey, 48, 56

Club-rush, Sharp, 14

Club-rush, Wood, 65, 210

Clupea harengus. See Herring

Clytus arietis. See Beetle, Wasp

coal, 8, 9, 66, 92, 118

Coal Measures, 7, 9, 42

Coalfish. See Saithe

coarse fish, 192, 193, 195, 197

coastal cliffs, 14, 48, 59, 141

cobble skears, 13

cobbles, 22

cobwebs, 264, 265

Coccinella septempunctata. See Ladybird, Seven-spot

Coccinellidae (ladybirds), 253

Coccothraustes coccothraustes. See Hawfinch

Cochlearia danica. See Scurvygrass, Danish

Cochlicopa lubrica. See Snail, Slippery Moss

Cock Cabin Wood, 112

Cock's-foot, 60, 78, 80, 96

Cockchafer, 252

Cockerham, 175, 176,

Cockerham Moss, 84, 124, 216, 301

cockles, 23, 29, 180

Cockle, Edible, 13, 26, 28, 31, 33

cockroaches, 258

Cod, Poor, 38

Coenagrion puella. See Damselfly, Azure

Coincya monensis. See Cabbage, Isle of Man

317

Index

Wildlife of
Lancashire

Wildlife of
Lancashire

Index

Mitre, Bishop's
(shieldbug), 221
mobile dunes, 52, 175
Mole, Common, 120, 258
Molinia caerulea. See Moor-
grass, Purple
molluscs, 33, 180, 203
Monosynamma sabulicola
(bug), 222
Monotropa hypopitys. See
Bird's-nest, Yellow
Montia fontana. See Blinks
Moor-grass, Blue, 72
Moor-grass, Purple, 8, 85,
278
Moorhen, 150
Morchella spp. (fungus),
114
Morecambe Bay, 5, 7, 13,
15, 22, 23, 29, 30, 32,
34, 35, 36, 37, 38, 39,
43, 45, 50, 59, 61, 68,
70, 71, 129, 130, 137,
139, 142, 143, 145, 146,
148, 176, 184, 212, 221,
231, 232, 234, 239, 264
Morecambe Bay Natural
Area, 13
morels (fungi), 114
morel, false (fungus),
114
Moschatel, 64
Moses Gate Country Park,
233, 288, 303
mosquito, 186, 238, 239
mosses (mossland), 57,
60, 84, 88, 93, 124, 159,
168, 263, 275
mosses (plants), 19, 42,
100–104, 217,
mossland, 10, 42, 94, 127,
137, 145, 153, 155, 156,
158, 176, 209, 212, 275,
278, 289
Motacilla flava. See Wagtail,
Yellow
moths, 106, 223–229
moths, china mark, 188
Moth, Cinnabar, 222, 223

Moth, Emperor, 8, 225,
226
Moth, Magpie, 224
Moth, Peppered, 106
Mother-of-pearl, 181
Mouse, Harvest, 120, 121
Mouse, House, 120
Mouse, Long-tailed Field,
120
Mouse, Wood, 120
Mouse, Yellow-necked,
120
Mouse-ear, Little, 55
Mouse-ear, Sea, 55
Mudwort, 92
Mugil cephalus. See Mullet,
Grey
mullet (fish), 38
Mullet, Grey, 36
Muntiacus reevesi. See
Muntjac
Muntjac, 133
Mus musculus. See Mouse,
House
Musca domestica. See
House-fly
Muscardinus avellanarius.
See Dormouse,
Common
Muscicapa striata. See
Flycatcher, Spotted
Mushroom, St George's,
112
mussels, 23, 29, 34, 179,
180
mussel beds, 13, 34
Mussel, Common, 13, 24,
26, 28,30, 31
Mussel, Pearl, 181
Mussel, Swan, 181
Mussel, Zebra, 181
mussels, pea, 181
Mustela erminea. See Stoat
Mustela nivalis. See Weasel
Mustela vison. See Mink,
American
Mustelus asterias. See
Smooth-hound, Starry
Mustelus mustelus. See

Smooth-hound
mycorrhizal fungi, 110,
111
Myer's Dike, 82
Myosotis spp. (forget-me-
nots), 48, 175
Myosotis laxa. See Forget-
me-not, Tufted
Myosotis ramosissima. See
Forget-me-not, Early
Myosotis scorpioides. See
Forget-me-not, Water
Myosotis secunda. See
Forget-me-not,
Creeping
Myosotis stolonifera. See
Forget-me-not, Pale
Myotis brandtii. See Bat,
Brandt's
Myotis daubentonii. See Bat,
Daubenton's
Myotis mystacinus. See Bat,
Whiskered
Myriapoda (centipedes &
millipedes), 260
Myrica gale. See Bog-
myrtle
Myriophyllum alterniflorum.
See Water-milfoil,
Alternate
Myrmeleotettix maculatus.
See Grasshopper,
Mottled
Mysticeti (baleen whales),
131
Mytilus edulis. See Mussel,
Common
Myxine glutinosa. See
Hagfish
myxomatosis, 122

Nabis rugosus. See Bug,
Common Damsel
Nacerdes melanura. See
Wharfborer
Nanogona polydesmoides
(millipede), 261
nanoplankton, 35
Narcissus pseudonarcissus.

See Daffodil
Nardia compressa
(liverwort), 104
Nardus stricta. See Mat-
grass
Narthecium ossifragum. See
Asphodel, Bog
Nasturtium, 231
National Trust, 232
Natrix natrix. See Snake,
Grass
Natural Areas, 14
Navicula (diatom), 35
Necrophloeophagus flavus
(centipede), 262
Nematocera (flies), 238
Nematoda (roundworms),
199
Nematus ribesii. See Sawfly,
Gooseberry
Nemertea (ribbon
worms), 184
Nemotelus uliginosus. See
Snout, Barred
Neomys fodiens. See Shrew,
Water
Neottia nidus-avis. See
Orchid, Bird's-nest
Nepa cinerea (water
scorpion), 185
Nephtys spp. (catworms),
25, 29, 34
Nephtys cirrosa, 24, 25, 27,
29, 31
Nerophis lumbriciformis. See
Pipefish, Worm
nestbox, 122, 166
Nettle, 100, 219, 230
Nettle, White Dead, 221
Neuroptera (insect group
including alderflies),
187
neutral grassland, 10, 40,
78, 79
New Zealand Flatworm,
203
Newt, Great Crested, 10,
12, 172–175, 290
Newt, Palmate, 172, 175

327

Index

Index

Vaccinium oxycoccus. See Cranberry
Vaccinium vitis-idaea. See Cowberry
Valerianella locusta. See Cornsalad, Common
Vanellus vanellus. See Lapwing
Vanessa atalanta. See Admiral, Red
Varroa (mite), 246
Venus spp. See shells, Venus
Vernal-grass, Sweet, 55, 78
Veronica agrestis. See Field-speedwell, Green
Veronica anagallis-aquatica. See Water-speedwell, Blue
Veronica beccabunga. See Brooklime
Veronica persica. See Field-speedwell, Common
Veronica polita. See Field-speedwell, Grey
Verrucaria manura (lichen), 33
Vertigo alpestris. See Snail, Mountain Whorl
Vertigo angustior. See Snail, Narrow-mouthed Whorl
Vertigo pusilla. See Snail, Wall Whorl
Vetch, Horseshoe, 69, 70
Vetch, Kidney, 54
Vetch, Spring, 55
Vicia lathyroides. See Vetch, Spring
Viola arvensis. See Pansy, Field
Viola canina. See Dog-violet, Heath
Viola palustris. See Violet, Marsh
Viola reichenbachiana. See Dog-violet, Early
Viola riviniana. See Dog-violet, Common

Viola tricolor. See Pansy, Wild
Violet, Marsh, 86, 232
Viper's-bugloss, 54
Vipera berus. See Adder
Vole, Bank, 120
Vole, Field, 120
Vole, Water, 10, 12, 116, 120, 121
Volucella bombylans (hoverfly), 241, 242
Vulpes vulpes. See Fox, Red
Vulpia fasciculata. See Fescue, Dune

Waddington Fell, 86
Wade Hall, 210
Wagtail, Grey, 8
Wagtail, Yellow, 138, 155, 156, 272
Wall (butterfly), 234
Wallflowers, 231
Walney Channel, 30
warblers, 139, 167, 218, 290
Warbler, Cetti's, 138
Warbler, Dartford, 138
Warbler, Garden, 166
Warbler, Grasshopper, 12
Warbler, Reed, 152
Warbler, Sedge, 156
Warbler, Willow, 166, 167
Warbler, Wood, 8, 11, 138, 166, 167
Warbreck Moor, 82
Warrington, 16, 17, 18, 21, 194
Warton, 48, 71
Warton Crag, 126, 133, 228, 231, 232, 235, 263, 266, 304
Warton Moss, 84
wasps, 241, 242, 244, 245, 247, 248
wasps, gall, 258
wasps, social, 247
Wasp, Field Digger, 247
Wasp, Median, 248
Wasp, Sand, 247

Wasp, Wood, 259
water quality, 182, 187, 191, 193, 194
Water-cress, Fool's, 84
Water-crowfoot, Common, 90
Water-crowfoot, Pond, 88
Water-crowfoot, River, 88
Water-crowfoot, Stream, 88
Water-crowfoot, Thread-leaved, 90
Water-dropwort, Fine-leaved, 90
Water-dropwort, Hemlock, 84
Water-dropwort, Parsley, 48
Water-dropwort, Tubular, 90
Water-lily, Fringed, 12
Water-lily, White, 83
Water-milfoil, Alternate, 88
Water-parsnip, Lesser, 84
Water-pepper, Small, 92
Water-plantain, Floating, 3, 12, 91
Water-plantain, Lesser, 56
Water-purslane, 92
Water-speedwell, Blue, 90
Water-starwort, Autumn, 92
Water-starwort, Common, 90
Water-starwort, Various-leaved, 90
Waterweed, Canadian, 90, 92
Waterweed, Nuttall's, 90, 92
waxcaps, 109, 113
Waxcap, Ballerina, 113
Waxcap, Crimson, 113
Weasel, 128
Weever, Lesser, 36
weevils, 254
Weevil, Grain, 254
Weevil, Rice, 254

Weevil, Vine, 254
Weil's disease, 122
Wenning, River, 121
Wesham marsh, 79
West Pennine Moors, 159, 160, 161, 164, 170
whales, 130
whales, baleen, 131, 132, 133
whales, toothed, 131
Whale, Fin, 132, 133
Whale, Humpbacked, 132, 133
Whale, Killer, 132
Whale, Long-finned Pilot, 132
Whale, Minke, 132, 133
Whale, Northern Bottle-nosed, 132
Whale, Sei, 132
Whalley, 114
Wharfborer (beetle), 255
Wheatear, 159
Whimbrel, 151
Whinchat, 9, 159, 160
White Coppice, 239, 304
White, Green-veined, 231
White, Large, 230, 231, 258
White, Small, 230, 231
whitebeams, 43, 59
Whitebeam, Lancashire, 7, 43
whiteflies, 218
Whiteweed (hydroid), 30
Whitlowgrass, Common, 55
Whitlowgrass, Glabrous, 55
Wigan, 15, 84, 92, 117, 141, 168, 176, 210, 213
Wigan Flashes, 92, 93, 149, 150, 152, 153, 192, 210, 213, 214, 288, 304
Wigeon, 14, 140, 144, 145, 149
Wildlife and Countryside Act, 173

336

Wildlife of
Lancashire

List of Subscribers

John K. Adamson
Jessie Addison
Val and Martin Alldred
Victoria Allen
John A. Almond
Willum Ashton
John E. Ashworth
Dr L. J. Ashworth
Hon. J. H. Assheton
Hon. Nicholas Assheton
　　C.V.O.
Hon. R. C. Assheton
Robert and Alison
　　Asworth
Nora H. Atkin
Reg Atkins
Charles R. Atkinson
Joan Baldwin
Vera Baldwin
Harry Ball
David Haig Banks
Kirsten Barger
David Baron
Mr and Mrs P. J. Bartlett
Donald Barton
M. A. Bateson
David Beattie
David Bell
P. Benson
Jack Benyon
Gordon Berry
Peggy Beverley
David Bickerton
W. A. Bickerton
Mrs Joan Bideau
John Birch
Mike J. Blackburn
D. Blackburn
Beryl Blackhall
Suzanne M. Blake
Miss Cherith Bland

Winefride Bleasdale
Heather Blunt
Meg Boak
Bolton Conservation
　　Volunteers
Eleanor Bowden
Doug Bowker
Mr R. and Mrs J. Boydell
Jill Bradshaw
Walter Breakell
Kane Brides, Young
　　Environment
　　Champion of the
　　Year 2003 for the
　　North West
Barry and June Brigden
Keith Briggs
Miss Elizabeth Brindle
Ian Brodie
Jean Brooks
Christine Broughton
Antony Brown
Jennifer Brown
Geoff Buffey
Mr B. Bulling
Colin Burford
Dr N. R. Burford
Richard Burkmar
Stuart A. Burnet
Gill Burrill
Norman Burrows
The Cameron Family
Tony Cameron
E. Campion
Norma Canty
Jessica Ruth Carey
Lennard Carroll
Peta Carter
Roger Cartwright
Richard Catlow
Mrs P. Cavanagh

Shirley and Jeff
　　Chambers
Mr and Mrs T. Chambers
M. J. Chappell
Ian Cheetham
Fiona Chippendale
Chorley and District
　　Natural History
　　Society
Mr Michael Clapham
Marie Cecile Clark
Jacqueline Clemingshaw
The Rt. Hon. The Lord
　　Clitheroe Dl
Carol and Bob
　　Colderley, Bolton
Rosslyn, Simon and
　　Joseph Colderley
Dr E. R. L. Cole
J. and L. Colling
Bill and Lesley Comstive
Brian and Jane Cooper
Mr Tony Cooper
Cecilia Coram
Eddy Cowen
Florence Cragg
Tania Crockett
Alan Cross
J. and P. Cundill
C. and T. Curry
Mr Allan Cutler
Bob and Diane Danson
Joanne Davenport
Susan and Michael
　　Davie
Arwel and Amanda
　　Davies
Eric and Emily Davis
C. Dawson
Mr and Mrs P. del
　　Strother

Dorothy F. Derry
Barbara Dickinson
Rosa Dietch
Lisa Dixon
Stephen Doel
Tony and Valerie Dorey
Rob Douglas
Denise Drinkall
Gordon and Brenda
　　Driver
A. S. Duckels
Mr T. V. Dudley
Mrs H. M. Duerden
Tom Duerden
Tony Duffey
Rob Dunford
Mac Dunsmore
Chris Dyckhoff
Phil and Rose Dykes
Mr B. Dyson
R. G. Eckersley
Peter Edmondson
Roy and Irene Ekins
Christine Elding
William and Shirley
　　Ellwood
Brett Entwistle
The Environmental
　　Action Group
Ron and Pat Fairweather
Sue and Roger Farrand
Jonathan Fenton
Mrs M. Fenton
Mr Philip Fermor
Carole and Les Fielden
Emma Fielden
David Finch
David Fisher
P. Fitzsimons
Marjorie Fletcher (Mrs)
Mark and Ros Flinn

Jon Follows
Jill Ford
James M Forrest
Derek Forshaw
The Francis Family
Jamie Fuller
Sally Furlong
Mr P. Gahan and Miss A. Kimpton
Peter Garland
Peter Gateley
B. H. and D. Gibbons
Mr Derek Gifford
Peter and Veronica Gilchrist
Barbara Giller
D. and B. Gillett
Mike Gittens
John Gofton
Dr Peter Golborn
Yvonne Golding
Rachel M. Goldring
Pamela Goode
Daniel Joshua Graham
John Greaves
Mr Ken Green
Mary Green
P. C. Green
Mrs Mary Greenwood
Mr and Mrs D. Gregory
Esmé Lillian Gregory
Anne Griffiths
Margaret Grimshaw
Mrs Margaret Grimshaw
Roy Grimshaw
Lynn and Graham Grindrod
Pat and Roy Grindrod
Pam Grundy
Cerys Rhian Hall
Mr and Mrs Hammond
Mr S. Hampson
Christine Hardy
Mr J. P. Harrison
Ken Harrison
Sharon Harrison
Ian and Diane Hartley
Peter Harwood
Ted and Enid Hawkins,

Chris Hawkins
Simon J. Hayhow
Alex Heede
Mr Graham Hickey
Geoff Higginbottom
Pat Higson
David John Hindle
Robert Hirst
Edward R. Hoare
Jeffery S. Holiday
Peter Holland
Mavis and Jack Hopkinson
Belinda Hornby
Peter J. Hornby
Dr M. D. and Mrs J. Horrocks
Ron Hothersall
John Houston
Scott Hughes
David and Valerie Hughes
James H. Ingham
Mr Stan Irwin
Keely D. Isherwood
Ted Jackson
Simon Jennings
(Miss) Elizabeth Johnson
Mary Johnson
Mrs and Mr S. Johnson
Mrs Rosemary Jolly
John Jones
Ray and Marjorie Jones
Rhiannon and Rowan Jones
Tony Jones and Tracy Gordon
David Kay
Tim Kaye
Barbara Kennedy
John Kenny
J. L. Kenyon
John Kilcoyne
Mr D. and Mrs J. Kippax
Ken and Ann Kitchen
C. A. Klinkenberg
Jeanne I. Knowles
Kathleen Knowles

John and Elsie Lamb
Lancashire County Museum Service (Natural Sciences)
Lancaster University
Alan Lancaster
Jill Lavis
Ken and Zoe Lawson
G. C. Lea
In Memory of Dr John Leather
Jim and Joan Leaver
Gareth Lee
Mark Lee
In Memory of Dr Mark Levy
Mrs M. Lord
India Amelie Low
Susan Lucas
Susanne E. Lunn
Robin Macdonald
Chris Marsden
Colin Marshall
Ian and Kim Martin
Richard Martin
Stephen John Martin
Stephen Mawdsley
Mark McAlister
Mr R. G. and B. B. McBurnie
Mr Kevin McCabe
Jake McCarthy
Norman Mccormack
Dr Helen McGarry
Peter Mcintyre
Dr S. L. McKinlay
Stefanie McLaney
Mr and Mrs D. G. McNamara
Mr and Mrs J. D. McNamara
In Memory of Mrs Rene Merritt
Liz Michael
Middlemarch Env. Ltd
Gill Midgley
Renée and Ray Miller
Barney and Andrina Mitcham

Cathy and Derek Mitcham
Leslie Mitchell
K. and M. E. Moore
Ann Morgan
Gwyn Morgan
Geoffrey Morries
Peter and Joan Morries
Professor Glyn Morton
Elizabeth Mosey
Philip Mulholland
Charles L. Mullin
Dorothy and Patrick Mulvenna
Tina Murray
Mr Robert and Mrs Sheila Myron
Jason Nash
D. A. Nicholas
Lesley Nixon
Julie and Richard Norman
Harry Noyes
K. and D. Nunnerley
Norman Nutter
Richard Nutter
F. D. and J. O'Brien
Miss Carol Ann Ogden
Harry Ormerod
J. R. and R. J. Owen
Mr R. and Mrs J. Owen
Mr W. J. Owen
Lucy Page
Walter D. Park
Dr David Parker
Jacqueline Parkinson
Mrs R. E. Parks
Vi Peacock
Nigel Penberthy
Joan Penney
A. J. Percy
Bob Pickup
Mrs Gillian Pierce
Hazel and Sethu Pillai, Witney
Enid Pimblett
Colin and Lisa Platt
Jill Player
Joyce Plumb

Dr and Mrs H. B. Pollock
Rev E. M. Pope
Edward J. Potter
Michael Potter
Mark and Karen Preece
Barry Prescott
E. and E. L. Prince
J. V. Pritchard
Andrew Procter
Ken and Anne Procter
Phil Procter
Stuart Procter
William Procter
Ruth, Jake and Odin
    Pryor, Canada
Mary Pye (Fulwood,
    Preston)
David John Quirk
B. J. Rafferty
Gavin Rainford
Stuart Rammell
B. Rawstron
Bob Read
Roger C. Rees
'Rehabilitation Home
    For Hedgehogs'
Mr Mark Reynolds
Ethel and Harold
    Richardson
Dr Irene Ridge
Terence John Rigby
Joyce Riley
Maureen and Simon
    Riley
Pamela A. M. Riley
M. Rimmer
Mr E. W. Roberts
S. L. and A. Roberts
Mr and Mrs J. Robertson
Andrew Robinson
Mike Robinson
Alan Roff
Rossall School
Anne-Marie Rotheram
Miss Ann Evelyn
    Rothwell
The Rowett Family,

Leyland
Miss A. C. Royden
Donald Rusling
C. I. Rutherford
Maxwell H. Scattergood
Mr J. K. Seabrook
Mr Eric Sefton
Mr J. J. Shackleton
Peter and Maureen
    Shakeshaft
Mavis Shannon
Dave Sharpe
Mr Jack Sharples
Harry and Renee Shaw
Mike and Barbara Shaw
Paul Shenton
Alan Shepley
Margaret Sherlock
Mun Ling Shields
J. R. Sillis
Mr R. Singleton
Christine Skelton of
    Norden and
    Tewkesbury
Slade Family, Ormskirk
Mr M. B. Slater
Mr R. and Mrs C. Slatter
Dr and Mrs R. W. Small
Frank Smith
Ida Smith
Mr Jack Smith
Jane Smith
Judy Smith
Loraine Smith
Phil Smith
Dave and Chris Sowter
Ian M. Spence
Joan Springett
Sue Stallibrass
Carl Startin
Gordon Stead
John Stead
Christopher Stell
Suzanne, Alan and Anya
    Stenhouse, Bury
Mr Gerry Stephen
Ted Stevens

Guy Story
Margery Story
Karl Sturge and Rebecca
    Pepper
Mr K. Sullivan
Allan Sumner
Ann Sutcliffe
Dr H. and Mrs B.
    Sutcliffe
Peter and Sylvia Swain
David Swinburn
David Talbot
Janet Tapley
Mrs A. M. (Maisie)
    Tarbuck
Mr J. Michal Tarbuck
Hon. Mrs R. Tarling
Margaret Tattersall
Clare Taylor
Cynthia and Kevan
    Taylor, Bolton
Mr Gordon Taylor
Penelope Taylor and
    Paul Miller,
    Manchester
Mr Alan Ternent
Richard and Janet
    Thomas
Richard David Thomson
Mrs M. F. Threadgold
Peter Tipping
Sal Tracey
Doug Trafford
A. W. Tranter
Duncan Turner
Enid Turner
George Turner
Aidan Turner-Bishop
Carole and David Wake
Mr and Mrs D. Wakefield
J. B. Waldron
James Malcolm Walker
Nathan Walker
Andrew S. Waller
Mr F. Walsh and Mrs B.
    Walsh
Mr and Mrs G. Walsh

Graham Walsh
Matthew Harry Walsh
Dr William Ward
John and Janet Warner
Rachel Waterhouse
John Watt
Terry Weight
George Arnold Welch
George Martyn Welch
Reg and Doreen
    Wharton, Bolton
Chris Whitehead
Mr H. Wickham
Brian Wilby
Wildlife After School
    Project (WASP)
Barbara Wilkinson
Harry James Wilkinson
Alex D. Williams
Derek Williams
J. P. Williams
J. R. Williams
Mr R. W. Wilmshurst
Mary Winder
Mr Donald Windle
Mr Michael Windle
Ian Wolfenden
Frank Wood
Thomas David Wood
Geoff and Jenny
    Woodcock
Barbara Woodruff
Gail and Peter Woods
Keith and Maria Woods
Pat and John Woodside
Dave Woodward
Mrs Dorothy
    Wordsworth
D. M. Worsley-Taylor
Jim and Wendy Wright
Lesley A. Wright
Alwyn Yates
Peter Yates
Jonathan D. Yeats
Edmund Yoxon